Praise

'*Scaling Conservation* is a marvel. Rich is a pioneer in the true sense of the word, and he is grabbing the opportunity to restore nature in Britain at scale. In this book, he describes passionately and eloquently how he is going about it.'
— **Ben Goldsmith**, Chief Exec, Menhaden PLC

'In this book and in his work, Rich Stockdale and his team are doing the incredible: they are making nature sexy again. Sexy in terms of breathless landscapes. Sexy in terms of the adventure of conservation. Sexy in terms of teamwork and the best place to dare and do. Sexy in terms of hope for our future.'
— **Elena Doms**, CEO, Earth Plus, and LinkedIn Top Green Voice

'A master textbook on how to turn nature restoration from optional nicety to economic necessity – and give us back the natural riches that we all deserve.'
— **Benedict Macdonald**, Founder and Director, RESTORE; author of *Rebirding*

'Rich Stockdale and his Oxygen Conservation team loom large in my mental map of emerging Green Swan innovators, with their efforts to scale both conservation and regeneration.'
— **John Elkington**, Founder and Global Ambassador, Volans; author of *Green Swans: The coming boom in regenerative capitalism* and *Tickling Sharks: How we sold business on sustainability*

'*Scaling Conservation* by Rich Stockdale is a must-read for anyone interested in significantly impacting the restoration of nature at scale. Rich's ability to connect the dots between different aspects of conservation makes this book a comprehensive and engaging read. His honest discussions on the trade-offs between finance and nature and his visionary approach provide invaluable insights for seasoned conservationists and newcomers. I highly recommend *Scaling Conservation* to anyone looking to deepen their understanding of conservation and how to create a world worth living in.'
— **Rob Gardner**, CEO and Co-Founder, Rebalance Earth

'Richard Stockdale and Oxygen Conservation are changing the world and, with this book, inspiring us all to do the same.'
— **Lisa Pinney** MBE, CEO, Mining Remediation Authority, and Chair, Birmingham & Black Country Wildlife Trust

'Stockdale, a man of immense energy and intellect, is a disrupter who you suspect won't take no for an answer. He understands the huge scale of the investment needed to address the climate crisis and biodiversity depletion, and is determined to change the way we view nature by proving that conservation is an investment, not a cost. His hypothesis is simple: show that nature is a bankable proposition and you can unlock huge capital flows which will scale conservation in a way never before seen. This collection of essays provides an open and honest account of his nature restoration journey and provides a call to action for anyone inspired to follow his lead.'
— **Andrew Hicks**, CEO, BNGx

'This book epitomises how Rich approaches life – leading with his chin into areas that he cares passionately about. It is as much an approach to building a business and a culture as it is to influencing how we can get over the humps in the road needed to make the changes in our collective approach to scaling conservation. This needs thoughtful, knowledgeable, and irrepressibly optimistic individuals and leadership to make the change. This is not easy. It requires engaging communication, conviction, and resilience, all of which you can see in spades in these essays.'
— **Jonathan Digges**, Chief Investment Officer, Octopus Capital

'Rich is a powerhouse – an unstoppable force of, and for, nature. In these transformative times, his is a voice that must be heeded. He is bravely honest about his mission and methods and, with real heart, he urges readers to rethink what they do and how they do it. I have had the great pleasure of working alongside Rich and have seen first-hand his unrelenting drive to create ambitious environmental and social impact and to enthuse and energise people to think bigger and to do and achieve more. I cannot think of anyone better placed, or more skilful, to hold the pen on rewriting the narrative on conservation leadership. I commend this book to all as a truly exhilarating read.'
— **Ross Simpson**, Partner, Burges Salmon

'Nature can deliver significant support to both climate transition and adaptation agendas – as demonstrated in this book. To ensure it does, we need visionaries like Rich Stockdale.'
— **Julius Pursaill**, Non Exec, NatWest Cushon

'Rich Stockdale probably knows more about the innovative future potential of natural capital in the UK than anyone else. That insight and knowledge is comprehensively contained amid these pages and makes for an enjoyable read. A necessary book.'
— **Merlin Hanbury-Tenison**, Founder, Thousand Year Trust, and author of *Our Oaken Bones*

'Rich Stockdale's *Scaling Conservation* is a captivating narrative, a personal journey, and a call to action. It's a testament to the power of one person's vision and the collective potential of many to heal our planet. Stockdale's authentic voice and candid reflections invite us to join him on his mission, empowering us to become agents of change in our own right. This book isn't just a great read; it's an invitation to a conversation, a movement, a revolution for a sustainable future.'
— **Cain Blythe**, CEO and Founder, Ecosulis and CreditNature

'Rich and the team at Oxygen Conservation are completely changing the game in conservation. It's high time someone did. This super inspiring book is a wonderful look behind the curtain. OC are disruptors through and through, and I for one am extremely excited to see what they do next. Interesting times ahead…'
— **Hector Hughes**, CEO and Co-founder, Unplugged

'Rich Stockdale's collection of essays brings together the challenges, triumphs, and dichotomies of restoring nature at scale, within the confines of a distracted and fragile economy. We are lucky to have a prolific writer in this sector, who writes confidently, frequently and with radical candour.'
— **Alexa Culver**, Legal Counsel, RSK Wilding

'Rich's passion for nature shouts loudly from every page of this glorious compendium of all things nature. Each chapter adds another layer to the biodiversity journey that Rich has invited us to join him on, all amounting collectively to the system that he will rightly have convinced you we need by the end of the book. My favourite parts are those where Rich chooses not to shy away from the trade-offs that our decision making often leads us to, particularly when it comes to our interactions with the complexity of biodiversity – in that lies this book's power.'
— **Eoin Murray**, Chief Investment Officer, Rebalance Earth

'This is an incredibly well-informed piece of work, which oozes passion for its powerfully put vision of nature recovery.'
— **Derek Gow**, author of *Hunt for the Shadow Wolf* and *Bringing Back the Beaver*

SCALING CONSERVATION

THE BUSINESS OF RESTORING THE WILD

DR RICH STOCKDALE

Re^ethink

First published in Great Britain in 2025
by Rethink Press (www.rethinkpress.com)
© Copyright Rich Stockdale

All rights reserved. No part of this publication may be reproduced, stored in or introduced into a retrieval system, or transmitted, in any form, or by any means (electronic, mechanical, photocopying, recording or otherwise) without the prior written permission of the publisher.

The right of Rich Stockdale to be identified as the author of this work has been asserted by him in accordance with the Copyright, Designs and Patents Act 1988.

This book is sold subject to the condition that it shall not, by way of trade or otherwise, be lent, resold, hired out, or otherwise circulated without the publisher's prior consent in any form of binding or cover other than that in which it is published and without a similar condition including this condition being imposed on the subsequent purchaser.

Cover image © Oxygen Conservation

Contents

Foreword   1

Introduction   5

1 Landscape Scale   15

Unveiling the Potential: Transforming a Blank Canvas   16

Contradictions and Compromises in Conservation   22

The Unsettling Truth About UK Land Use   29

Birds, Bees, Butterflies, and an Explosion of Voles   39

Why We Buy Land   43

The Greening of the Glen: A New Era in Scottish Estate Ownership   48

2 Building The Best Team In The Conservation Industry — **61**

Building the *Edie* Team of the Year — 62
Lessons Learned from the NFL Draft — 70
Just Coasting — 77
Beginning a Career in Conservation — 84
Experience Is Overrated — 93
Ruining Recruitment — 102
Recognition — 112
The Best Job in the Natural Capital Economy? — 117
We Got It Wrong — 124

3 Engagement — **129**

We Will Always Listen.
We Won't Always Agree. — 130
The Privilege of Criticism — 137
Can We Go Beyond Self-Interest and Embrace True Environmental Conservation? — 146
The Politics of the Environment — 152
Fear. Hope. And Hate. — 157
Rebranding Conservation – Our Thinking So Far — 163

4 Oxygen Conservation's Process — **171**

Networking Nature: How We Are Pioneering the Natural Capital Economy with Silicon Valley Strategies — 172
Adventures in Safety — 182
Taking the Risk Out of Risk Taking — 194
How We Buy Land — 203

Embracing Change	211
Green Is the New Black	219

5 Peak Performance — 227

The Untold Truth of High-Performance Environments	228
Radical Transparency	238
Business Athletes: Learning from the track, the road, and the hillside	243
There Are Five Quarters of Performance	254
Unsung Heroes: Recognising the Domestiques of Business	260
Calendar Defence	267
Oxygenating Your Time	274

6 Green Finance — 283

The Business of Conservation: Why Conservation for Profit Is a Sustainable Approach for the Planet's Future	284
The New Paradigm of Natural Capital Investment	291
Creating Pathways for Private Finance	296
Navigating the State of UK Environmental Data	302
Crediting Nature	312
The Best Carbon Credits (Quality Matters)	321

7 Breaking Barriers, Shifting The Paradigm — 333

Tearing Down the Red Book: Growing a Greener Valuation Standard	334
Why Rainforests Are Worthless	344

The Oxygen Conservation Recruitment Process	350
Adventure with a Purpose: Oxygen Conservation's Mission to Scale Conservation	363
The Urgent Call to Be Kind: Battling Climate Change, Biodiversity Crisis, and Our Collective Concerns	370
Please Choose My Backyard	375

8 The Interconnectivity Of Solutions — 383

Let's Talk About Lying	384
Hold Strong Opinions, Loosely	387
Building a Sustainable Future	395
Patient Urgency	402
Wind vs Wilderness	406
Education in Conservation	418
Wild Camping, Wild Places, and Wildlife	428
Oxygen Escapes: Ecotourism Conservation	435

9 Call To Action! Navigating The Future — 445

The Green Revolution: How Natural Capital Is Emerging as the World's Most Important Alternative Asset Class	446
Activist Leaders and Green Businesses	452
Will We Be the Generation That Saved or Killed the World?	459
Hope Is Just a Four-Letter Word	469

Conclusion	475
Bibliography	483
Acknowledgements	491
The Author	493

Foreword

Dr Bevis Watts, Chief Executive, Triodos Bank UK

Here in the UK we live in one of the most nature-depleted countries in the world. Precious wildlife and biodiversity that enrich our lives – and are essential to our wellbeing – are being lost. The latest *State of Nature* report, published in 2023 by a coalition of wildlife and research organisations, offers a stark picture of our country's wildlife. Since 1970, UK species have declined by 19% on average, and nearly one in six species (16.1%) is now threatened with extinction (State of Nature Partnership, 2023). Restoring our depleted natural environment and reversing biodiversity loss is vitally important to our wellbeing and will help to mitigate the effects of the climate crisis.

Oxygen Conservation is pioneering a brand-new approach to protecting and restoring nature and is leading the way through its commitment to deliver positive environmental and social impact, while generating a sustainable financial return.

In *Scaling Conservation* Dr Rich Stockdale draws from the learnings and experiences Oxygen Conservation has encountered so far on its nature restoration journey. As well as offering an insight into the challenges these projects face, he explores the scale of what can be achieved and the many reasons this work is so vital. We need books like this to show what nature-based solutions look like in action, and to offer both hope and guidance to others who may be inspired to follow in Oxygen Conservation's footsteps.

Triodos Bank has been operating in the UK for thirty years, financing organisations we believe have the potential to change society and make the world a better place for future generations. Without losing sight of the intrinsic value of nature, we have been developing nature-based solutions since 2017, and this has become an important focus for us. We're extremely proud to have worked with Oxygen Conservation on a groundbreaking loan facility to scale its work. I hope that what we've achieved together is just the start.

Oxygen Conservation's aim to generate a positive economic return as a result of its work, not as its purpose, very much aligns with our own values as a bank. And just as Rich is doing here, we want to share our experience in the nature finance sector in the hope that others will follow. This book isn't being published for profit and we hope that by sponsoring its publication we can help to put copies into the hands of those who can take these learnings forward.

The scale of investment needed to address nature depletion is huge. In the Nature Markets Framework for England, published as part of the government's Green Finance Strategy in 2023, Defra (the Department for Environment, Food and Rural Affairs) estimated that at least £500 million of private finance is needed annually by 2027 and more than £1 billion by 2030 (Defra, 2024). In considering this investment, it's right that we acknowledge the risks of bringing nature into our broken economic system. However, I believe that redirecting the flow of capital in all its forms – including support for the natural world – as a force for good is essential in tackling the multiple crises we face.

Private sector investment in restoration of our natural environment is not yet a recognised commercial proposition, but it can be part of a new nature-connected economy. What Rich and the team at Oxygen Conservation are doing is a strong example of how this can work in practice.

We hope *Scaling Conservation* will awaken others to what's possible.

Introduction

Has anyone ever asked you how you think? Not just *what* you think, but the mechanics of your thoughts – how ideas spark, collide, and evolve inside your mind? For some, thoughts might be linear like a London Tube map, or smooth and long-formed like a sound wave. For me, it's like a firework display. Give me a single suggestion, idea, or even an object, and my brain explodes into a thousand possibilities. It's exhilarating, exciting, and sometimes tiring; but it's how my mind works.

This mental cacophony is mostly a blessing but occasionally a curse. It's brilliant for running scenarios, evaluating consequences, and imagining the impossible and improbable (Oxygen Conservation being a case in point). When I want to truly grapple with something complicated – to dive deep, unpack the nuances, and challenge my own real thoughts – I turn to writing. Writing forces my thoughts to order, align, and present themselves in a structured form I can easily share with others. Abbey Dudas, my wonderful editor at Oxygen Conservation, often jokes that she can tell when I'm especially passionate about a subject because I start missing words – typing simply can't keep up with... speed... thoughts.

Writing about our work, and specifically about Scaling Conservation, has been a journey of clarity. It's one thing to believe passionately in the mission. It's quite another to begin to articulate the *Why*, the *How*, and the *What next* to others.

At Oxygen Conservation we're doing what has previously been thought impossible. We're building an entirely new asset class – making the market for natural capital and Scaling Conservation, as a movement, a mindset, and a measurable impact.

The environment sector operates under a level of scrutiny most industries can scarcely imagine. Every intention, every action is dissected and debated. Successes are rarely celebrated, but mistakes or reluctant compromises are always criticised or attacked. Expectations are stratospheric, but that's OK – it's the arena where we've chosen to perform. The environment sector has to lead by example, proving not only that conservation is essential but also that it can be equitable, transparent, and scalable. Our work isn't just about Oxygen Conservation; it's about reinventing and scaling the entire sector.

What we're attempting is hard. It's complicated. And it's essential.

Conservation needs to evolve from being the purview of the volunteer or the retiree into a mainstream force. It needs to be woven into the fabric of economic, social, and cultural systems. We need to make it easier for the next wave of conservationists to go further and faster, building on what we've started. By doing this, we can foster a virtuous cycle: Scaling Conservation while creating space for innovation, competition, and collaboration.

This book is about the ideas, experiments, and lessons learned on the road, in the field, and in the boardroom. It's about the people who think differently and bigger, the moments that tested our resolve, and the milestones that transformed a vision into a reality. It's about the landscapes we've nurtured, the revival of ecosystems we're witnessing, and the partnerships that have propelled us forward. Most importantly, it's about: the power of people, the possibility of change, the potential of collaboration, and the promise of a future where conservation and prosperity coexist

As you turn these pages, you'll step into a narrative of ambition and action, of lessons learned, and of horizons expanded. You'll discover that this narrative is encapsulated in articles written at times relevant to each project and development, with recent reflections added at the end of each article. From the foundational ideas and inspiring people that seeded our mission to the incredible portfolio that now spans tens of thousands of acres, across the entire country, this book is not just the story of Oxygen Conservation. It's a call to action for anyone who believes in the transformative power of the environment, innovation, and adventure.

Before that, I'd like to lay the foundation by answering one of the questions I get asked most often: *How on Earth did Oxygen Conservation happen?*

Oxygen Conservation: The origin story

Oxygen Conservation was founded on the belief that conservation could be reimagined as a transformative force, propelled by innovation, ambition, and purpose.

Inspired by a passion for proving the impossible possible, the relentless drive for excellence from my time in high-performance sport, and an unwavering commitment to making a meaningful impact, we set out to redefine the entire environment sector.

Conservation, for us, has never been a passive act. It's a dynamic, data-driven platform for measurable positive impact – delivering tangible benefits for nature, communities, and economies.

The seeds of change

The beginnings of Oxygen Conservation can be traced back to a number of convergent inspirations. The first of these occured six years before this book was published.

I was living in the South West of England and leading the Environment Agency in Devon and Cornwall when I was introduced to Oxygen House, an incredible group of people (and businesses) committed to rapidly driving large-scale solutions that make a significant impact on pressing global challenges. That first introduction set in motion many of the events that follow in this book.

A global inspiration

Another pivotal moment in the development of our story was a visit to South America by the founding members of Oxygen House, a close likeminded group of friends and colleagues. They visited the Tompkins Conservation Foundation in Argentina – a large-scale conservation initiative that had turned barren landscapes into thriving ecosystems. Witnessing what could be achieved on a massive scale was deeply inspiring. It made the visitors

INTRODUCTION

wonder: Could something similar be done in the UK? Could they use their investment to Scale Conservation?

From vision to greenprint

The leap from concept to actionable strategy came through the creation of the 'Greenprint' – a 30,000-word proposal on the future of conservation in the UK. This document outlined the framework for a business that prioritised environmental and social impact alongside profit, recognising that this would lead to long-term, genuinely risk-adjusted returns on investment. It was a radical yet necessary departure from traditional models, challenging the notion that profitability and purpose are mutually exclusive.

None of this would have been possible without the backing of those who believed in the mission from the start. The Oxygen House Group – led by Dr Mark Dixon and supported by friends and family (you'll hear more about these people later) – played *the* instrumental role in providing the financial backing to turn this vision into reality. Their belief in the power of change, their belief in me, and their willingness to provide the adventure capital (the original term for venture capital) allowed us to establish Oxygen Conservation on 2 June 2021. Nothing has been the same since.

The early days: The foundation of Portfolio One

Oxygen Conservation's early years were defined by speed – decisive action and bold investments. We focused on acquiring land that could serve as a foundation for transformative conservation projects. We started building our first portfolio in the South West of England, acquiring estates like Leighon (861 acres) on Dartmoor and forming a partnership with the lovely family at Wood Advent (428 acres) in the Exmoor National Park. From there our portfolio expanded to include sites across the UK such as Swineley (496 acres) in Yorkshire, Esgair Arth (304 acres) in West Wales, and part of the Firth of Tay (546 acres) in Scotland.

These acquisitions were not about accumulating land; they were about identifying opportunities where we could restore, protect, and enhance natural ecosystems. We sought landscapes that held potential for biodiversity uplift and carbon sequestration, always guided by the belief that conservation and economic sustainability must go hand in hand. You can't be a good business if you're not in business.

Landscape-level ambitions and acquisitions

As we grew, so too did our ambitions. In the next phase of our journey, we expanded further, acquiring significant landscapes at Invergeldie (11,701 acres), in Perthshire, and Blackburn and Hartsgarth (11,407 acres), from the Buccleuch Group in the Scottish Borders. These large-scale investments exemplified our approach: to secure and restore landscapes in ways that could generate both environmental and financial returns. The generation of high-quality carbon credits (with other nature-based credits planned for the future) became an essential part of our strategy. These estates also provided us the opportunity to explore the development of onshore wind farms, introducing us to the challenges that come with these large infrastructure projects.

These acquisitions were supported by our friends at Blue & White Capital, the family office of Tony Bloom, renowned entrepreneur and the owner of Brighton &

Hove Albion FC. We're delighted that this has led to the increasing involvement of Adam Franks, Chair and Chief Investment Officer at Blue & White Capital, and now also an investor in Oxygen Conservation.

Further developments

One of our most important accomplishments was proving that conservation could be a bankable proposition. Our groundbreaking, debt-funding partnership with Triodos Bank was a pioneering effort that showed conservation could attract institutional capital, helping to establish a market for sustainable investments. One of our key goals is to make the market for nature an asset class, and making these products and services bankable is a key step on that journey.

Balancing the portfolio

As the portfolio grew, we recognised the need for balance – integrating diverse geographies and revenue streams to ensure both environmental impact and financial resilience. This led us to acquire Mornacott in Devon (777 acres) and Manor Farm in Shropham, Norfolk (696 acres). These estates allowed us to diversify the portfolio:

- **Mornacott:** We added opportunities for regenerative agriculture and enhanced sustainable tourism.

- **Manor Farm:** We supplemented the magical Wild With Nature glamping property with an opportunity to create biodiversity net gain (BNG) units, now a regulatory requirement for all new developments in England and Wales.

Both sites reflected our evolving vision of harmonising restoration efforts with increased community engagement and sustainable economic development.

Scaling Conservation

In 2024 we added Siblyback (968 acres) on Bodmin Moor in Cornwall, where we're supporting temperate rainforest restoration; and the majestic Dorback Estate in the Cairngorms, bringing another 15,014 acres to the portfolio in one of the most ambitious geographies in the UK for environmental restoration. Across our now more than 43,000 acres, we're delighted to provide connectivity to more than 500,000 acres of land, managed with conservation-minded objectives that help to Scale Conservation way beyond our own boundaries.

As we closed out chapter one of the Oxygen Conservation story, we were also delighted to welcome as our Chairman the brilliant Benny Higgins – whom we first met during the acquisition of Blackburn and Hartsgarth. Benny is also currently the Chairman of the Buccleuch Group, the National Galleries of Scotland, Markerstudy, and Edinburgh Fringe.

Adventure and collaboration

What makes Oxygen Conservation so special is the culture we've built. Conservation is an adventure, and from exploring potential acquisitions to tackling complex environmental challenges, our work is fuelled by a commitment to environment, impact, adventure, and togetherness. None of what we do would be possible without the people who make it happen – our investors, our team, our partners, and the local communities who work alongside us. We've always believed that conservation needs to be inclusive to be successful. Through effective collaboration, we amplify our positive impact and create initiatives that benefit people and wildlife alike.

Throughout this book you will meet some of the most exceptional people who will one day almost certainly put their stories on paper too. Our team is the most amazing that you can know, and we are blessed to be working in the golden age (or perhaps 'green age' is more appropriate) of natural capital.

Looking ahead

As we continue to grow, our sights are set firmly on the future. We are committed to Scaling Conservation in a way never before seen and, in doing so, setting a new standard for nature-based investments. Our goal is ambitious: to be managing £1 billion worth of land for conservation by 2030. We're driven by a belief that conservation is not a cost but an investment – in the planet, in people, and in the possibility of a future.

This adventure has been remarkable, and it's been possible only because of the dedication of so many people – from our early funders, especially Dr Mark Dixon and supportive friends and family, to the growing team of incredible people who are making our vision a reality.

Together, I believe we have and will continue to redefine what is possible in conservation. I'm often asked what I want our legacy to be. Firstly, I'm not that old yet; and secondly, I think that if we're successful in achieving everything we hope, we will leave no legacy at all.

Just like walking through a beautiful temperate rainforest, we should try to not even leave footprints. Instead, we should aim to leave only ideas, stories, and maps to help guide the far more meaningful achievements of the next generation. After all, that is who we're doing it for.

This is the first part of our story and one we're delighted to share.

ONE
LANDSCAPE SCALE

Unveiling the Potential: Transforming a Blank Canvas

Written winter 2023

Our mission is to Scale Conservation, delivering positive environmental and social impact. Generating a profit as a result of what we do, not the purpose.

One of the best investments we've made to date was the acquisition of the nearly 12,000-acre Blackburn and Hartsgarth Estate, close to Newcastleton in the Scottish Borders. This expansive canvas provides:

- Enormous potential for positive environmental and social impact, principally through the capacity for the development of one of the biggest onshore wind farms in the UK*

---

* This represented our ambitions at the time. After learning more about the Estate, we have significantly scaled back our estimate of the area that is likely to be suitable for turbines, with early studies indicating a maximum of twenty turbines.

- Storage of up to 750,000 tCO2e (tonnes of carbon dioxide equivalent), through native broadleaf woodland planting and peatland restoration
- Creation of one of the biggest and most exciting conservation projects in the UK

It also offers the potential for the Blackburn and Hartsgarth Estate to be the home to several returning iconic species, including perhaps one day the Eurasian lynx.

We believe that the area surrounding Newcastleton in the Scottish Borders is often a missed feature of the UK. It provides remarkable impact potential and investment value, essentially offering a location, climate, topography, and atmosphere similar to those of the Lake District but for a fraction of the price. Please don't tell too many people, though – we so often spoil the most precious places and spaces.

Our blank canvas

The landscape here has gone through several environmentally and culturally painful transactions, following large-scale community clearance in the 1790s. The remaining agricultural land has been intensively grazed for far too long, the legacy of which offers little biodiversity and heartbreakingly little bioabundance, meaning key indicator species are largely absent. There have been far too many sheep for much too long, plus too many deer (to the point now where numbers are diminishing due to a lack of food), and generations of aggressive focus on sporting pursuits have burned, browsed, and broken this landscape.

Potential for impact

There are significant opportunities to restore degraded peat, using innovative and non-synthetic, site-won materials. This includes applying proven river restoration techniques to peatland recovery, integrating the addition of large wooden debris. Following numerous fact-finding trips to ancient peat bogs in northern Scotland, we have observed naturally occurring examples of large wooden debris (think tree trunks and stumps) acting as nuclei for the damming and coagulations of materials within especially deep and wide peat hags. We intend to explore the use of these techniques to help nature kick-start its own peatland recovery.

We are desperate to see trees back in this place. By restoring native, broadleaf woodland – initially in gills and cloughs – we can create new habitats and improve water quality in the headwaters of multiple water bodies. This will also help to regulate water temperature and build the area's resilience to the impacts of climate change.

The impacts of flooding are all too real for the communities in and around Newcastleton, and the absence of vegetation from the hills and upper slopes is a key part of this problem. We want to help, and we believe the planting of extensive, native broadleaf woodland will:

- Increase interception
- Increase the natural storage capacity of the uplands
- Slow the flow of water

This will help the rivers and their flood plains operate in the way nature intended.

We are committed to bringing structural and ecological diversity to the moorland fringe habitats, to support the reintroduction of even the most common examples of UK wildlife. This includes birds, bees, and butterflies; and, maybe even one day, more iconic keystone species such as the Eurasian lynx, blue hare, and pine marten.

Above all, we believe the greatest impact we can achieve will be through working in partnership with the local community.

Social impact

Earlier this year we had the opportunity to meet many local residents and members of the community at our welcome event, immediately following the acquisition of the site. The openness, kindness, and hope that we were met with was genuinely humbling.

One of the leading members of the local community council explained to me that his son and young family had moved away to find work, fearing this often forgotten place offered little in terms of opportunity. He said we were the ideal buyers of the landscape and that we had given him hope that, while he'd lost one son from the community, he didn't want anyone else to lose another.

We fundamentally believe that if we help restore the very building blocks of nature, the wider environment and the community can be built on these foundations. We want to create opportunities for more people to visit, live, and work in and around Blackburn and Hartsgarth. Our current plans are as follows:

- We will work to create wilderness-based sustainable tourism experiences and opportunities and have already partnered with leading wild camping specialists CampWild to offer incredible nature-based adventures. These will include embracing the unique dark skies and spellbinding celestial performances of this area.

- We will explore the development of renewable energy potential so we can not only restore nature but also reenergise the local community.

- At Hartsgarth Farm and Blackburn Farm we will invest in the redevelopment of significant rural properties, exploring ways of improving the environmental performance of these homes and buildings, which are sadly no longer serving an active role in the community.

Brush strokes

Blackburn and Hartsgarth is a superb blank canvas of a landscape, offering perhaps the most potential for positive impact of all the estates in the Oxygen Conservation portfolio.

Landscapes, like the canvas of the original impressionist painters, are so rare and precious that they should never be considered used, done, or finished. Instead, with time, patience, passion, and determination, we will continue to partner, innovate, and iterate until we've delivered genuinely positive impact for people and wildlife.

UNVEILING THE POTENTIAL: TRANSFORMING A BLANK CANVAS

On reflection

I'm writing this reflection on my way back to visit Blackburn and Hartsgarth with the wonderful team at Triodos Bank that helped us build the world's largest conservation-focused debt-funding package that made this acquisition possible. You can read more about that later in the book.

When I think back on this piece, I realise how much we've learned in so little time. That includes appreciating the careful balance that needs to be struck between being honest about the state of the natural world and respectful to the people who see things differently. What is ecologically desolate from our perspective might be perfectly balanced to those passionate about sheep farming and preserving their way of life. People can look at the same thing in a number of different ways.

The interest we've enjoyed at Blackburn and Hartsgarth has been fascinating. We've appeared on the front page of the local newspaper regularly, including attracting a headline that caused the team great hilarity – 'Oxygen Man and the Trailing Ban' – when we declined permission for people to trail hunt across the land.

Contradictions and Compromises in Conservation

Written May 2023

In today's complex world the challenges of climate collapse, biodiversity crisis, and our relationship with the natural world demand our immediate attention. Recognising this complexity, we all still strive for simplicity. This means we often oversimplify the intricacies of environmental issues, leading to a loss of meaning and limiting our effectiveness in achieving progress, never mind finding actual solutions. Conservation efforts in particular require us to constantly grapple with contradictions and compromises.

The ever-present contradictions

In this article we will explore several examples (experienced at Oxygen Conservation) that highlight the delicate balance we must strike between competing priorities in environmental conservation.

Balancing access and preservation

Ensuring that the environment is accessible to all while also protecting its delicate ecosystems presents a significant challenge. We want everyone to enjoy nature, but the presence of people, vehicles, and recreational activities can damage flora, fauna, funga, and the very composition of the ground. Consequently, we face the dual imperative of making the environment more accessible to a broader audience while also safeguarding it against potential harm. This is one of the reasons our national parks and their leadership teams have a virtually impossible task. Some of the main challenges are outlined below.

The tree dilemma

The importance of planting more trees is indisputable. However, finding suitable land for afforestation becomes increasingly challenging when we consider competing needs such as agriculture, conservation of existing habitats, and energy generation and development. Additionally, the use of plastic tree guards – often required for securing grant support – contradicts our efforts to reduce plastic waste and prevent its breakdown into microplastics, which can infiltrate our water systems and food chain.

Managing invasive species

The ethical dilemma arises when we acknowledge the need to manage non-native invasive species that pose a threat to our most precious ecosystems. While we believe it is wrong to harm living creatures, addressing the impact of invasive species like mink on river systems, especially on water voles and other small mammals, becomes imperative.

Striking a balance between ecological preservation and the management of invasive species requires careful consideration and the collection of compelling data. There almost always has to be a compromise somewhere.

Native flora and chemical intervention

Removing invasive plants such as rhododendron, to promote the growth of native flora (especially around our incredible Atlantic rainforest), often necessitates chemical injection or mechanical excavation and burning. However, these methods conflict with our commitment to organic land management and our obligation to reduce carbon emissions.

Finding a solution that allows native woodlands to recover without compromising environmental and health concerns becomes a complex trade-off.

Agriculture and environmental impact

Farming plays a critical role in ensuring food security, but conventional practices often harm the environment, destroying wildlife and impacting soil health. Paradoxically, these conventional practices increasingly jeopardise the very food security we strive to protect.

Balancing the need for sustainable farming practices with environmental preservation is essential for achieving a harmonious coexistence, but this requires landowners and farmers to compromise and change.

Preserving heritage and ecosystems

Historic weirs and structures in rivers, like those found in Bath and Ludlow, are cherished for their cultural and architectural significance. However, these structures act as barriers to migratory fish and hinder the attainment of good ecological status in our rivers. Removing them could improve the natural environment but would have significant cultural and, very likely, structural implications. Finding common ground between conservation and cultural heritage preservation remains a challenging task, especially where the obvious compromises would almost certainly have worse consequences. The installation of engineered fish passes would require vast amounts of natural resources and produce significant carbon emissions. It would also lock these passages in place as a result of the additional public funds likely used to install them.

The sad truth is that these structures rarely work. Where they do, their success is short-lived and possible only under a narrow range of flow conditions.

Respecting local perspectives

Respecting local people's views and opinions regarding the natural environment is crucial, but defining what *local* means and reconciling diverse perspectives within communities can be daunting, and sometimes even impossible. The truth is also that in many communities it is local land management practices that have resulted in environmental damage and ecological loss. An example is the burning of moorland to support upland grazing (or, more accurately, to access or profit from subsidies). Practices such as this can hold cultural importance yet have adverse ecological consequences, exemplifying the intricate balance required when managing conflicting interests.

How do we find the compromise in the apparent contradiction? I'm still working on that one.

We greatly appreciate those people that take the time to reach out to us and offer their views, whether this is via our website or social media channels, by email, or in person. We won't always agree, but we will always listen.

Sports and biodiversity

In my opinion, engaging in activities that involve raising, stocking, and killing living things for sports is inappropriate. These activities do, however, hold a significance importance for some, particularly in rural communities. The creation of environments optimised for specific species like grouse or pheasants inevitably have significant negative ecological implications.

The custodians of these landscapes are absolutely committed to the preservation and conservation of the environment that they feel is appropriate for the landscapes. From an environmentalist perspective, this is perhaps the greatest contradiction, as we would welcome the restoration of natural processes over the forced management of a landscape. Recognising the importance of cultural heritage while promoting biodiversity recovery requires navigating many similar contradictions and searching for compromises inherent in this context.

The complexity of organic farming

Raising awareness about the benefits of organic farming has become increasingly important in recent years, and we're committed to all our land becoming organic.

However, the transition to organic practices often comes with its own set of challenges and contradictions. While organic farming promotes biodiversity and reduces reliance on harmful chemicals, the process itself can sometimes contribute to a higher carbon footprint. This applies especially during the transition period, when supplementary feed might be necessary and only available from further afield.

Organic farming requires careful management to ensure that the ecological gains outweigh the potential environmental trade-offs. It is essential to find innovative solutions to minimise carbon emissions during the transition phase and maintain sustainable practices in the long run.

Moving forward

The examples provided above are merely a glimpse into the myriad of contradictions and compromises faced on a daily basis by environmentalists and conservationists. In the realm of environmental conservation, absolute rights and wrongs are rare, while navigating complex trade-offs becomes the norm. Balancing the competing demands of accessibility and preservation, native flora and chemical interventions, cultural heritage and ecological integrity, and various other dilemmas requires constant dialogue, critical thinking, and a commitment to collaboration.

Acknowledging these contradictions and compromises does not mean succumbing to inaction or accepting defeat. Instead, that acknowledgement is an invitation to engage in thoughtful conversations, evaluate the potential consequences of our actions, and seek innovative solutions. The path towards sustainable environmental conservation will undoubtedly involve difficult choices and compromises, which might themselves appear contradictory.

The reality

In the environment sector, contradictions and compromises are a constant reality. Achieving long-term sustainability and conservation goals requires us to navigate the complexities and challenges posed by competing interests. By recognising and addressing these contradictions, we are trying to develop strategies that strike a balance between often conflicting priorities (and apparent hypocrisy, often including our own).

Although there are few easy answers or universally agreed-on solutions, our commitment to delivering positive environmental impact for people and the environment will continue to shape our guiding principles in our mission to Scale Conservation.

On reflection

Navigation of the many contradictions and compromises continues to inform every day at Oxygen Conservation. In reality, however, very few absolute rights and absolute wrongs remain in a world far too complicated for simple solutions.

The Unsettling Truth About UK Land Use

Written October 2023

Almost every week we encounter versions of the same argument: that there is no room for conservation, and that we need all the land we have for feeding people.

These discussions – usually accompanied by claims that conservation, especially tree planting, is displacing farming – are often voiced by the very farmers looking to sell their land. They argue that conventional farming is no longer economically viable, and that the next generation isn't interested in pursuing it. Still, though, they blame conservation.

To address this debate, we've delved into the existing literature this month to understand the realities about land use in the UK.

At Oxygen Conservation our ambition is to manage at least 250,000 acres (just over 0.4%) of the UK to Scale Conservation and deliver positive environmental and social impact. Let's think, though, about how might this affect overall land use, and whether it could unintentionally affect our ability to feed ourselves.

Land use in the UK

The United Kingdom boasts approximately 60 million acres of diverse land types. In England, for example:

- 23.5 million acres (63.1%) are allocated to agriculture
- 7.5 million acres (20.1%) are designated as forestry, open land, and water
- 3.25 million acres (8.7%) are developed
- 1.8 million acres (4.9%) serve as residential gardens (DLUHC, 2022)

Somewhere within this patchwork mosaic, approximately 1.3 million acres (4% of England) are dedicated to grouse moors (Shrubsole, 2016), of a total 2.6 million acres (almost 8%) across the UK (Macdonald, 2019). Nearly 700,000 acres (1.8%) are allocated to golf courses (Allen, 2016).

As I write this article, with these figures in mind, I can only assume that many farmers are also challenging traditional sporting enthusiasts and golfers about their impact on agriculture.

It's important to note that land use figures in the UK can vary, and the sums provided are illustrative. Finch et al (2023) use the figure of 60% for agricultural land (35.8 million acres), while Defra (2023) suggests 71% (42.7 million acres), and Savills (2019) claims 72% (43.5 million acres). These disparities often stem from whether and where certain land types like heather, bog, and fen are included (Heal et al, 2023).

Agricultural land breakdown

Agricultural land in the UK is broken down roughly as follows:

- 72% of agricultural land is covered in grass, 26% in cropland, and the remainder set aside or left fallow (Defra, 2023).
- Arable land consists of 60% cereals, with wheat accounting for 54% of this category.
- Grassland accommodates 1.6 million dairy cows and their followers with an average herd size of approximately 140 cows.

Additionally, there are 1.4 million breeding beef cattle and their followers, with an average herd size of 80 cows, along with 15 million breeding sheep and their average flocks of 275 ewes. The UK is home to around 192,000 farms, many being family-run units, with only 20% exceeding 250 acres and approximately 50% comprising fewer than 50 acres. Despite this, the larger farms cover three-quarters of the farmland (Savills, 2019).

The decline of UK farmland

The country's total agricultural area has decreased by approximately 64,000 acres per year over the past two decades. This decline can be attributed to factors such as transport infrastructure, property development, woodland expansion (more than doubling over the past twenty years), non-agricultural uses (eg, golf courses, grouse moors, mineral extraction), and land lost to the sea (Savills, 2019).

We treat our soils like dirt

It's not only alternative land uses that are eroding our agricultural land but also agriculture itself. A 2023 report (Defra, 2023) identified that almost 10 million acres of soil are at risk of heavy compaction, severely impacting its capacity to support food growth, sequester carbon, and capture water during intense rainfall. Another 5 million acres of soil are at risk of erosion. This results in nearly 3 million tonnes of soil being lost from agriculture annually, most of which finds its way into rivers and waterways, destroying habitats and endangering wildlife (Environment Agency, 2023).

Food flow in the UK

The UK imports around 46% (Defra, 2023) to 48% (GFS, 2022) of its food from various countries, none of which contribute more than 11% of total imports. In 2020 the UK imported £48 billion worth of food, drink, and feed (yes, for animals), while exporting £21.4 billion (Defra, 2023).

Defra (2016) claims that the UK, based on its production-to-supply ratio, is 76% 'self-sufficient'. This figure would be higher if not for exports (Defra, 2023). Defra recognises the greatest threats to domestic production as climate change, soil degradation, deteriorating water quality, and biodiversity loss. Conservation, rewilding, and land use change don't appear on the list.

For instance, in 2020 wheat yields plummeted by 40% due to heavy rainfall and untimely droughts during the growing season. Although they rebounded in 2021, this demonstrates the potential impact on future food production of increasingly erratic weather patterns, exacerbated by climate change (Defra, 2023).

As a result, I'm left wondering if failing to dedicate sufficient land for nature and conservation – which would help address the challenges caused by climate change and the biodiversity collapse – is not a far bigger risk to agriculture than that perceived by land use change.

Food waste in the UK

When challenged on the impact of land use changes for conservation on agriculture, we often ask the challengers for their thoughts on food waste. To my surprise, this aspect is frequently dismissed as irrelevant or inconsequential, largely because it doesn't fit with the more comfortable narrative that conservation is to blame.

Let's delve further into this perspective. In the UK:

- Approximately 13 million people (nearly one in five) struggle to access sufficient food (The Food Foundation, 2023).

- Around 6.4 million tonnes of edible food, valued at £19 billion and equivalent to 15 billion meals, go to waste each year (House of Lords Library, 2021).

- Of the 6.4 million tonnes of food wasted, roughly 3 million tonnes never even leave the farms on which they are produced (WWF-UK, 2022).

A study by Porter et al (2018) revealed that up to 31% of fruit and vegetable produce is discarded on farms merely because it doesn't meet aesthetic standards – that's ludicrous! Additionally, British farmers have reported that crops are often left unpicked because market prices don't justify the expense of harvesting (Bowman and O'Sullivan, 2018).

If this edible food that never left the farm was no longer wasted, it would represent the equivalent of an additional 2.3 million acres of food production that could be available to benefit the UK population. For context, this is equivalent to additional land, half the land area of Wales, being made available for agriculture, with no additional environmental impact or emissions.

On-farm food waste also contributes roughly 10% of greenhouse gas emissions from UK farming (WWF-UK, 2022). The root of many issues related to climate change and biodiversity collapse lies in our choices and behaviours. We've developed unrealistic expectations regarding the aesthetic appearance of food and are unwilling to pay the true cost of food. This undoubtedly results in excessive food waste and unpicked produce, contributing to many farms becoming economically unviable.

In a broader context, Jeswani et al (2021) found that:

- About a quarter (13.1 million tonnes) of the 58.7 million tonnes of food consumed in the UK is wasted each year throughout the entire supply chain.
- Almost half of this waste (46%) occurs at the consumption stage, with about a third (28%) being lost in the primary production stages.
- Manufacturing and distribution contribute 17% and 9%, respectively, to the total waste.
- Despite accounting for only 10% of overall food waste, meat and fish have the most significant

impact on total life cycle environmental effects. This waste results in 5.9% of national greenhouse gas emissions (27 million tonnes of CO_2 equivalent per year).

Household food waste in the UK is responsible for 3% of greenhouse gas emissions (Chapagain and James, 2011) and 6% of the nation's water footprint (WRAP, 2015). Almost half of avoidable food waste (48%) is discarded due to not being used in time; 31% is thrown away because of large servings and leftovers, 14% due to personal dislikes for certain foods, and 4% due to accidents such as freezer failure (WRAP, 2013).

Creating space for conservation

Finch et al (2023) assert that to achieve net-zero emissions by 2050, the land area allocated for farming must shrink by an additional 22% (around 5 million acres). This reduction is necessary to make space for woodland creation and peatland restoration. Meeting the net-zero target also necessitates up to 17% of land currently used for livestock feed to be transitioned to produce food for humans. This shift would require substantial reductions in food waste and a more significant adoption of plant-based diets. For instance, to approach net zero, we'd need:

- A 37% decrease in beef, lamb, and dairy consumption

- A 29% reduction in pork, poultry, and egg consumption

- A subsequent 13% increase in plant-based product consumption (Finch et al, 2023)

It is important to note that land use choices don't have to be binary, and we recognise that a conservation-focused approach to land management can (and in many places should) also include regenerative agriculture. At Oxygen Conservation this will most commonly include a small number of organic, rare-breed grazing animals, as well as organic arable and agroforestry enterprises. The commercial viability of each of these enterprises remains challenging and is often reliant on highly skilled, experienced individuals working in these rural businesses. We're fortunate to partner with some of the very best, but the environment sector needs many more of these people. How we help find, develop, and support them is an article for another day.

Changes of this type and magnitude are understandably unsettling to many, especially to people later in life or those who enjoy their current lifestyle. The reality is that if we don't make the choices to prioritise the natural world, the choice will no longer be ours. The floods, the fires, the failures of entire ecosystems, and eventually the collapse of our economic system are coming, and they are coming quickly.

Cause and effect

The responsibility for achieving net zero and halting the biodiversity crisis should not be levied on any individual group of people or any one industry. Instead, we must all look in the mirror and challenge our daily decisions and choices because, in so many ways, the challenges we face are of our own making. Many of us waste too much food. Many of us – including me – eat too much meat. Many of us don't pay the real costs for the food we eat; in fact, virtually none of us do, if we're honest with ourselves. That said, archaic subsidy schemes have incentivised production at all costs and resulted in significant declines in the rural environment, landscape, and economy. Now these subsidies are being taken away, rendering a commercially unviable industry completely fucked. Perhaps, then, it isn't all our fault – the supermarkets and the government hold some of this responsibility too.

Whether we can articulate it as such, we are all scared about the effects of climate change and the impacts it will have, in one way or another, on our way of life. The same goes for environmentalists and farmers.

Nature-based solutions

Land use change and nature-based solutions are not a threat to food production. They're a solution for a more regenerative future for people and wildlife. If we do not create more space for nature, for people, and for wildlife, our entire agricultural system and ecosystem will collapse under the weight of our own ignorance, incompetence, and arrogance.

Unfortunately, the government has set largely unambitious targets for nature in its twenty-five-year environment plan, and yet they clearly don't even intend to hit those targets! They claimed they would dedicate a further 1 million acres for conservation by 2030, and they won't. They aren't even going to try. I can assure you that we are!

On reflection

It must be a terribly scary time to be a farmer. The subsidy systems that have provided an element of certainty are rapidly disappearing, and the effects of climate change are becoming all too real. At the time of writing, it has rained almost continually across the UK so far in 2024, and this could quite possibly (though I hope not) be followed by summer droughts. Farmers are scared, and they're angry – angry at the supermarkets, angry at the food system, and angry at the government for not doing anything to help. They're also increasingly angry at environmentalists for highlighting the truth they don't want to face: the truth that all our lives have changed as a result of climate change and the biodiversity crisis.

The arguments about food security, together with the ridiculous claims that alternative land uses like conservation or renewable energy will mean the end of food production in the UK, unfortunately won't help, as they're just not true.

We are living through increasing levels of obesity, and we waste more food than ever before – the equivalent of more than 2 million acres of food production every year. This isn't about food security. It's about fear – fear of the loss of a way of life we've loved and have now lost.

It's a fear we will all face at some point in the not-too-distant future. We either change the way we live or have change forced on us. At Oxygen Conservation we're choosing to be an agent of change.

Birds, Bees, Butterflies, and an Explosion of Voles

Written July 2023

Earlier this week I had the opportunity to visit Swineley Farm in Widdale in the Yorkshire Dales for the first time in almost a year.

When we purchased the farm a little over eighteen months ago, we found a landscape that perfectly encapsulates much of the Yorkshire Dales. The fields were overgrazed by too many sheep, the meadows were decimated, the wetter areas were eroding, trees were almost completely absent, and the environment sat silent.

A transformation

Our return visit could not have been more different, thanks to the excellent work of the Oxygen Conservation team, led by our estate custodian and senior ecologist, Simon Stainer. The land was once again alive in every way.

The process

Our commitment when we acquire a new site is always to look, listen, and learn as much as possible. This includes working in partnership with local landowners, groups, and specialists to establish ecological, social, and economic baselines. At Swineley this includes: extensive ecological assessments, soil sampling, and peatland mapping.

Once those were completed, much of our initial work focused on removing barriers to natural processes, giving nature the space and time it needs to recover. The great news is it needs much less time than we might have thought.

We have removed the significant grazing pressures, including sheep from the hillside. We also removed artificial chemical and fertiliser, decades of discarded material, and significant lengths of redundant fence lines. The very act of removing these barriers began the process of ecological restoration. Only once you've removed the bad can you begin to offer assistance towards a better environment.

Our work has included:

- Working in partnership with Natural England on the design and development of a new, improved countryside stewardship scheme

- Partnering with the neighbouring landowner to graze the hay meadow site of special scientific interest; in the process supporting the production of wonderful, high-quality local produce

- Creating extensive buffer strips around the Widdale Beck and planting 5,000 trees to help control water temperatures and create new habitats and havens for wildlife, in partnership with the Yorkshire Dales Millennium Trust and the Woodland Trust

We have plans in place to plant a further 60,000 trees in the autumn to create fantastic areas of wood pasture as we help nature create its own mosaic of habitats across this remarkable part of the Yorkshire Dales.

The outcome

Our work across the landscape has also seen scrapes and hollows naturally fill with water again, keeping much-needed water within the landscape, thereby creating places for birds, bats, and bugs of every kind.

When we returned to Swineley earlier this week, the place could not have been more different. It sang, danced, jumped, and flew with birds, bees, and butterflies. Barn owls swooped across the hills, feasting on the explosion of voles, which were rapidly darting through the tall grasses. All of this was watched on by the cattle grazing in specific compartments where the land needed that most.

Everything – the look, feel, smell, and sound – was transformed. You could hardly believe this was the same Swineley we visited just a few months ago.

On this fabulous adventure that is Oxygen Conservation, I never fail to be amazed by just how quickly wildlife returns and nature begins to restore itself, if only we give it a chance.

On reflection

Swineley continues to change, and for the better. We've now successfully planted more than 60,000 trees in this formerly forgotten landscape, targeting the riparian corridor to provide shelter and structural diversity to the watercourses that criss-cross Swineley Farm. We've also added more wetland scrapes and, following the discovery of white-clawed crayfish, created a unique arc site. This is an offline refuge for the threatened and protected white-clawed crayfish that call the Widdale Beck (part of the Ure Catchment) home.

None of this would have been possible without the spectacular leadership of Simon Stainer, our former Senior Ecologist, who for almost two years achieved so much for the environment across the Oxygen Conservation portfolio. Simon has now moved on to his next adventure to ensure he can reduce his travel burden and spend more time at home with his wife and daughters. My only wish is that we could have had the opportunity to work with Simon earlier in his career and for much longer.

One final story before we leave Swineley: we almost lost this acquisition when I was misidentified as Chris Packham! The selling agent called us late in the process to ask that we officially confirm that I was neither Chris Packham nor acting on his behalf. I've never met Chris, but I do know that he's sixty-two years old and 6ft tall, weighs 72kg, and is clean-shaven. I am forty years old, 5ft 7in, 105kg, and have a full beard!

Why We Buy Land

Written spring 2024

Our work is about delivering positive environmental and social impact. Generating a profit is a result of what we do, not the purpose.

Why buying land is integral to our ethos and practice

We're often asked if we will consider leasing land in support of our mission to Scale Conservation, and our answer is always the same: we only buy land. Here are the seven main reasons why:

1. Long-term commitment to positive impact
2. Time and space for restoration of natural processes
3. Holistic approach to land management
4. Development of natural capital as an additive
5. Investment returns and downside protection

6. Simplification of landscape-level change

7. Respect for others' choices

1. Long-term commitment to positive impact

Environmental restoration and social impact are not overnight phenomena. They are gradual processes that unfold over years, if not generations.

Buying land allows us to commit fully to these long-term goals without the constraints of lease terms or the shifting priorities of different landowners. Our ownership ensures continuity in our efforts to nurture and protect the land, aligning with our vision of enduring positive change.

2. Time and space for restoration of natural processes

Restoring natural processes, for example by rewilding landscapes or rehabilitating ecosystems, demands both time and space. These processes cannot be rushed.

Owning the land gives us the freedom to allow natural processes to evolve at their own pace, free from the pressures of lease expiration dates or the need to show immediate results to landlords.

3. Holistic approach to land management

When we own land we can manage it holistically, considering all aspects of the ecosystem.

This approach ensures that every decision we make is in the best interest of the land and both its human and non-human inhabitants. As landowners we can plan for the long term, implementing sustainable practices that balance ecological improvements with community needs and financial return.

4. Development of natural capital as an additive

Owning land allows us to focus on developing natural capital in ways that enrich the landscape and benefit rural communities.

This approach sees the land not just as a resource to be used, but as a living, breathing entity that contributes to the wellbeing of the ecosystem and the people who live within it.

5. Investment returns and downside protection

From an investment perspective, owning land offers tangible returns and provides a safeguard against potential losses as natural capital markets develop.

As custodians of the land, we can ensure its value is enhanced through regenerative practices, increasing its worth not only economically but also ecologically and socially.

6. Simplification of landscape-level change

Owning land simplifies the process of making significant changes at the landscape level.

Without the need to negotiate with landlords or adhere to the restrictions of a lease, we can implement large-scale environmental improvement more efficiently and effectively.

7. Respect for others' choices

Purchasing land achieves and respects the wishes of those who have owned and cared for it before us. Many landowners are emotionally attached to their land and the way it's used, which has often developed over many generations.

Supporting a landowner's wishes to sell respects their right as an asset owner, offering them the opportunity to pursue the next chapter of life. It also avoids the emotional challenges that might arise from seeing the land used differently under a lease.

In short: Why we buy land

Our commitment to buying land is rooted in our dedication to long-term positive environmental and social impact. It allows us the time, space, and flexibility needed to:

- Restore natural processes
- Develop natural capital
- Implement significant landscape-level changes

This approach not only benefits the environment and rural communities; it also aligns with our investment strategies. By owning the land, we become genuine partners with nature, working towards a regenerative and, hopefully, flourishing future.

On reflection

We're committed to Scaling Conservation and believe that owning land is the only way of achieving the scale and pace of change we need in the battle against climate change and biodiversity collapse. It's that simple.

The Greening of the Glen: A New Era in Scottish Estate Ownership

Written spring 2024

The rolling hills and rugged landscapes of Scotland have long been the canvas for tales of history and tradition. Integral to this narrative are Scotland's large estates, often spanning many thousands of acres. For generations these estates have been the bastions of the wealthy, who sought them for both leisure and as status symbols.

Don't believe me? Just ask Evelyn Channing, the fantastic head of rural agency at Savills, who has an almost unparalleled thirty-five years of experience of living, working, and playing among this magnificent landscape. During her recent *Shoot Room Sessions* podcast recording session (Stockdale, 2024a), when asked how the market for large Scottish estates had changed in recent years, Evelyn said:

> 'Extraordinarily! … It is the biggest change I've seen. … Estates are being repurposed. During the 90s and 00s the fund manager with their city

bonus was prevalent in the market. Perhaps some questioned the merits of owning an estate with all the complexities of its management when they could rent the sport as an alternative and sun themselves in the Caribbean! The world has become a much smaller place in which to spend one's leisure time.'

Evelyn added:

'To have a new style of buyer in the market with different motives has been transformational. We used to joke about valuing rock and fresh air – now there is value attached to that rock and fresh air! It is exciting – land potentially is one of the solutions to the climate crisis and biodiversity loss.'

As the world enters a new era of climate consciousness and environmental awareness, the profile of Scottish estate ownership is undergoing a significant transformation.

Traditional Scottish estates: A legacy of leisure and perceived luxury

Historically, Scottish estates have been synonymous with luxury, decadence, and traditional sporting pursuits. Purchased by the affluent, these lands served as retreats where the elite engaged in hunting, shooting, and fishing. They symbolised a blend of wealth, tradition, and social status. The typical owner was often a high-profile banker or businessperson, using their substantial annual bonuses to invest in these vast tracts of land as little more than a plaything. In the words of Bob Dylan: the times, they are a-changin'.

The turning tide: Environmental awareness and land stewardship

The twenty-first century has ushered in a heightened consciousness, not only about the climate but also more generally – an ever-growing awareness of the environment and our role in preserving it. This global shift in perspective is increasingly evident in the way large estates are viewed and managed. Where once the emphasis was on sport, now there is a growing focus on conservation, biodiversity, and sustainable land use.

Traditional sporting activities and associated land management practices are no longer considered appropriate or acceptable to many – killing for fun is increasingly viewed as brutal, barbaric, and backward. A 2024 poll found that only one in ten Britons (10%) support allowing hunting for purely recreational purposes, while trophy hunting is seen as acceptable by just 4%, with nine in ten Britons (92%) viewing such behaviour as unacceptable (Difford, 2024).

The new guardians: Conservationists and environmentalists

The demographic of Scottish estate owners is changing rapidly, and in the last few years it has become markedly different. The new generation of estate owners are more concerned with the future of their lands and its impact on people and wildlife.

Conservation groups, environmental NGOs, individuals committed to ecological causes, and exciting new businesses focused on growing and protecting natural capital (yes, including Oxygen Conservation) have objectives to:

- Protect and restore natural habitats, including peatlands
- Reintroduce native wildlife
- Promote ecological diversity

Many of these groups recognise the complexity of these landscapes, in seeking to help rewild the land. This approach marks a significant departure from the traditional management of these estates.

Transforming landscapes: From hunting grounds to havens of biodiversity

The shift in ownership is transforming the Scottish countryside. Estates that were once manicured, manipulated, and mutilated for shooting parties are now being rewilded. Native broadleaf woodlands are being created, peatlands restored, and native wildlife species reintroduced. The transformation is not just ecological; it is reshaping the cultural and social landscape, helping rural Scotland realise its potential to become the natural capital capital of the world.

For too many years Scotland's rural communities have seen an exodus of talent, as the brightest young people have been forced away by the absence of opportunity, investment, and ambition. This has been exacerbated by the loudest, protectionist few seeking to stop any form of progress or development, instead opting to enjoy their vision of the slowly decaying communities and rapidly decaying landscape.

This was very much the sentiment of the incredibly talented Chloe Finlayson, chief creative officer of the leading natural capital marketplace platform Kana Earth. Born and raised minutes away from our wonderful

Invergeldie Estate in Perthshire, Chloe moved away for university and later found herself relocating to London for career advancement and opportunity. Chloe shared how she felt it was impossible to maintain the status quo and also ensure young people both wanted to and were able to remain part of small rural communities.

Chloe was, however, much more positive when stating that a shift to a natural capital economy could provide the aspiration, inspiration, and opportunity these places and communities require.

Visiting Invergeldie recently for her own *Shoot Room Sessions* podcast interview (which we unfortunately could not release due to technical difficulties), Chloe said; 'I think in a modern-day world you need change. Everything isn't the same anymore. There are new industries, new ways of farming. I think people need to be open to that change to get younger people to stay. Everyone young thinks they have to move away to the city. They think they must move to London or to Glasgow. To keep them, there must be more industry, and that requires change.'

Chloe added, 'We need change. The way we have been growing businesses as usual isn't working anymore. The climate is changing right in front of us. Even in my lifetime, which doesn't seem that long, it has changed.'

In Scotland a remarkable transformation is underway as traditional estates evolve to embrace ecological conservation and community-focused initiatives. This shift is not only about land management. It also represents a profound change in values and a reimagining of the role these vast tracts of land can play in the twenty-first century.

The next generation of owners

Alladale Wilderness Reserve

One of the most notable examples of this transformation is the Alladale Wilderness Reserve, spread across 23,000 acres in the Scottish Highlands. Once a typical hunting estate, it has been re-envisioned by owner Paul Lister as a haven for wildlife and a centre for ecological restoration. The reserve's ambitious plans include:

- Reintroducing native species such as wolves and bears, long absent from the landscape
- Actively engaged in habitat restoration, including regenerating native forests and revitalising peatlands and river systems
- Serving as a hub for research and education, hosting various scientific studies and educational programmes focusing on conservation

Langholm Moor

Langholm Moor, where a community group has successfully purchased a large area from the Buccleuch Estate, provides another inspiring story. This initiative marked a significant shift in landownership, from private hands to community stewardship.

The community's primary goal is to manage the land for the benefit of both the local population and wildlife, emphasising sustainable practices like peatland restoration and woodland creation. This move towards a community-led approach to managing and benefitting from natural resources is a testament to the changing perception and value of land in Scotland.

Carrifran Wildwood

Another example of community-led land purchase is the Carrifran Wildwood near Moffat. In 1993 this was conceived by the Wildwood Group, primarily local volunteers, and later became the Borders Forest Trust with a land purchase completed in January 2000.

Now Carrifran is a leap back in time. Trees thrive from the valley floor to the sub-montane zone, flowers have moved downhill from crags and scree without the pressure of grazing, and the valley breathes with new life. It is a staggering achievement in so short a time, led and driven by a few people with vision and an attitude of *Yes, we can do this*.

Dundreggan Conservation Estate

Trees for Life's Dundreggan Conservation Estate in the Highlands offers a different perspective on ecological restoration. This estate is being transformed into one of Scotland's most significant rewilding projects.

The focus here is on restoring the Caledonian Forest, which once covered much of Scotland but is now limited to fragmented remnants. Trees for Life is actively involved in planting native trees, restoring natural habitats, and reintroducing native species. The estate serves not only as a conservation area but also as an educational resource, offering volunteer opportunities and educational programmes to involve the community and visitors in the rewilding process.

These cases reflect a broader trend in Scotland, where large estates – traditionally seen as symbols of sporting decadence – are increasingly recognised as vital resources for conservation and community development. This shift has significant economic and social implications:

- Economically, it opens up avenues for regenerative revenue through ecotourism, rewilding, and renewable energy initiatives.
- Socially, it fosters a deeper sense of shared ownership and stewardship of the land.

The movement towards eco-focused estates in Scotland is a pioneering example of how private land can contribute to the public good, blending tradition with a vision for a regenerative and more inclusive future.

This paradigm shift is not without its critics. Traditional estate activities, especially game shooting, are often reported to provide significant revenue generation in rural communities, although this is often challenged:

- Many local communities argue that the only people that benefit are the estate owners themselves, with limited economic spillover into the local economy.
- Critics point out that, while estates may employ local staff and contribute to certain local businesses, the overall impact is frequently less substantial than portrayed.
- The seasonal nature of traditional estate activities often results in inconsistent and unreliable income streams for the local workforce.
- There's the contention that large estates, focused on game shooting, can monopolise land use, restricting opportunities for broader community-based economic activities such as ecotourism, agriculture, or renewable energy projects, which might offer more sustainable and widespread benefits to the local population.

This debate highlights the complex and multifaceted impact of traditional estate activities on rural economies and communities, suggesting the need for a more nuanced understanding and balanced approach to land use and economic development in these areas.

Moreover, the concept of land ownership for ecological stewardship is often at odds with traditional views on land use, sparking debates over land rights and management practices. There are a vocal few who want to see the land continue to be bent to their will, grazed, beaten, and burned, to produce a patchwork landscape for hunting, giving little thought to the environmental, ecological, or economic cost of doing so. When asked why, the two most prevalent answers I've personally heard are *Because we've always done it* and *Because I don't want things to change*. What we've always done and not wanting things to change are also two of the main reasons our climate is in chaos and biodiversity is collapsing!

Future development

The future buyers of Scottish estates are likely to be even more diverse, encompassing not only conservationists and environmental NGOs but also a new wave of entrepreneurs and investors, who understand the intrinsic value of natural capital. This new breed of owners is expected to prioritise sustainability, ecological restoration, and community involvement.

Technological innovators and eco-entrepreneurs

We are likely to see a rise in interest from technology entrepreneurs and green innovators. These individuals and groups, driven by a passion for sustainable living and ecological innovation, may view Scottish estates as ideal grounds for experimenting with and demonstrating green technologies such as renewable energy sources, sustainable agriculture, and ecological monitoring systems.

Global investors with a green focus

The increasing global focus on environmental issues will likely attract international investors interested in contributing to global conservation efforts. These buyers might see Scottish estates as opportunities to invest in large-scale rewilding projects or carbon-offset initiatives, aligning their financial interests with global environmental goals.

Community cooperatives and collaborative ownership

A significant shift might occur towards more communal forms of ownership. Community cooperatives, where local residents collectively own and manage estate lands, could become more prevalent. This model promotes local engagement, ensuring that the benefits of land stewardship directly impact the surrounding communities.

Educational and research institutions

There may be an increase in ownership by educational and research institutions seeking living laboratories for studying environmental science, conservation, and sustainable land management practices. These institutions could use the estates as sites for groundbreaking research and as educational resources for students and the public.

A sustainable legacy for Scottish estates

The future of Scottish estate ownership is set to be dynamic and diverse, reflecting broader global shifts towards sustainability and environmental responsibility. The estates of tomorrow will likely be managed with a keen awareness of their role in ecological preservation, carbon sequestration, and community engagement.

Rewilding and rewriting the narrative of Scottish estates

The changing profile of Scottish estate owners is more than just a shift in property deeds. It represents a deeper change in values and priorities, reflecting a growing global consciousness about our relationship with the environment. As this trend continues, Scottish estates are poised to become exemplars of how private land can contribute to the holistic public good, helping Scotland become the natural capital capital of the world.

On reflection

There is much discussion about community land ownership in Scotland at the time of writing, and a new piece of legislation is entering the Scottish Parliament that will make it harder for private investment to acquire land to deliver positive environmental and social impact. While I recognise the significant value in community engagement and discussion, I'm yet to see a community ownership model that can operate with the vision, capital, and agility required to deliver meaningful change in the face of the climate collapse and the biodiversity crisis.

My fear is this approach will again see an increasing exodus of the brightest young people, forced away from Scotland by the absence of opportunity, investment, and ambition. This would be a result of the loudest, protectionist few seeking to stop any form of progress or development.

Scotland has a choice to be bold, be ambitious, and aspire to be the natural capital capital of the world. It can be the natural capital economy's Silicon Valley, launching and incubating incredible new businesses (like TreeStory and Caledonian Climate Partners), training and developing the environmentalists of the future, and fuelling this new economy with completely renewable energy.

The predominant thing Scotland needs to do is to choose to give the next generations an economy, a country, and a world to live in and to lead.

TWO
Building The Best Team In The Conservation Industry

Building the *Edie* Team of the Year

Written April 2023

Almost two years ago, Oxygen Conservation was founded with the mission to Scale Conservation, delivering positive environmental and social impact, and generating a profit as a result of our work, not the reason we do it.

Over the last two years, we have built the country's largest genuine environmental investment fund, deploying tens of millions of pounds for the acquisition of almost 30,000 acres across ten different sites, in eight counties and three countries.

It continues to be my belief that if we can grow natural capital and create a genuinely new alternative asset class, we could mobilise the investment we need to save a little of the world. In the process, we could find nature-based solutions to climate change and the biodiversity crisis.

Teamwork

Our success thus far has been possible only because we have assembled the most fantastic team of people – a group of unique high performers from a wide range of backgrounds and experiences. These people are aligned in our mission and united by our culture, despite being geographically disparate.

I'm delighted that their hard work has been recognised, with the team being named in 2023 as the *Edie* Team of the Year. We also know that we're just getting started.

In this article I'm going to tell you how we built the team of the year by focusing on:

1. Vision
2. Talent
3. Commitment to excellence
4. Accountability and feedback
5. Radical transparency
6. Continuous improvement

1. Vision: Create an inspiring ambition

People want to do something that matters. Climate change and the biodiversity crisis are among the most important challenges of our time. As a business, we are therefore fortunate to have an ambition that is inherently inspiring and fundamentally good. We want to Scale Conservation – not just Oxygen Conservation, but the entire movement, market, and industry. The most talented people want an inspiring ambition and to be given the opportunity to embrace it without fear. I love the line from the famous advert: 'Don't ask if your dreams are crazy. Ask if they're crazy enough' (World Class Advertising, 2023).

We have combined our passion for the environment and our love of data and tech, setting our goal to become the world's first conservation-focused unicorn company. *That's one with a valuation of over £1 billion.* The world needs hope, and if we can build our unicorn, the market (and society) will have moved forward so much that we might have a chance of giving the next generation a future on this planet.

We've been fortunate to find people who view these wild ambitions as inspiring and have committed their time, effort, and passion to working towards making it a reality.

2. Talent: Only recruit people better than you

To Scale Conservation, we need to find ways of attracting the most talented people to be part of our team. We need to continuously be recruiting. I'm always on the lookout for brilliant people that can help our business, and we need to compete for them by creating an environment where they can be exceptional and love what they do. This doesn't mean talent is everything, but it is one of the most important things. Another is that we need each team member to be a great person – a concept we've adapted from the New Zealand All Blacks (Kerr, 2013). Our colleagues need to be humble and recognise that no one person is more integral than the collective. They also need to understand that bringing a poor attitude or reacting negatively to their circumstances can have a catastrophic impact on our team's culture and, as a result, our performance as a business.

My rule when it comes to recruitment is for me to recruit only people better than me, in a meaningful way. Being better doesn't need to relate to education, exams, or experience in conservation. This is about recruiting people that challenge themselves and me, push the boundaries, and push themselves to be the best they can be in their field (pun intended).

This approach to recruitment has to be the most obvious thing in business – surely if you're not doing this, you're actively getting worse. We never, ever sacrifice our performance bar. If we don't find an exceptional person, we won't appoint anyone. We owe it to every exceptional person already on our team to find only brilliant people to work alongside them.

3. Commitment to excellence: How you do anything is how you do everything

We have an absolute commitment to excellence and hold ourselves to the mantra *How you do anything is how you do everything*. This doesn't mean we create fake productivity, putting things on the to-do list just to tick them off. It means that if something is important in the pursuit of our ambition, we do it to an exceptional standard. Every detail matters; every decision matters. As soon as you sacrifice the quality of any aspect of your business, you're telling your team, partners, customers, or clients that you will tolerate lower standards and you will compromise. Who wants to work with businesses that operate in that way? We don't.

Let's not pretend this is easy or comfortable. It isn't. It takes time, effort, and sacrifices, but if we're trying to be the best in the world at what we do, or do what many people say is impossible, we have to be prepared to do what others haven't done and aren't prepared to do.

This commitment to excellence is an incredibly powerful self-selection tool when recruiting. We're completely honest about our expectations and the realities of what it means to be part of our team. To make this possible, we involve as many of the team as we can in the process and make the decision as one.

4. Accountability and feedback: Hold everyone to account

We have committed to creating a high-performance culture, so everyone – especially me, as CEO – needs to be held to account.

People often avoid giving challenging feedback or calling out poor performance. While this is easy in the moment, it's cowardly, immediately sacrifices your credibility as a leader, and is a death knell to the performance of a team. It's also often the moment when your highest performers realise the business doesn't share their ambitions and question if they will soon need to leave to fulfil their potential elsewhere.

As a business and as individuals, we are receptive to the opinions of others (even if we don't always agree) and recognise the importance of listening to help us learn, not just to respond.

I know I can only ask the team to work extremely hard if I'm prepared to outwork them. Throughout my career, this has been one of the two consistent performance advantages I've found; the other is continuous learning. I learned these rules from my time playing international sport. I simply had to outwork and outcompete everyone to earn my place on the team, and playing contact sport gave me instant, impactful feedback. I learned lessons fast or spent a lot of time getting up off the floor.

I've carried this principle into business by striving to provide immediate, honest feedback. I've learned from experience that I need to provide this as soon as possible, but only when the other person can hear it and benefit from it. Feedback has to be passed gently, not thrown viciously, and it has to work both ways. We have to immediately praise effort, learning, innovation, and success. Where possible, it's also important to celebrate the response to failure (when trying something new) and sharing the learning that can come from these experiences. This can hurt – sometimes it is mentally and emotionally painful to fail and then review that failure in order to learn. It's only through these experiences, though, that we develop and adapt, similar to how muscles hurt after a workout.

Success is hard. Change is difficult and not often popular, but it's necessary if you want to do something incredible.

5. Radical transparency: Share everything with the team

We share everything with the team, with the only exceptions being where it would be inappropriate to do so, for example due to medical conditions, family situations, or an individual remuneration package. Many of the team choose to share their personal circumstances with their colleagues due to the supportive culture we have built, but that has to be their choice.

How do we achieve this? We open each week with our Mondays at a Blackstone-inspired team call (Blackstone, 2016), where we discuss:

- Every potential acquisition
- The performance of every business (every individual estate)
- All the issues and challenges for the week ahead

Everyone is welcome to join the team call, and all views are equally valued. Ultimately, we tend to reach a consensus, which means I rarely have to overrule the majority with my decision. When I do need to do that – which has, I think, happened only twice in two years – I nonetheless recognise the team's valuable input and am clear that I am responsible for the decisions that have been made.

I cannot expect my team to make great decisions if I'm not going to share the information and the context they need to put their expertise into action. Also, how can I ask people to grow and develop if I don't expose them to new ideas, information, and experiences and make it safe for them to fail forward?

My final transparency rule is that anyone can request anything, as long as the other person has the right to say no. I will answer anything the team asks, but if I say 'I'm sorry, I can't tell you that', they know not to push further.

6. Continuous improvement: Learn from the best

At Oxygen Conservation we're never satisfied and are always looking for ways to improve everything we do. The best way to do this is to borrow ideas from the best in every different field, apply these ideas and concepts to our context, and continue to develop on these ideas and concepts. We constantly take inspiration from high-level sport, iconic businesses, and industries, and awesome individual people and performers.

We believe in making this as easy as possible. We encourage everyone to absorb as much as possible – from physical books, ebooks, audiobooks, video subscriptions, and any other means information can be consumed – and are delighted to pay for those materials. In any business, if a team are asking to learn and improve, largely in their own time, it's vital to buy them whatever they need to do so and to thank them.

Achieving the impossible

Creating and working in a high-performance culture is hard. It's painful emotionally, mentally, and sometimes physically, especially in sport (or where significant travel to our estates is required), but it's necessary if you want to do something incredible.

I'm grateful that over the past two years, we have used and stuck to these principles to build the best team working in the environment sector, united by the shared goal to Scale Conservation. I'm extremely excited to see what they will achieve over the coming months and years. We all need this team to achieve the impossible.

On reflection

Reflecting on this piece, a little over a year after it was first written, I've massively overcomplicated the process.

It's really very simple: we simply needed to hire brilliant people, and we have!

Every day I find myself saying how much I love our team, and I am so grateful they all agreed to come and be part of this adventure.

Lessons Learned from the NFL Draft

Written April 2023 in collaboration with Head of People, Andrew Dewar

We (Oxygen Conservation Head of People Andrew Dewar and I) always loved the NFL draft (NFL, no date), in particular:

- The incredible number of potential permutations
- The fact that a transcendent talent can change the fortunes of an NFL team and an entire city
- The nuance and detail associated with finding that right fit
- The data and information about every aspect of the player, and trying to project that in a different system and context

In our world that translates directly to recruitment. It's the battle to find, attract, and retain the best and the brightest people that fit our system and also help push us forward, improving what we do and how we do it.

Adapting the NFL draft

In some ways, we wish we had the simplicity of the NFL draft: the same structured approach to the process, all data and information available to everyone, and shocking amounts of game tape that we can study and watch to pick patterns to project forward for future performance. We realised, though, that this isn't significant. We'd then just work harder to find ways around that process too, to find opportunities in the system others haven't seen. Here are some of the lessons we've learned and applied to building the team at Oxygen Conservation:

1. Slow recruitment processes
2. First-round picks
3. Character over talent
4. Value others don't see
5. Our own game
6. Unlimited first-round picks

1. Slow recruitment processes

In the NFL, the entire process takes several months (if not years) and includes the whole previous playing season. It looks like this:

- Predraft process (application process)
- NFL combine (interview)
- Visit to the team facility (meetings with the wider team)
- Draft day (job offer)

The process needs to take time because the risk of making a mistake is potentially catastrophic to a team or a business. In terms of the offer, both the NFL and we celebrate the chosen pick (new team member) and work hard to make them feel as excited as possible about the adventure ahead.

Peyton Manning, Andrew Luck, and Trevor Lawrence are all examples of this slow process. They were spotted early; heralded as transcendent talents; and anointed first overall picks, from high school through college and into the NFL.

2. First-round picks

We're a scaling startup, having grown from an idea to almost twenty people, and every one of these people is a first-round pick – the best of the best. They're all special, unique, and could work anywhere in the environment sector. We therefore don't take risks on first-round picks. We don't reach for a player or a role we need, and we definitely do not sacrifice our performance bar. We only select people better than us, in a meaningful way, and we work hard to create an environment (playbook) to make these talented people even more successful.

There are so many examples in the NFL of players over-drafted at positions of need. Most notable are Jamarcus Russell, first overall to the Raiders in 2007; and Ryan Leaf, second overall to the Chargers in 1998. We will see it again this year with a team overreaching for a position of need instead of waiting for a real talent with great character.

3. Character over talent

Every year, super-talented NFL prospects slip down the draft board, losing millions of dollars in the process, because of character or work ethic concerns. Of course, we target incredibly talented people, but not at the expense of character and work ethic. If you're not prepared to work in a high-performance environment and push yourself harder than you've ever worked before, Oxygen Conservation isn't the place for you.

Put simply: talent gets you an interview, character gets you an opportunity, and work ethic keeps you in the team.

For instance, just as the Seattle Seahawks prioritised Russell Wilson's character and leadership qualities when they drafted him in the third round of the 2012 draft, or Jalen Hurts was picked by the Philadelphia Eagles in the second round of the 2020 draft, we look for team members who possess not only talent but also the right character and work ethic to thrive in our organisation.

4. Value others don't see

In the NFL draft everyone wants the prototypical player in terms of height, weight, speed, and where they played football in college (most often the South Eastern Conference). We so often see these same prejudices in business. People want to see a linear path via Oxbridge or Russell Group universities, MBA, or similar; or increasingly in the environment sector, the expectation of several years' volunteering/unpaid work experience.

Just as the New England Patriots found value in late-round picks like Tom Brady and Julian Edelman, we look for hidden potential in unconventional candidates who may bring unique perspectives and skills to our team.

5. Our own game

We don't follow the crowd. We want differences but won't sacrifice our performance bar to get those. Our recent internship programme (December 2022) was explicitly targeted at finding 'the misfits, the rebels, and the crazy ones' – people that want to change the world. We found four brilliant people with completely different backgrounds, experiences, interests, and passions. We have already benefitted from their involvement in so many different ways. If those people are reading this, thank you again!

In the same way that a talented prospect may fall to the later rounds of the draft, in business it's often possible to attract brilliant people with unique backgrounds earlier in their career, at great value to the business, while providing them with a reward package that works for them and that they're delighted to accept.

Do what others don't to find the value others won't.

For example, the San Francisco 49ers traded a considerable number of future picks in the 2021 draft to select Trey Lance, likely overreaching for a talent, likely costing the team several championships if they'd used those same picks on talented players that could have improved the wider team. Fortunately, however, they selected Brock Purdy with the final pick in the final round of the 2022 draft, making him known as that year's 'Mr Irrelevant'. Lance, on the other hand, was traded for a significant loss in picks. Having cost millions while playing only four games in two entire seasons, Purdy won ten games in a row and led the team to the championship game, all while making the league minimum for the next three years until he was eligible for his contract to be renegotiated.

6. Unlimited first-round picks

We are especially glad that we're not limited on the number of top talents – first-round picks – we can take. We want only exceptional talents – people that are better than us, in a meaningful way. In this way our approach most closely mimics that of the famed USC Trojans Team of the 2000s (eleven players drafted in 2006 and 2009); the LSU Tigers of 2020 (with fourteen players drafted); and today's Georgia Bulldogs, with every position filled by a first-round talent (fifteen draft picks in 2022 alone).

We're delighted to say we've got a team full of first-round picks and are in the process of recruiting even more.

If you believe you have what it takes to help us Scale Conservation, we would love to make you our next incredible draft choice.

On reflection

We're constantly looking for ideas, opportunities, and advantages to apply to Oxygen Conservation. High-level sport has always been a powerful teacher, and we will continue watching and learning. This year I've read a lot about the NFL, cricket, football, and F1, learning something different each time.

SCALING CONSERVATION

Reflecting back on this piece, written in partnership with Andrew, I still love the following line. It is as true today as it was when first written.

Put simply: talent gets you an interview, character gets you an opportunity, and work ethic keeps you in the team.

Just Coasting
Written August 2023

Every business talks about culture. Far too often, though, culture is no more than a set of corporate buzzwords, retrospectively pieced together in the boardrooms and corner offices of senior people, so far away from the actual realities of a business that at best it's a distinct memory of the company they once hoped to be.

Cynical? Yes.

Accurate? You tell me.

The Oxygen Conservation culture

When I dreamed about Oxygen Conservation, I wanted to build a business that was about impact, environment, and adventure. I wanted to build a business that borrowed from the best companies like Patagonia, Google, Apple, and Tesla and apply their learning to our purpose: to Scale Conservation.

I've learned first-hand, especially during my time playing competitive sport, how culture is built through shared adventures, experiences, achievements, and hardships.

As I thought about the process of scaling the team, alongside our mission to Scale Conservation, I had a list of shared experiences I believed would create opportunity to develop an authentic culture committed to impact, environment, and adventure.

While we're a completely remote team, we are fortunate to have access to some of the most spectacular natural landscapes the country has to offer, and we are sure to make these a feature of everything we do. We've e-biked alongside the peatland of Perthshire, free-dived in Cornwall, wild swum under waterfalls in the Borders, forest-bathed in the rainforests of Dartmoor, hiked up endless hills, and bagged many a Munro.

I know that many senior leaders, especially in traditional businesses, are working hard to encourage everyone back into the office. I'd caution you to think about this, especially about what the next generation of super-talented people want from work. I've heard from those people that they want purpose, adventure, freedom and flexibility, and opportunities to develop. We want Oxygen Conservation to be the aspirational place to work in the environment sector and beyond, so we're working to provide exactly that.

At Oxygen Conservation, working remotely is a feature – not a bug – of what we do, and we use brilliant shared experiences to build and maintain our culture.

Oh, and by the way, we're recruiting!

The latest in our list of incredible experiences was a day spent coasteering in the stunning Pembrokeshire Coast National Park. This experience gave us so much more than we could ever have imagined. Here are some of the highlights:

1. Living locally
2. Time in the environment
3. Sense of adventure
4. Facing fears
5. Shared adversity
6. Decision making
7. Fun

1. Living locally

At the time of writing, we're fortunate to have ten estates, in eight counties and three countries, each intentionally unique. Each estate has its own unique environment, geography, topography, ecology, and culture, and we take every opportunity to spend time living, working, and playing within these special places. Following a fantastic local engagement event at our Esgair Arth Estate, we travelled along the coast to extend our stay in this special part of Wales and make the most of the time we spent in the environment.

2. Time in the environment

The dark-grey, giant shards of rock that rose from the cool, blue waters of the Pembrokeshire coast created the most spectacular amphitheatre for our laughter (and the occasional scream). Our performance featured opportunities to climb over cliffs; crawl through caves; dive from rocks; and swim among the many birds, fish, and plentiful jellies that call this breathtaking place home.

Connecting with the purpose of what you do in a meaningful way is one of the most powerful ways to engage and motivate people. At Oxygen Conservation we are working hard to Scale Conservation for the benefit of people and wildlife. That commitment is attracting super-talented people that want to make a positive impact, and it was an absolute pleasure to see our team thrive in this environment.

3. Sense of adventure

The anticipation and excitement that comes from experiencing something new has fuelled my career from the beginning – so much so that I wanted to make adventure a key feature not just of what we do but also of how we do it.

The anticipatory trek down the secluded coastal path to meet our guides, before clambering over the saw-toothed boulders to enter the water, foreshadowed the adventure ahead. One amazing highlight was swimming into complete darkness through a cave network, before emerging into a beautiful natural staircase of clambers, climbs, and jumps. Many of us faced new fears head on – quite literally, for those inclined to perform a penguin dive.

4. Facing fears

One of the most fantastic parts of our time coasteering was seeing people facing their fears – swimming through rough waters, traversing rocky outcrops and cliff faces, and jumping from heights they never would have thought possible.

Seeing the team support each other with patience, kind words, gentle encouragement, more laughs than you can imagine, and cheers of heartfelt celebration was truly special.

5. Shared adversity

The weather was cold, dark, and grey, and the winds picked up as we got colder and became more tired. As the winds rose, the seas became choppier. Together, we had to swim hard against the tide, climb out of the water, and cross the barnacle line, then cling on to the razor-sharp ridges as we felt our way back along the shore.

The adventure was not without adversity, and nor should it be, but it is these shared experiences that are so powerful in creating a lasting culture.

6. Decision making

Another fantastic learning experience that presented itself in the sea off Pembrokeshire came in the many opportunities to practise decision making under pressure. Much of our work is about this real-time decision making and risk management, often with limited information.

Experience is so important in effectively managing yourself and the situation in high-pressure scenarios, and coasteering provided constant exposure to that opportunity. Deciding where to put your hands, feet, elbows, and knees; considering when to jump, and from where – all while in an increasing state of cold and tiredness – was incredible training. It was also wonderful to see everyone looking out for each other, and offering a hand or support – physically and emotionally – whenever it was needed. That's how a team comes together. As a leader, you can't make it happen, but you can create opportunities for it to occur and be patient enough to not unnecessarily insert yourself into the process.

7. Fun

I don't believe in work–life balance – that presupposes a battle. Instead, we're trying to create an industry, business, and team that offer everyone the opportunity to live a wonderful life – one where work only makes life better. Coasteering was such a special way of showing that fun can be the best conductor of cultural reinforcement, relationship building, and experiential learning.

We're just coasting

A note on cost: The day's coasteering costs £50 per head, including an amazing team of local instructors. It was bolted on to a day when we all needed to be in Wales to deliver key local engagement to minimise the environmental impact of travel. We try and look for opportunities like this for team events, and we appreciate that time away from family and friends isn't free – it often leaves debts that require repayment to partners and other loved ones.

Next time you're booking a team event or training day, remember how you do anything is how you do everything, and live the culture you want in your business.

Some people accuse us at Oxygen Conservation of working incredibly hard and demanding an incredibly high standard. I disagree. I think we're just coasting.

On reflection

When I think back to our time coasteering, the interactions between different members of the team make me smile the most:

- Elly Adams, our brilliant FD, failing to tell anyone she was a former high-board diver, before throwing herself from the highest levels.
- Andrew Dewar, our performance psychologist PhD, kindly offering support to the super-talented Esme Evans (one of our first interns, who was so talented we couldn't let her leave), only for her to spin round and firmly say, 'Don't psychology me, Andrew!'
- Our resident genius in chief, Chris White, screaming as he jumped/fell from the lowest of the three jumping spots; and then, having been correctly placed in a high-visibility buoyancy aid (as the only one wearing yellow), slowly disappearing out to sea as he momentarily forgot where and perhaps even how to swim!

It is an absolute joy to share adventures with these and every other member of the Oxygen Conservation team.

Beginning a Career in Conservation

Written August 2023

I'm in the fortunate position of having one of the best jobs in the world: helping an amazing team of people to Scale Conservation. As a result of our work and the culture we've built, we are regularly approached by people wanting to be part of the Oxygen Conservation adventure, or asking for advice about beginning a career in the environment sector.

Conservation career tips

While it's always lovely to hear from people that have been inspired by our journey, it's just not possible for us to speak to each and every one of the people that reaches out, but I do endeavour to reply to every message I receive.

In an attempt to offer some advice to those I can't meet with as they begin their efforts to find a career in conservation, here are some things you might like to consider:

1. Following your passion

2. Being relentless
3. Adopting a growth mindset
4. Working incredibly hard
5. Asking for help

1. Following your passion

My advice for anyone thinking about their career is *don't*. Instead, think about the life you want, and focus your time, efforts, and energy on what you love. Find a way to do more of that and be the best in the world at doing it. Find the thing you'd pay to do, and then in time figure out a way to get paid to do it. Imagine the professional surfer – do we tell them to surf less? No; we say what an amazing adventure that must be!

If you're a professional surfer, please do put that on your CV. I always read the last part of the CV first. I want to see adventure, environment, and impact in what you're doing. If you've achieved amazing things in any aspect of your life, it tells me that you can and will achieve something you decide you want to. It doesn't matter if that's elite sport, music, adventure, or academics – just being exceptional in what you do will make you stand out.

It so important to be authentic about your passion. Today, working in the environment sector is increasingly popular and one of the sexier career paths to follow. The realities of the competition, sacrifices, and hard work you have to endure to succeed really test whether you're following your real passion or someone else's.

If you love being outside – if you long to climb hills, swim in rivers and lakes, and wake up with the sun – then the world of conservation has some fantastic career paths. You're just going to have to work exceptionally hard to get one of these rare opportunities.

2. Being relentless

Once you find that passion, become obsessed about it. Spend every minute surrounded by nature, taking every opportunity you can to get involved in every aspect of the subject. Be relentless.

We are surrounded by information on every subject possible. Read everything that inspires you, listen to everything that excites you, and watch everything you can in any time that remains. If you don't choose to consume everything you can about the subject, someone else will. You'll then need to reach out and ask them for help about a career in conservation, because they'll be living your dream.

The level of relentlessness you need extends to the fact that, unless you're super-talented *and* lucky, you will experience a lot of setbacks. Your CV will be ignored before it's even rejected, and you'll have to fight to receive feedback. That feedback will feel harsh and somewhere between unfair and unpleasant. You'll have to smile and pick through the bones of that uncomfortableness, with the feedback likely coming from someone not qualified to help you learn and improve your materials. You'll have this very same process through screening interviews, panel interviews and presentations, pitches, fireside chats, and a whole range of random, likely disconnected experiences. Finally, you'll be offered an unpaid volunteer opportunity, where you'll be expected to work extremely hard, likely for little or no pay.

Did I do this? Yes.

Should I have done it? Probably not.

Will it help your career? Potentially.

Unpaid work is one of the worst things about the environment sector and one that I don't recommend you do, at least not without careful consideration. Working without pay, in a job that is presented as a volunteer opportunity, will undermine the entire sector and disrespect your time and efforts. We do not offer unpaid internships at Oxygen Conservation – if you work, we pay you, and we pay you fairly.

This doesn't mean you shouldn't gain unbelievable experiences and adventures – please do. As I've said, these are the things that jump off a CV and make a recruiting manager or an interview panel want to meet with you.

One final great piece of advice comes from our exceptional ecologist, Esme, who started with us an intern before securing a permanent role with the team:

> 'Make sure you stay in touch with a "dream company", even after a rejection. If you've been warm and humble, welcomed feedback, and acted on it, then be relentless too in your pursuit of the company. If it truly is a company you want to work for, then a position may open up in the future, and staying in contact will put your name at the top of their list.'

3. Adopting a growth mindset

One of the many contradictions I'm going to recommend here is that, while being passionately obsessed about what you do, you must also be open to a range of ideas, opportunities, and experiences. It is only by gathering a wide spectrum of different experiences that you can begin to develop your own unique offering in any role and really add value.

The easiest way to do this is by consuming information, having conversations, and listening to people that know more than you, and then applying these learnings to your passion. Early in your career, you're going to need to pick up books, listen to podcasts, and watch YouTube clips, following inspirational people in the industries where you want to work. Open your mind to their ideas, challenging your own, and collaborate with others as you develop your thinking. Beg, steal, and borrow everything you can from everyone. Listen to it all, pick and choose what you think will help, and let the rest wash over you. I assure you, though, there will be some gold in all of others' shared wisdom, even if you just aren't yet ready to see it.

As you learn more, revisit your CV, your interview preparation, your LinkedIn profile, and the way you see the world, constantly seeking to grow and improve. If you want to build a career in one of the most competitive sectors, you need to be your own marketing team.

4. Working incredibly hard

I will always remember reading a quote from Leigh Halfpenny, former Wales and British Lions fullback. His grandfather – also an international rugby player – apparently taught Leigh: 'You don't have to put in the work, but someone else will!'

I'm that someone else. As much as I might have liked to be the best athlete on the teams I played in, the reality is I never was. The part I could control was how hard I worked, and I've simply outworked everyone else I've ever been around. That has given me a lot of opportunities and, in the process, increased the surface area for luck.

In finding an opportunity in the environment sector, your willingness and ability to work hard will be tested in so many ways.

I'm writing this piece in the back of a vehicle, while travelling back from a week on the road with the team, during which we visited potential acquisitions, spent time at our own sites, and helped in a series of interviews for new roles in the team. The hardest workers stood out. These people were prepared, they researched Oxygen Conservation hard, they were relentless in their planning, they were passionate about what they wanted, and they could articulate effectively and enthusiastically. They had ideas about how they would contribute to the team, to help us progress to the next level, and they knew and understood the realities of what that would take. They had discussed the compromises and sacrifices they would have to make and discussed these with their partners and families.

This commitment to hard work must continue once you get an opportunity. Unless you're in a very unusual situation, you'll have to do many of the low-value, routine tasks, which will be a long way away from the fun and excitement you might imagine. Throughout this period, remember you're learning how to succeed in this context and environment. Every one of the team at Oxygen Conservation started at the bottom of their particular industry; they took the bins out and continue to do so today. By outworking everyone else in the room, they've risen to the top of their respective specialisms and (literal and figurative) fields.

Here are the minimum requirements you need:

- A LinkedIn profile
- A well-prepared and visually attractive CV

- Five interesting stories or experiences, and the ability to talk about them confidently and inspiringly – these are about you, and you are the world's leading expert on you

- Answers to the questions *What do you want?* and *Why you?*

- A willingness to jump at an opportunity, including something you don't yet know how to do

5. Asking for help

You will almost certainly need a great support network around you. Some people are lucky enough to have supportive friends and families; unfortunately, others aren't. This doesn't mean you can't build that support network. Some people talk about virtual boardrooms; others say mentors, coaches, or trusted advisers. I prefer to call them *friends*.

My advice to anyone early in their career is to give a lot more than you expect to receive and do lots of favours for lots of people, making friends as you go; and be selective about the people you keep close to you over time. The reality is that as your career progresses, time is the most limited resource you have. The US Navy Seals talk about being selective about who you let into your boat – you're going to have to paddle hard for them, and you need to know that they will paddle for you too (McRaven, 2017).

As well as your support network, if you've followed each of the steps above, then you're in a good spot to ask for help from experts in the conservation sector. Reach out to the people you respect and admire, tell them why you're approaching them, and ask for any thoughts or advice they would offer you from their perspective. Make this approach only once you're prepared, make it relevant to the individual personally and professionally, and be open to them being too busy to respond quickly, if at all.

Throughout this journey, you will have to become resilient along the way. Learn how to see positives in each rejection, setback, and failure. Don't be afraid to ask for help in this process too, but do so knowing that everyone else is fighting their own battles that you know nothing about – they might not have the time to help right now, but they might in the future.

Earlier this year, I received a LinkedIn message from someone that had inspired me. I'd messaged them years earlier and never received a reply. It wasn't until they contacted me that we were both reminded of the message I'd previously sent. My message had been polite and complimentary, but it wasn't sent at the right time. It is now the right time, though, and I'm excited to share ideas and opportunities with this person moving forward.

Good luck!

Let's include one more key point: *luck*. I've been hugely lucky in my career so far. Anyone that has been even a little successful will tell you that – despite all the hard work, the miles, the sacrifices, and the failures – we all need luck along the way.

On reflection

At the end of 2023 we launched our second internship campaign, providing an opportunity for people to begin a career in conservation. Only one year after our first intern campaign, and thanks to the brilliant work of our dedicated marketing team, we achieved a 500% increase in the number of applicants.

That was more than 500 people applying for only four potential roles.

The conservation sector and the wider natural capital economy are becoming some of the most in-demand places for people to work, and the standard of applicants is growing exponentially as a result. The competition for roles is becoming so challenging that regularly our directors and heads of department comment how they don't think they would make it through the selection process if they were starting their career again today.

If we're all honest, that's how it should be, and in fact how we need it to be. If not, we're not making anywhere near the progress we need as a business and a sector. Solving the dual challenges of climate change and the biodiversity collapse is going to need innovation, creativity, and environmental engineering beyond which we can possibly imagine. I'm extremely grateful that the very best people want to be part of the solution for the greatest challenge of our time.

Experience Is Overrated

Written September 2023

The world is at a critical juncture, where the need for conservation and regenerative practices has never been greater. To address this pressing issue, we must be not only stewards of the environment but also challengers of the very way Oxygen Conservation does business.

Talent strategy

We recruit for the ceiling, not the floor.

We're currently in the process of developing our talent strategy, evolving the way we attract, develop, and launch the future careers of the most talented people.

We'd like to share a little of this developing thinking now, including the source of some of our inspiration. We're going to write about:

- The importance of our mission
- The culture we've built

- Our commitment to targeting the most talented people
- Providing opportunities to early-career professionals
- Our commitment to identifying talent and offering unparalleled development opportunities
- The fact that we are willing to compete and do so financially for the most talented early-career professionals

In doing so, we'd love to encourage those very same talented early-career professionals out there to give us their thoughts and feedback, ahead of our 2024 internship campaign, which will launch this autumn.

We have the most inspiring mission: Scale Conservation

INSPIRATION: TESLA

Tesla, the electric vehicle and clean-energy company led by Elon Musk, embodies an inspiring mission in the commercial sector. Tesla's mission is to 'accelerate the world's transition to sustainable energy' (Tesla, 2023). This vision has not only attracted top talent in the fields of engineering, renewable energy, and automotive innovation; it has also garnered a massive following among environmentally conscious consumers. Tesla's audacious goal to revolutionise transportation and energy production aligns with the urgent need for a more sustainable way of life. It has inspired a global community of employees and supporters dedicated to reshaping the future of transportation and energy consumption.

Our mission is to Scale Conservation, delivering positive environmental and social impact. Generating a profit is a result of what we do, not the purpose. Every member of our team is inspired by the idea that their work directly contributes to protecting and preserving our planet for future generations. We see this as one of the most inspirational missions possible for the next generation of talented people.

Our culture is about environment, impact, and adventure

INSPIRATION: PATAGONIA
Patagonia's corporate culture embodies environmental consciousness, integrity, justice, and a refusal to be bound by convention (Stanley and Chouinard, 2023). They not only produce high-quality outdoor clothing and equipment but also actively promote sustainability and conservation in everything they do – even so far as telling people to boycott Black Friday and not buy Patagonia products if they're not needed. Patagonia employees are encouraged to participate in environmental activism and take paid time off to engage in grassroots efforts (Patagonia.com, no date). This culture has not only attracted passionate employees but has also built a loyal customer base that shares their values – growing the business by delivering a superb product in a more regenerative way.

Our culture is a unique blend of environmental consciousness, meaningful impact, and the adventure of making a difference. We provide a way to genuinely align people's passions with their work in a way that makes a measurable impact on the world around them.

The culture isn't for everyone. It's highly dynamic, demanding, and fast-paced. The team are all highly committed to our mission, and they demand that same commitment from each other, constantly pushing and supporting one another to be better. That type of high-performance environment is quite simply addictive. We are radically transparent about what we do and how we work, creating a remarkable number of interactions and opportunities for collaboration, allowing us to produce work together that we could never do alone.

If you want to be comfortable, content, and average, this isn't the place for you. However, if you are super-talented and you want to know how good you can be, Oxygen Conservation could be your ideal place to work.

We will attract the most talented people

INSPIRATION: GOOGLE
Google, the tech giant known for its innovative projects and global impact, has consistently drawn in the most talented individuals across various fields. Google's mission to 'organize the world's information and make it universally accessible and useful' (Google, no date) resonates with professionals who are passionate about technology and information accessibility. The company's reputation for fostering a creative and inclusive work culture, combined with opportunities to work on groundbreaking projects like self-driving cars and artificial intelligence, has made Google a magnet for top-tier talent in the tech industry. We are committed to becoming that same magnet for the environment sector.

To make a significant impact, we need the most talented individuals. We will proactively seek out and attract top-tier talent by showcasing our mission, culture, and opportunities for personal and professional growth.

We will only ever recruit people better than us, in a meaningful way, and are delighted to have continued to find increasingly talented people to help us Scale Conservation. Four of our previous interns are now permanent members of the team and are thriving in a culture that challenges and supports their development in equal measure.

We prioritise early-career talent

INSPIRATION: THE NORTH FACE

The North Face, a prominent player in the outdoor industry, is committed to prioritising early-career talent. The company understands that fresh perspectives and a passion for the outdoors are crucial for innovation in their field. North Face offers various programmes, such as internships and entry-level positions, aimed at recruiting and developing young talent (The North Face, no date; Rane, 2023). These opportunities allow early-career professionals to immerse themselves in the world of outdoor gear and apparel, work on exciting projects, and learn from seasoned experts. North Face's dedication to nurturing emerging talent reflects their commitment to advancing the outdoor industry and continuing their legacy of exploration and adventure. We want to have the same impact on the entire environment sector.

We recognise that fresh perspectives, energy, and a disregard for the status quo are crucial for innovation. We will therefore prioritise recruiting and developing early-career professionals, providing them with opportunities to grow within our organisation.

We have been fortunate in attracting an incredible senior team of national experts in their respective fields, which allows us to target our future growth to Scale Conservation with early-career talent.

Our work is extremely demanding and requires absolute commitment, extensive travel, and flexibility. We also want people who are committed to lifelong professional development. We recruit for a person's ceiling, not their floor, and we care less about experience than we do about potential. As a result, we prioritise early-career professionals that rarely get the opportunities, access to information, and development opportunities they deserve. They will get all of that and more at Oxygen Conservation.

We believe in our ability to identify talent and coach

INSPIRATION: FC BARCELONA'S LA MASIA ACADEMY

FC Barcelona's La Masia Academy is a shining example of believing in the ability to identify and coach talent to reach its full potential. The academy, renowned worldwide, has consistently demonstrated its ability to discover and nurture promising young footballers (Kuper, 2021). Notable talents like Lionel Messi, Xavi Hernandez, and Andres Iniesta emerged from La Masia's ranks, representing the pinnacle of Barcelona's talent identification and coaching efforts. This dedication to recognising and cultivating talent has not only led to on-field success but has also solidified FC Barcelona's reputation as a global footballing powerhouse, showcasing their belief in unlocking an individual's full potential. We will do everything in our power to achieve that same process at Oxygen Conservation.

We love recruitment and back our ability to identify and develop the most talented people. We have a brilliant person, with a background in performance psychology, in post as Head of People; and a unique team of exceptional experts in their respective fields. This, combined with a radically transparent culture, offers the most talented early-career professionals unparalleled access to information and development opportunities.

We will also coach, mentor, and challenge everyone in ways that allow them to thrive, from experiential learning to exposure to everything we do across the business. This is supported by a constant commitment to find new and exciting learning materials.

This autumn we will launch our 2024 intern campaign, led by our amazingly successful interns from 2023, helping to identify the next wave of talent to join Oxygen Conservation. Hopefully, some of these people will find roles as part of the Oxygen Conservation team, but if not, we know their experience throughout the process will help them in securing almost equally wonderful roles in the wider environment sector.

We will compete for talent

INSPIRATION: VIVOBAREFOOT

Vivobarefoot, the trailblazing footwear company, beckons talented young individuals with a compelling vision and unwavering values. At its core, Vivobarefoot champions sustainability, minimalism, and foot health, igniting the passion of environmentally conscious and health-focused young minds (Vivobarefoot, no date). Vivobarefoot's appeal transcends shoes, though – it's a beacon of sustainability, practising what it preaches by using eco-friendly materials and fostering a culture of wellbeing. This company stands as a symbol of transparency and ethical practices, enticing talented people who desire meaningful work with a positive impact.

Vivobarefoot is a community of likeminded individuals who are passionate about making a difference. By embracing inclusivity and a strong sense of belonging, they create an atmosphere where young talent feels valued and empowered. The brand's global presence opens doors to projects with far-reaching impacts, offering young professionals the chance to leave their mark on a worldwide stage. Vivobarefoot doesn't just attract talent; it also nurtures it, investing in the growth of individuals who aspire to lead, innovate, and contribute to a more sustainable future. It's a place where values align with vocation, where transparency meets trust, and where community fosters creativity. For the young and the bold who seek to shape a world of purpose, Vivobarefoot shines as a company that not only talks the talk but walks the walk, leaving an inspiring footprint for the generations to come (Wedgwood, 2025).

We will work incredibly hard to create roles that allow the most talented people to succeed in our overall system and company culture. That extends to competing financially for the best talent. When it comes to reward – and, specifically, financial reward – the same does not mean fair. The most talented people can demand and deserve to be paid accordingly. We therefore believe in competing for that talent, offering well-paid internships and reward packages that people are delighted to accept. We recognise that if we truly back our ability to identify and develop real talent, this will be a great investment.

Launching the 2024 intern campaign

As we continue this exciting journey of reshaping the future of conservation and environmental impact, we draw inspiration from visionaries like Tesla, Patagonia, Google, North Face, FC Barcelona's La Masia Academy, and Vivobarefoot. Just like these pioneers in their respective domains, we are committed to our mission and culture. We are also dedicated to attracting the most talented early-career professionals, prioritising fresh perspectives, and believing in our ability to identify and coach talent; and yes, we are willing to compete for the brightest minds.

As we gear up for our 2024 intern campaign, we invite the most talented individuals out there to join us in the adventure that is Oxygen Conservation.

If you're looking to make a real impact and thrive in an environment that's anything but ordinary, you've found your home with us.

On reflection

Looking back over this piece, I think it's important to recognise that the reason talent is more important than experience at Oxygen Conservation is because we're building a new type of business, in a developing economy and asset class.

It has also perhaps been helpful to emphasise the importance of creating the environment to allow the most talented people to be successful. While I still think experience is widely overrated, if your business or culture isn't one where feedback flows freely and constantly, and where coaching isn't a genuine feature of everything you do, then talent is nowhere near enough. In those environments, experience, resilience, and independence are the more important (survival) skills to have.

I've worked in places like that, and they're horrible.

Ruining Recruitment

Written February 2023

I love recruitment. I've always loved recruitment. This passion first started when I was glued to my TV on football transfer deadline days. Latterly, I have become obsessed with every aspect of the NFL draft and college recruitment. I love finding ways to attract the most talented people and considering how different people will fit into a new culture or how they could create a positive impact beyond their own position or role.

Throughout my career, I've been involved in literally hundreds of recruitment processes and sat through many interviews on both sides of the table. Sadly, throughout many of these, I've seen what should be an inspirational and transformative experience (for everyone) ruined by HR departments.

At Oxygen Conservation we are privileged to be an extremely well-supported startup that gives us the opportunity to combine absolute freedom to push the boundaries in our recruitment exercises with forward-thinking, meaningful HR support. Operating in such a special environment, I've been reflecting on the differences between the impact of the bad and the best HR departments.

Bad and best HR departments

I've listed my top five observations from the bad and the best. I've also invited some of the wonderful people we work with to share their stories and experiences in relation to some of these observations.

Five things bad HR departments do to ruin recruitment:

1. Lacking ambition and avoiding mistakes
2. Over-focusing on processes
3. Insisting on vanilla and lazy campaigns
4. Irrelevant assessments and criteria
5. Misrepresenting the culture, the company, or the role

1. Lacking ambition and avoiding mistakes

Bad HR departments lack ambition and are focused on avoiding mistakes (bad hires and potential blame) as opposed to trying to find a brilliant person that could change the business or maybe even the world.

> 'Bad HR departments are disconnected from the business; finding candidates and filling the role is seen as the objective, finding the right candidates and filling the role with the right person is often overlooked.'
> — Ben Bulger, MD, Oxygen House

2. Over-focusing on processes

Bad HR departments develop processes for their department and insist on using them for ease of administration, even where they make things harder or more arduous for the candidates. This narrows down the attractiveness of the role and makes it less accessible, especially for the most talented candidates. The best performers are too busy, and simply won't commit the time required, to complete generic application questionnaires and tasks.

> 'Recently, I've been involved in recruitment with blind CVs. I hate them! Picture this: you've spent hours honing your CV, looking at every word, obsessing over formatting so it all fits on two pages, and you finally have something that makes you proud and you start to think you're a good candidate. So, what does a prospective employer do? Ask you to ignore all that hard work and remove a lot of useful information. It's also the first – but I'm sure not the last – time an organisation tells you they don't value your time. The same is true of filling out forms that span eight screens and ask you where you lived for the last five years. We can do better. It starts with thinking about the candidate.'
> — Dr Andrew Dewar, Head of People, Oxygen Conservation, and performance psychologist

3. Insisting on vanilla and lazy campaigns

Bad HR departments recycle the recruitment materials they've always used and focus on avoiding potentially upsetting one person, at the cost of possibly inspiring hundreds or thousands.

'When we've recruited, we like to include attention-catching first lines that attract the candidates we were looking for, while showing boldly what we are about. Being clear on what makes your mission and/or the way you operate unique and special means your message will not resonate with everyone, but that's a good thing, as it lets candidates think about whether your USP excites them as much as it does you. Those are the people you want to hear from!'
— Colin Hegarty, CEO, Sparx, and Founder, HegartyMaths

4. Irrelevant assessments and criteria

Bad HR departments create (often complex) assessments and criteria that don't relate to the business or the specific role. Instead, generic criteria or capabilities boxes can be ticked – boxes that HR have decided are important and that all managers should want.

'So often, there is an assumption that someone who's being "doing the job for twenty years" is the best to lead an interview panel or process. This is rarely the case. Techniques, methodologies, understanding, and best practice change – often rapidly. An old-school approach doesn't get the best out of anyone, nor does it create an environment that inspires prospective candidates to be excited about taking the role. The best teams are made up of the best people. It's time to inspire and enthuse the next generation of environmental custodians.'
— Dan Johnson, Head of Environment, Oxygen Conservation

5. Misrepresenting the culture, the company, or the role

Bad HR departments fail to accurately describe the expectations of the role, the amount of travel involved, and perhaps the culture or complexity of the organisation. Increasingly, HR departments want to portray woke utopias, when the reality might not exist. This isn't fair on the candidates or the team.

> 'Every time I've written a job advert in a corporate company, it's been changed to remove personality, be more generic, and become less inspiring. The applicant is looking for somewhere they will fit the culture and will be motivated to perform at their best. Vague, uninspiring language won't help them find that company and role.'
> — Dr Andrew Dewar, Head of People, Oxygen Conservation, and performance psychologist

Five things the best HR departments do to make recruitment successful:

1. Saying *Yes!*
2. Asking great questions
3. Understanding that their perspective is one of many
4. Always learning
5. Recognising exceptional talent

1. Saying *Yes!*

This is how you can achieve what you set out to do for the candidate, the team, and the business.

'Having a positive and supportive HR department is crucial to a successful recruitment process. It's easy to find ways to say no, but that's often the wrong response, because it shuts down an idea and an opportunity to do something new. Saying yes supports the vision of the company and projects this confidence onto potential recruits. An award-winning external expert recently offered us help with a specialist recruitment, yet previous HR teams I have worked with would have said, *No, that's too difficult*. With the help of Sarah Felfel and the team at Oxygen House, we were able sort within twenty-four hours, making the process even better for the candidates and the team. The best find a way to say *Yes!*'

— Dave Keir, Head of Operations, Oxygen Conservation

2. Asking great questions

The best HR departments ask questions to understand what recruiting managers need and what help they need in achieving that.

'I have so often seen HR departments undertake a tick-box approach when it comes to recruitment, not truly understanding what the company needs. They are often so disconnected from your team and the company, and not even caring. It's only recently that I have seen this turned on its head, and already I have seen the impact this can have. A supportive, passionate, and caring HR department that's directly intertwined with the recruiting manager and wider

team allows the company to continue to grow (but wait for the key word here)... successfully!'
— Ell Steers, Head of Storytelling, Oxygen Conservation

3. Understanding that their perspective is one of many

The HR department's perspective isn't more important than that of the team or the hiring manager. HR are a partner, not the police.

> 'The *best* have learned the importance of *being available* in the widest sense – for the candidate throughout their experience, for the manager, and for the team. Making sure they are true partners to the business rather than one element and ticking the box.'
> — Sarah Felfel, Head of Group HR, Oxygen House Group

4. Always learning

HR need to keep learning by being at the cutting edge of psychology, sociology, and business. They need to always be asking how we can improve the way we recruit, suggesting ideas to creating inspirational campaigns to attract the most talented people, and giving all candidates a fantastic recruitment experience.

> 'The best departments look to do something more than CVs, cover letters, and interviews, and try to make the process itself something that is rewarding for everyone involved. The best recruitment I have

been a part of was our recent internship programme advert to look for people "crazy" enough to think they can change the world.

'We got a huge response from enthusiastic candidates who loved the sense of mission, our playful advert, and the encouragement to apply, no matter their background or skills. After longlist interviews, each shortlisted candidate was invited to visit the team and have dinner at our offices in Exeter then taken out for a day exploring one of our incredible rainforest restoration projects in Dartmoor to ask questions, share their ideas, and challenge our approach. It felt like each step of the process had been designed thoughtfully and in a way which provided something unique and meaningful to everyone involved. I can't wait to start working with our final four interns this year!'
— Chris White, Director of Natural Capital, Oxygen Conservation

5. Recognising exceptional talent

The best HR departments recognise exceptional talent is just that – exceptional. They understand that the best candidate's needs and expectations are likely to be different or unique. They are imaginative about creating an offer that the ideal candidate is delighted to accept, appreciating that the best people disproportionally improve any team's performance.

> 'Finding unicorns (often for newly invented roles) often comes down to timing and luck. What good recruiters and companies do is increase the chances of being lucky through their actions. The whole company and how all the team act are a key part of

recruitment. If you get it right, it creates gravity – the only force that transcends space and time.'
— Matt Gingell, General Counsel, Oxygen House Group

If you don't love recruitment, and if you're not attracting transformative talents that you're desperate to invite to join your team, perhaps try and add one of the key points from the best HR departments to your process. If you can't – if the culture where you work is committed to all or maybe even any of bad things listed above – I'd like to apologise to your current employer, because you should probably close this article and click on the LinkedIn job listings pages.

On reflection

Recruitment continues to be particularly important, and attracting transformative talent is perhaps the most positively impactful thing you can do for your business. Since first writing this article, we've continued to evolve the way we advertise. We have also recently published the *Oxygen Conservation Recruitment Playbook*, a summary of which you can find in Chapter Seven.

Two of the changes that have had the possibly biggest positive impact on our recruitment process – for the candidates and for the quality of appointments – have been in:

- **Selection:** Our brilliant Head of People, Andrew Dewar, steps out of the process following the first round of interviews, having provided a shortlist of candidates for the final interview process. This forces Andrew to make a definitive yes/no decision on each candidate and allows him to provide feedback, coaching, and support for all candidates. Each candidate benefits from elite-level coaching by a highly qualified performance psychologist, and this process also allows us to assess their willingness and ability to respond to feedback.

- **Contracts:** We negotiate and agree outline deals with each of the shortlisted candidates ahead of the interview process. This provides candidates with clarity on the offer and allows them to consider whether the total package works for them. It also provides us with informed decisions about the cost of each hire, allowing us to make an informed comparison between candidates. The added benefit of this approach is that, when we place the call to offer the successful candidate the role and make the first step on what we hope will be a fantastic, long-term partnership, they will hopefully jump to say *Hell, yes!*, knowing what they're being offered. This has also allowed us to share contracts within twenty-four hours of the offer, removing a significant amount of wasted time from the process. This is especially important when we might have to wait three to six months for a talented senior hire.

I love recruitment; it's like Christmas Eve!

Recognition

Written September 2023

In the dark days of my career in the public sector, I was advised by a long-serving senior manager to not be so complimentary to my team because they would get accustomed to it. At the time I remember thinking that was why that manager was largely disliked and why people didn't speak to him honestly about – well, anything. With time and experience, I realised he was referring to a psychological concept known as the Kano model (Kano et al, 1984). This is essentially based on the belief that over time our expectations shift, such that today's praise becomes tomorrow's expectation. My solution, however, is not to stop recognising great people and great performance but to continue finding meaningful ways of recognising effort, achievement (and failure), and above all, improvement.

Effort, achievement (and failure), and improvement

Here are some of the ways you can offer recognition and help encourage the behaviours you'd love to see in your business:

1. Say thank you.
2. Share that thank you.
3. Send a gift.
4. Recognise those who made it possible.
5. Invest in the person (equipment and resources).

1. Say thank you

It's important to say thank you in the way the person would want to receive it. This can be via a phone call, a Teams message, an email, a video message, a voice note, a handwritten letter, or any other mechanism you choose to use. The key is to remember to do it. We're all super-busy, and while this takes time and effort, trust me: it's worth it. If you aren't going to recognise your amazing people, someone else will!

2. Share that thank you

When it's appropriate to do so, share your thanks widely, not only with the person you're thanking but with others, too, perhaps including close colleagues, a line manager, or other senior managers in the communication. The intent and consideration here are key. Think about what you're trying to achieve and how those people might like to be thanked. If you're not sure, ask for advice from colleagues and friends. Celebrate their achievements and successes in a way that elevates the team. In the process, you'll be modelling the behaviours that you'd like everyone else in the team and beyond to adopt.

3. Send a gift

I love sending gifts. (If my wife's reading this, I love receiving them too, while appreciating I'm extremely hard to buy for!) I think my absolute favourite gifts to give others are books – giving another opportunity for learning and development. Having been fortunate enough to put a lot of books on the read shelves over the past few years, I can usually quite quickly think of the right book that would connect with a person I'd especially like to recognise.

Again, it's important to remember this isn't about you – it's about the person receiving the gift. Sometimes the right gift is food- or drink-based – something especially meaningful or locally produced. It could be flowers or, increasingly from us, it's a beautiful, limited-edition photograph of one of our estates. The key point here is that the gift needs to be meaningful and thoughtful, not generic (don't bother if it's generic!), but it absolutely doesn't need to be expensive – just unique.

4. Recognise those who made it possible

One of the things we've made an effort to do more lately is recognise the efforts of those who have supported our amazing team in achieving special things. Often, it's a partner or the family of our team, and as such we have paid for the entire family to go out for dinner or have sent gifts that are meaningful to all. Most recently, we sent vegan chocolates to one of our team after a medical procedure, including a note that said half were for the them and the other half were for their partner, for putting up with them being a 'nightmare' to look after when bored. This was reinforced in the days immediately following, when they asked for additional audiobook and podcast recommendations because they were, as predicted, already bored.

5. Invest in the person (equipment and resources)

Where a person has achieved great things, we will always try and push the boundaries of what's possible with the equipment and resources that mean the most to them. By knowing our team as individuals, we can understand when a specific vehicle, IT equipment, a specific chair, or – unusually – PPE might make them feel especially recognised. The same is true of learning and development opportunities, training, conferences, or resources. This highlights a key principle in my thinking around recognition and reward – the same does not mean fair.

We have recently recognised the remarkable potential of one of our team by supporting their advanced professional qualifications, helping them move from high performance in one specific discipline into a new area of the business. They are already thriving in that new area. It's important to distinguish that this isn't a benefit – it is the person receiving something they need to do their job. By pushing the boundary of expense or uniqueness in this regard, though, you can demonstrate that you have recognised their achievement and performance by investing in that person. You will also find that this additional investment has an excellent return rate culturally, emotionally, and in terms of future performance.

Finding ways to say thank you

These are some of the many ways we try and recognise the efforts of our team and also our external partners. Reflecting on that same (terrible) advice I was offered earlier in my career, that was actually the ideal learning opportunity, pushing me to continue trying to find new and increasingly meaningful ways to say thank you.

Thanks for the advice!

On reflection

It gives me such pleasure seeing the tools and techniques we teach within the team being applied and evolving over time. When you see others in the team share recognition without your involvement, you know you've built an incredible culture made up of super-special people. I'm lucky to have exactly that at Oxygen Conservation.

Big shoutouts go to Ashlee and Ell for being the absolute best gift givers!

The Best Job in the Natural Capital Economy?

Written December 2023

In the midst of the emerging natural capital economy, a transformative prospect beckons individuals committed to improving the environment, delivering positive impact, and embracing a sense of adventure. The role of Estate Manager – often synonymous with traditional sporting estates or large-scale farming enterprises – is changing. From the shadows, the most exciting opportunity is emerging.

Journey towards regenerative land management

The contemporary Estate Manager, positioned at the forefront of the natural capital economy, now oversees a portfolio that extends far beyond the traditional guns on the peg, sheep on the hill, and a huge amount of tweed. This role has transformed into a strategic opportunity for professionals to contribute to sustainable practices and environmental conservation, marking perhaps the most pivotal shift in estate management in decades. Let's look at some of the main developments:

1. Expanded responsibilities
2. Ecosystem management
3. Regenerative agriculture
4. Ecotourism development
5. Community engagement
6. Purpose-driven leadership
7. Innovative stewardship
8. Holistic connection with nature
9. Global environmental impact
10. Professional opportunities unearthed

1. Expanded responsibilities

In stark contrast to conventional estate management, the Estate Manager of the future will have a much wider set of skills and responsibilities. We hope this will attract a much more diverse range of applicants, who will expand the role through their own innovation, creating more elements of the role that will have profound positive ecological and social impact.

2. Ecosystem management

As stewards of biodiversity, Estate Managers play a pivotal role in implementing comprehensive conservation programmes and wildlife management strategies. Collaborations with environmental experts are paramount to ensuring the sustainable coexistence of diverse flora and fauna within the estate's boundaries. No longer will this be limited to a few target species such as pheasant, grouse, or stag. Instead, it will be about people and wildlife across the landscape.

3. Regenerative agriculture

Where it is the right thing for the landscape, Estate Managers will be at the forefront of adopting and promoting regenerative farming practices, from championing organic farming methods to embracing conservation grazing. Estate Managers will contribute to a legacy of responsible agriculture that harmonises with the environment, recognising the interconnectedness of agricultural practices and ecosystem health.

4. Ecotourism development

By developing and promoting ecotourism, Estate Managers will carefully balance the drive to welcome more people to the natural environment with ensuring its improvement and long-term protection. This extends beyond mere attractions, as Estate Managers craft moonlight safaris and respectful wildlife watching, providing guests with immersive experiences, sharing their unique perspectives and knowledge to bring these experiences and places to life. This demonstrates the estates' natural beauty but also underscores our commitment to conservation and experiential environmental education.

5. Community engagement

Building meaningful partnerships with local communities – especially those that live on or in the immediate neighbourhoods of properties – is integral to the contemporary Estate Manager's role. Those people need to work collaboratively, to create opportunities for consultation and two-way conversation, allowing neighbours to be active collaborators in the pursuit of ecological preservation. This is crucial, especially for deer management in large upland landscapes; and for the control of invasive species, where that control can be successfully delivered only at a catchment or landscape level and in partnership with local communities.

6. Purpose-driven leadership

Estate Managers find themselves at the forefront of our work to deliver positive environment and social impact, where each decision made is inextricably tied to the overarching goal of preserving and enhancing the environment. This elevated sense of purpose transforms daily tasks into a mission, contributing to a greater calling – that of saving a little of the world for the next generation.

7. Innovative stewardship

The dynamic landscape of sustainability provides Estate Managers with a vast canvas for creativity. Experimentation with novel conservation initiatives becomes not just encouraged but essential, allowing for the implementation of vibrant and effective ecological practices that set benchmarks for the industry. As every estate is different, the challenges and opportunities vary. Towards the Highlands of Scotland, the focus may be on bracken control, tree planting, and deer management. In the South West of England we need to work in partnership with other landowners to rescue and recover precious areas of Atlantic rainforest and create a sensitive sustainable tourism experience that allows people to contribute towards their resurgence.

8. Holistic connection with nature

Immersed in a profound connection with the land, the challenges and triumphs of Estate Managers are rooted in the beauty and vitality of the ecosystems they protect. This intimate bond with the natural world becomes a source of constant inspiration, fuelling an enduring dedication to the cause of conservation and shaping Estate Managers' decision-making processes. This is not without its emotional challenges – we will often all be required to accept contradictions and compromises in our mission.

If we are to make conservation commercially viable, we may have to persist with current land use during a transition phase. This is in addition to welcoming new ways of fuelling the rural economy that will almost certainly not be perfect but will be progressive.

9. Global environmental impact

As leaders in the natural capital economy, Estate Managers find that their influence extends far beyond their immediate surroundings. Estate Managers become (electric) torchbearers, setting an example for global environmental management. Their impact reaches beyond estate borders, contributing to a broader discourse on environmental sustainability that reverberates across industries and regions. We truly believe this country's work on conservation and – by extension – the emergence of the natural capital economy will be our next greatest exports.

10. Professional opportunities unearthed

For experienced professionals, seeking purposeful work and also innovative challenges and a profound connection with nature, the role of Estate Manager in the natural capital economy offers a unique and exhilarating career path, unrivalled in its potential impact. For early-career professionals, the role of Estate Manager offers the ideal entry point into the environment sector and a potential rocket ship to future development and career progression.

In the rapidly emerging natural capital economy, the role of Estate Manager offers an excellent opportunity, calling the bold, the brave, and the adventurous – whether seasoned or early-career professionals – along a transformative and exciting career path. It is an opportunity to be genuinely involved in regenerative practices and environmental conservation, charting a course whereby responsibilities transcend mere management and become a strategic and purposeful endeavour.

As Estate Managers step into the forefront of this dynamic field, they become key players in shaping the future, where environmentally focused land management is not just a responsibility but also a career and a calling. This professional evolution offers a unique and compelling path for those ready to answer the resounding call of progress in estate management, ushering in an era in which purpose and impact intersect in our landscapes of profound significance.

Is the role of Estate Manager set to be the best job in the natural capital economy? At Oxygen Conservation: absolutely!

THE BEST JOB IN THE NATURAL CAPITAL ECONOMY?

On reflection

The recruitment of talented Estate Managers has been one of the most challenging aspects of building the Oxygen Conservation team. We have some wonderful Estate Managers and estate teams, including Charles, Archie, Lyall, Rowan, Ben, Adam, Esme, Ashlee, and Mel, but in the years to come we will need many more.

In the next article, you can read about the mistakes we made in recruiting for these roles and learn how we've applied the Oxygen Conservation approach to redefining the role and the recruitment of the next generation of incredible Estate Managers.

We Got It Wrong

Written January 2024

We've always been passionate about recruitment and are extremely grateful to have built an amazing team of wonderfully diverse people, united by our collective commitment to Scaling Conservation. In the last two years, we've had more than 2,000 applicants for less than twenty permanent roles. We intentionally recruit the 1% of successful candidates – the very best people living and working in the UK to deliver positive environmental and social impact.

Getting it right

Our journey in attracting the most talented individuals has been marked by creativity, adaptability, and a commitment to radical honesty and transparency. We care about every aspect of the recruitment process, seeking to give candidates a positive experience from start to finish, and we are especially happy when we receive positive feedback from them.

We deviated from this approach, though, in our recent recruitment campaign for Estate Managers, and that campaign didn't work. In this piece I'll describe what we did wrong and what we're going to do about it.

The power of unique job titles

We've prided ourselves on using unique job titles as a way to stand out from the crowd and quickly communicate our culture. From 'Head of Storytelling' to 'Terrain Detective', our titles have been a testament to our creativity and distinctiveness. We've even invited 'the misfits, the rebels, and the crazy ones' to become our interns and are delighted that three of these interns are now incredibly important members of the team.

This approach was intended not only to attract candidates who are excited by our mission but also to demonstrate the importance of innovation, adventure, and playfulness within our business.

Adaptability: Listening and learning

The journey of Oxygen Conservation has also been one of adaptability, and we've always committed to listening to others, even though we won't always agree with them. Feedback from our interactions with Estate Managers across the country revealed that our playful approach to job titles might not resonate with people within this sector. As a result, we launched campaigns titled for and targeted at existing and experienced Estate Managers. We were also encouraged to prioritise recruitment from areas as close as possible to an estate, so we worked hard to advertise within local geographies.

However, while the great advice of recruiting like-for-like replacements of existing Estate Managers might work for other companies, we haven't found it effective for Oxygen Conservation.

Diversity of opinion and experience

We realised that we were seeking advice and guidance from people experienced in living and working in the environment of the past, not of the future. We were also talking to people living and working close to the estate at the time of those conversations, many later sharing that they had relocated or moved for their dream roles. Unfortunately, due to the low population densities of remote locations, this approach also results in a very limited applicant pool.

Finding the right balance

The challenge we faced with Estate Manager recruitment was a great opportunity to re-evaluate and improve our processes. Despite overwhelming responses for literally every other role, we saw a significant reduction in the number and diversity of applicants. This outcome, along with a critical analysis of our processes, helped us realise that we had strayed from the essence of what makes Oxygen Conservation unique.

Forward-looking: Learning from our mistakes

Our reflection and analysis have been invaluable. We now understand the importance of not only focusing on local candidates, as every role is local to someone and somewhere. We also recognise the need to broaden our perspective beyond traditional skills, to include future environmentalists and land managers as well as Estate Managers. This realisation excites us, as it opens doors to new people, personalities, and possibilities.

What's next for Oxygen Conservation

As we move forward, we're thrilled to apply these learnings to our recruitment process. We're committed to maintaining our unique culture, while also being more overtly open to a wider range of different perspectives and backgrounds. This balance will enable us to continue making significant impact in environmental conservation and to build future careers for people in the rural economy and communities.

On reflection

Wow, did we reinvent our process! We called for the professional adventurers that wanted to transform their lives and the environment for the better, launching the campaign with a week-long countdown and a spectacular recruitment video (you can see that video here: youtu.be/watch?v=HCt9ME4lwpQ).

The impact of this campaign was so large and so immediate that it caused LinkedIn to suspend our post because it was attracting too much interest on the unpaid platform. We broke LinkedIn!

In the latest round of recruitment, we attracted 129 applicants for two Estate Manager roles. We achieved this by applying our own authentic approach to recruitment to a role and an industry that is desperately in need of innovation and modernisation.

THREE
Engagement

We Will Always Listen. We Won't Always Agree.
Written March 2023

We are hugely fortunate to own and manage a portfolio of special landscapes across England, Scotland, and Wales, and we recognise that we cannot and will never be experts in each of these unique environments. We are therefore committed to listening and learning from the people who know these places best: the local communities.

I'm often challenged on what I mean by *local*. I'm happy to admit it's an evolving definition in my mind, and I cast a wide net with respect to space and time. Of course, *local communities* includes the people living and working on our estates and areas neighbouring them. It also includes those that regularly visit the area or place, experts in the types of natural and built environments, and those that aspire to be part of that community in the future.

Open-mindedness

My intent is to be open to an especially wide spectrum of thoughts and opinions, crowdsourcing intelligence and experience that can help inform our vision for the future of each individual estate.

We cannot speak individually to everyone, we're not politicians, and we're not going to start knocking on doors. We wouldn't appreciate that imposition so don't want to impose ourselves on others who might not be interested in our work. However, we greatly appreciate those that take the time to reach out to us and offer their views, whether this is via our website or social media channels, by email, or in person. We won't always agree, but we will always listen.

Open communication

Our approach to seeking these views is to be as open as possible. You can contact us through our website or our social media channels, or you can email us directly at hello@oxygenconservation.com. We want to hear your views.

We love to hear your positivity, enthusiasm, and praise – who wouldn't? We also want to hear your challenges and your criticism, even those that sometimes seem unfair or hurtful – please remember we're all people too. We recognise, though, that we learn the most from challenge and criticism, and we will sometimes change our minds and our approach as a result of that feedback.

Reaching an understanding

In seeking such a diverse range of views, it is of course impossible to find consensus. In fact, we're not even looking for a consensus, as this so often leads to mediocracy and inertia. We simply don't have time to miss our opportunity to save a little more of the natural world. While I appreciate public sector bodies and charitable organisations must strive to find compromise, the truth is that we – as a private organisation – don't. We work with contradictions, and we prioritise impact. We will always do what best helps us Scale Conservation, and yes, that means generating a financial return as a result of our work, not as the purpose.

The vast majority of the time, we have found agreement with many people in many places. We strive to focus on the things that unite us, not those that divide. However, here are some of the things we've considered in the face of challenge, criticism, and negativity, and where we – despite careful thought – hold completely different views and perspectives.

- **Profit:** Some feel conservation should be the purview of charitable organisations, and others have told us the concept of natural capital itself is inappropriate. However, we believe that, by demonstrating it is profitable to protect and improve the natural world, we can mobilise the trillions of pounds needed to undo the terrible harm the human race has done to the planet.
- **Preservation:** We have been criticised for not killing badgers, foxes, mustelids (stoats and weasels), and even hedgehogs. However, we believe it's not the role of a conservation company to kill living things.

WE WILL ALWAYS LISTEN. WE WON'T ALWAYS AGREE.

Where we have to manage non-native and invasive species, we will do this reluctantly and with consideration and care.

- **Access:** We believe there are certain parts of the natural world too rare, too precious, and too delicate to allow regular public access; for example, temperate rainforests. Some think this is private landowners locking away the countryside.

- **Rate of change:** We take time to baseline, measure, monitor, watch, and listen to a landscape. We have been criticised that we're not changing things fast enough, while others think we're changing things too quickly. Perhaps both sides of the debate are correct.

- **Farming restrictions:** We are very supportive of farming and believe the best farmers are brilliant conservationists. We don't, as some do, believe every piece of land should be farmed, nor that it should be farmed in a certain way.

- **Organic farming:** We believe all land should be organic and have been criticised that this reduces the amount of food that can be produced from an area of land. We also know that organic farming is the route to long-term commercial viability, especially in the absence of subsidy payments.

- **Livestock:** We are committed to lower stocking numbers across our estates to ensure our impact on the natural world through agriculture is regenerative. We have been criticised for that belief by those who consider livestock to be a historical and cultural feature of the countryside.

- **Food pricing:** Others maintain that food needs to be available as cheaply as possible, regardless of environmental impact. We believe food is too cheap, as we are yet to truly factor the environmental cost of production into the price of food. We think increasing food prices as necessary is the route to a better future for wildlife and for people, including farmers and producers.

- **Food security:** Some believe that the solution to food security is to produce more food. We believe food waste is a bigger challenge to food security than conservation, because failure of biodiversity will lead to a complete collapse of the global food system.

- **Woodland:** We've been criticised by foresters for not planning to plant commercial timber, by farmers for planning to plant any trees at all, and by environmentalists for not planning to plant enough trees. We believe there should be more native woodland in the natural environment. We are committed to maintaining the right trees, in the right place, at the right time.

We want to hear your views about the places and spaces that mean the most to you. Again, while we won't always agree, we will always listen.

On reflection

Local engagement is one of the most difficult challenges we face, and it is one that I face personally from a leadership perspective. While we recognise it's impossible to change things without upsetting some people in the process, the criticism directed at the team and myself personally is sometimes hard to take.

Our experience is that successful local consultation is largely impossible, which is likely why most private landowners avoid engaging at all with the process. Everyone has a different opinion; everyone wants to be consulted more and in a uniquely specific way; and most people think their version of the future is correct, regardless of them not being the underlying landowner nor an expert in a particular discipline. This is perhaps magnified as we're investing in rural landscapes where people are often inherently more adverse to change of any kind.

One example of this is where, with the purchase of an estate, we became responsible for a historic, decrepit private water supply to properties across the estate, some of which had been sold by previous owners. Significant investment was required to upgrade the infrastructure, to provide clean and safe drinking water to all properties. Inevitably this led to some unavoidable short-term disruption, but we received a remarkable amount of criticism and attack for many aspects of this necessary and costly project.

The reason the relentless, vocal minority are particularly challenging is that it threatens the very commitment we've made to being as transparent, accessible, and engaging as possible. If every time we share anything about our work we're attacked about a specific issue, species, or location (often unrelated to the work), it makes the team question the value of being so open and transparent.

In seeking to provide some balance, the investment in local engagement can help highlight some important learnings. At a recent Native Woodland Planting consultation, we receive some wonderful feedback, alongside the random array of criticism. That criticism ranged from not consulting about changes on an estate we don't own or have any involvement in, to not starting a venison sale or gifting business to the local community, and to challenges that the government's guidance on consultation didn't constitute consultation from one person's perspective.

Our favourite and most valuable criticism was regarding the ideal position to place gateways for hill walkers, to ensure access to the landscape, where new fences will need to be erected to protects trees against deer browsing and feasting. We've taken this feedback on board and will adjust the planting plans to make this possible.

We know engaging openly and regularly is the right thing to do, and it makes us the company we want to be, but it's not always easy.

The Privilege of Criticism
Written July 2023

We've worked incredibly hard for the opportunity to deliver positive environmental and social impact. When you're seeking to create change, though, you have to recognise that you are inviting critique, criticism, and sadly even attack.

Working in the environment sector is a true privilege, and waking up every morning knowing that you're doing something meaningful is special. For some, though, it can mean also carrying a heavy weight. If you're actively working on the climate emergency and biodiversity crisis, the realities of what is happening right now and the knowledge that the worst is yet to come can weigh heavily.

For many, especially those early in their career, this weight can be exacerbated by the criticism they receive at every step, even though those steps are being taken in an attempt to achieve positive improvement. This criticism often arises because it threatens the status quo enjoyed by others, which may have – at least in part – contributed to the climate and biodiversity emergency we now face.

Positive action

I don't know if this will help those of you who face similar challenges, but our brilliant Head of Operations, Dave Keir, has a valuable perspective that has stayed with me for many years. It's one that is particularly applicable to the battle against climate change (as well as any challenge in general): *We don't have to hear criticism – we get to hear it!*

For too long we have collectively taken too much from the planet, with little to no regard for the impact we're having, and the sad reality is that most people are unknowing of their own impact. I'm sure we at Oxygen Conservation aren't perfect in this regard. This last week has been one where we've been privileged to receive a range of challenge and criticism, but thankfully, we know this means we're having impact and we have even more potential to create positive change. We therefore need to keep moving forward.

Here are some examples of the recent criticisms we've received and the positive impact we hope to deliver by taking the positions we have:

1. Estate management
2. Transparency
3. Fox hunting
4. Hound trailing
5. Game bird shooting
6. Bracken
7. Sheep
8. People
9. Trees
10. Finance

1. Estate management

We've been criticised for managing estates differently from how our tenants and local private landowners are used to, or how they would manage the estates themselves were they in our position.

Positive impact: More families are living in the rural environment as a result of us opening up properties for rent. Ultimately, our work is intended to deliver significant longer-term benefits for them personally as well for the environment and the wider community. It's certainly not easy, though, and we're not suggesting that we've been perfect in our delivery.

2. Transparency

We've been criticised for not sharing more information with our neighbours about our plans for the estate over the months, years, and decades to come.

Positive impact: We will always listen to local opinions, but we won't always agree. We also can't share information we don't have, especially about decisions we haven't yet made. Despite being a private landowner, we are and will continue to be committed to radical transparency by sharing as much as we can as soon as we can with those people who have expressed an interest in helping deliver positive impact.

3. Fox hunting

We've been criticised for not allowing activities such as fox hunting on our land.

Positive impact: Our ownership of land has removed opportunities for unsustainable hunting or sporting activities. We are finding new ways for people and wildlife to thrive in the rural environment. However, we recognise the need for and will undertake conservation-focused deer and goat management as part of our environmental restoration plans.

4. Hound trailing

We've been criticised for not supporting hound trailing.

Positive impact: We believe in removing damaging activities from our land. These include hound trailing because its inconsistent with our conservation objectives. By doing so, we will ensure more land can support the restoration of natural processes, giving flora, fauna, and funga the time they need to recover from the negative environmental impact.

5. Game bird shooting

We've been criticised for not supporting the shooting of pheasants, grouse, and other associated 'game' birds.

Positive impact: We're a conservation company and we don't believe in killing things if it can be avoided. We've stopped grouse shooting on the hills of two of our large Scottish estates and transitioned away from a 25,000 pheasant shoot in Devon.

6. Bracken

We've been criticised for not supporting the burning of bracken on a hillside.

Positive impact: We believe in restoring natural processes and do not support the burning of bracken as it causes significant damage to everything in its path. We have stopped burning across our entire portfolio, most notably on Dartmoor and in the Scottish Borders and Highlands. The reality of climate change is that we will see more wildfires in this country and across the globe. Our work will focus on reforesting and rewetting the landscape, keeping more life in the land rather than burning it away.

7. Sheep

We've been criticised for 'hating farmers' because we plan on reducing sheep numbers across our estates.

Positive impact: Over the last two years, in the process of acquiring significant landholdings across the country, we have also assumed responsibility for over 4,000 sheep. While we're greatly supportive of local produce, we have found that large-scale sheep farming at our estates is environmentally and economically unviable. We're therefore committed to reducing sheep numbers and, as a consequence, hope to create opportunities for new entrant farmers to manage high-quality, organic animals and increase growing space that can supply local communities in more regenerative and sustainable ways.

8. People

We've been criticised for not welcoming enough people onto our estates, and also for welcoming too many.

Positive impact: We believe that for people to truly connect with nature and become champions of the environment, they have to experience it. We're also committed to creating special opportunities for people to holiday at home rather than abroad, thus reducing plane travel and lowering the carbon footprint of adventure and relaxation. We have wonderful ecotourism offerings in Devon and Norfolk and are exploring an exciting collaboration with an organisation advocating sensitive wild camping. The reality, however, is that too many people (and this number can be very small) can cause significant damage. We are therefore seeking the right balance between accessibility and protection.

9. Trees

We've been criticised for planting too many trees and also not enough trees.

Positive impact: We have planted around 10,000 trees so far. Our ambition is to plant millions of trees in the coming years on land we own and manage for conservation activities. We are not alone in recognising the exceptional value of trees in the natural landscape. Every government across the UK now has extensive tree-planting targets they're not hitting. We're committed to planting more trees but equally committed to planting the right numbers and species of trees in the right places and for the right reasons. While we recognise the need for more

UK-grown timber, we're not foresters and will only plant native biodiversity-led woodlands. We would appreciate it if the respective regulatory bodies helped us a little more as we try to help them achieve their own targets.

10. Finance

We've been criticised for not being a charity and for being unwilling to fund things for which we are not responsible or that will not provide an impactful outcome.

Positive impact: Oxygen Conservation was founded with the mission to deliver positive environment and social impact, delivering a profit as a result of – not the purpose of – what we do. We are fortunate that our investors have committed significant capital at their risk to help us to achieve this goal. It is only by demonstrating that conservation activities can generate a positive financial return that we can encourage others to mobilise the investment we need to protect and improve at least a little of the natural world. Charity has done so much, and in many ways we're standing on the shoulders of giants, but now we need business to do more!

We *get* to hear criticism

If you're out there trying to do what you can for people and the environment, and if that pressure is weighing heavy, please try and remember that you don't *have* to hear that criticism – you *get* to hear it. You get to hear it because you're changing things, because you're challenging the status quo, and because you're trying to be part of the solution.

If you can meet the criticism with kindness, compassion, and understanding, there is often the potential to learn from those with a different set of lived and learned experiences. There is also the chance to find new and interesting ways of engaging with the very people we need to influence the most.

If it all weighs a little too heavy, remember that you are part of a fantastic, growing community of environmentalists ready to take a call, reply to an email, or meet for a coffee.

Thank you, criticism – it's a privilege to receive you!

On reflection

My opinion remains the same today as it did when I wrote this piece – it's a privilege to receive criticism and, even more so, constructive feedback. However, over the last year we've had to develop approaches to managing and responding to attack and persistent complaints.

Wonderfully, just as I wrote in the article above, when we reached out for advice from those that have unfortunately had much more experience of being attacked, the environment sector was so helpful. The advice I was given and will share is to respond to every genuine observation, thought, and question. I still respond personally to everyone that emails me.

When criticism becomes persistent, incoherent, or offensive, though, it can be better not to respond – the majority of these people just want attention. When we visited one of our estates with some local people recently, we talked about our experience of a persistent complainant. We didn't mention the person by name, but the others immediately guessed correctly. We subsequently learned that this person is known to be the village complainer and has an array of grievances, including a passionate anti-vaccine stance. Yes, that issue was raised repeatedly at one of our public events!

For a long time I was reluctant to block anyone on social media, as we are genuinely committed to being open and transparent. When interactions become relentless, incoherent, and abusive, though, I'd encourage you all to hit block and delete. Focus your attention instead on those wanting to be part of the solution.

Can We Go Beyond Self-Interest and Embrace True Environmental Conservation?

Written June 2023

Everyone we meet claims to love the environment, wildlife, and conservation. The reality is that this passion – while usually a genuinely held belief – often reflects a perspective of the world viewed through a single, self-interested lens.

Motivation factors

We frequently come across people who want to 'optimise' the environment for something that is of particular importance to them. Peeling back the layers, though, tends to reveal a use of the environment to facilitate their business or personal interests – a means to an end – as opposed to delivering positive environmental and social impact for the planet as a whole (as their primary objective).

Let's explore some examples.

Food and farming

Many farmers are genuine lovers of nature, but in trying to find a route to the economic viability of their businesses, they seek to maximise yields often in the short term at the expense of wildlife, their soil system, and water quantity.

Farmers and associated interest groups will argue passionately about food security while refusing to consider the impact of biodiversity loss. They also often disregard the irony that pesticides used to protect certain crops (neonicotinoids) decimate pollinators, presenting a much greater threat to food security than conservation ever will. Other groups argue for the importance and cultural heritage of certain types of farming, most often sheep farming, while simultaneously lamenting the damaged state of the natural environment and the losses they've seen in flora, fauna, and funga that result from over grazing.

Sporting enthusiasts

Stalkers, hunters, fans of game shooting, and even fishermen seek to maximise their enjoyment of the natural world by bending and distorting it to suit their preferences. This can include burning the hillside (*swaling*, or *muirburn*); releasing invasive species in vast numbers; killing competitor species; and medicating target species to increase populations of deer, grouse, or stocked fish. This is all at the expense and to the detriment of the surrounding environment.

Despite being architects of these focused ecosystems, passionate sporting enthusiasts will honestly and wholeheartedly contend that they are conservationists and environmentalists.

Perhaps most troubling is the significant number of local communities wanting to continue the barbaric act of fox hunting across the landscape due to its claimed historical, cultural, or social importance, again in the name of their version of conservation. Having heard this time and again, my interpretation of this narrative is that *They just don't want anything to change.*

Specific species (most often birds)

Some of the most ardent environmentalists are those that feel a particular affinity to birds, often specific bird species. This can result in people seeking to 'optimise' a landscape for a specific species at the expense of a much wider range of wildlife.

This drastically limits landscape recovery and sentences many parts of the uplands to a barren and ecologically sparse future. In our experience, this is particularly the case in Yorkshire and the Lake District. There we have seen first-hand how the preservation of curlew (a wonderful and musical wading bird, which of course should be protected) being solely prioritised, to the expense of all other ecological species and indicators, can deny an opportunity for real environmental improvement at scale.

Gardeners

One of the most surprising encounters we've had is with passionate botanists, who are committed to a zero-tolerance approach to invasive species, except for the 'pretty' ones they like to see.

This has presented itself most starkly in respect to rhododendron, which is suffocating and threatening broadleaf woodlands and increasingly rare areas of Atlantic rainforest across the country. Groups have still campaigned for its place in the landscape for a range of reasons, including cultural heritage, historic record, diversity, and because *We think the flowers are pretty* (for the short period each year when they are in full bloom).*

Energy producers

Developers, landowners, and proponents of hydropower choose to espouse the need for that form of renewable energy to mitigate climate collapse and the biodiversity crisis, but they choose to ignore its resulting catastrophic impact on our river systems.

The presence of artificial barriers – most notably dams – is one of the principal reasons for the serious decline in aquatic species, because dams limit access to spawning grounds. As a result, our children may in later life no longer see wild salmon in the UK.

Of course, we need to generate increasing amounts of renewable energy and, while recognising that they also have impacts on the natural world, we're advocates for

---

* I have to add a note on possibly the most unexpected complaint we've received to date. This came from a person living several miles away from one of our estates. Our plans to remove large areas of invasive rhododendron were met in horror, with the challenge, 'Don't you know there's a war on?' After seeking further clarification, this person explained that the Russian invasion of the Ukraine was already putting enough sadness into the world that removing this invasive species – miles away, on private land – represented a step too far. I'll admit that wasn't a line I was expecting!

both wind and solar power as better options for achieving a net-zero transition. In our opinion, hydropower is a price too high to pay, especially when other technologies are so readily available.

We will always listen

In each of the above examples, the individuals or groups in question genuinely and passionately believe they are environmental champions. The reality is that their campaigns promote their version of conservation, which tends to be preservation of the status quo in a way that allows them to enjoy or profit from nature.

This level of cognitive dissonance is so severe that these groups are arguably greenwashing themselves. On an individual level, this is probably for the better. I've witnessed first-hand a farming patriarch realising the long-term impact of conventional agriculture on the land he was passing to his son. I've also seen an experienced sportsman recognise the need to change his way of interacting with the land and understanding that, despite his decades of hard work, his legacy was fewer grouse and a declining landscape. This was clearly painful for both these people. With it coming at a point in their lives when they could do little to make amends, perhaps it would have been better if they hadn't realised what they'd done to the natural world.

Oxygen Conservation will always listen to the opinions of groups whose views differ from ours, to constantly understand their perspectives and challenge our aspirations for the natural world. To me it is obvious that the next generation, should we leave them a world to look after, will almost certainly prove our thinking wrong and be lost as to how we – me very much included – made so many mistakes. This is why we will never seek to optimise any landscape for one single purpose. We engage with as many different perspectives and opinions as possible – listening to learn, not just to respond.

Over time we will craft a masterplan for each of the estates we are fortunate enough to manage that maximises positive environmental and social impact. We will generate a profit, crucially as a result of what we do, not the purpose. We know that we will have to adapt our plan as the climate changes, and we intend to continue learning, and to implement better ways of protecting and improving the environment for people and wildlife.

On reflection

Reflecting back on my time working in the environment sector, the conversation has continued to change.

If I'd wanted to talk about natural capital five years ago, it would have been a lonely endeavour. If I'd sought to talk about climate change and biodiversity decline, there would have been much more debate about whether it existed rather than about the potential solutions, challenge, and consequences of acting or not.

Instead, today we're now having much more informed discussions and debates.

Are we where we need to be? Absolutely not, and self-interest still dominates the discourse. We are without a doubt moving forward, though, which has to be considered a positive.

Perhaps we could just all work together to do it a little faster.

The Politics of the Environment
Written August 2023

The environment is clearly set to be some kind of weird battle line, drawn between the Conservatives and everyone else leading into the next general election.

We have the Tories sinisterly arguing that anyone who is against new licences for fossil fuel exploitation is pro-Russia, and that anyone who doesn't think small children should die of poisoned air in our cities and towns is anti-business. This is set against the hottest month the planet has ever recorded, so much so that the UN have declared that we've entered a period of global boiling.

Ironically, the sad reality is that it's a positive the environment is at least being talked about. Perhaps that's a step too towards genuine discussion and engagement on the subject. As the climate worsens, the more acutely we all feel the impacts. Appreciating that those impacts are in no way felt proportionally by all, the more aware, the more agitated, and the more angry people – especially young people (and those with young people) – will become.

I'm therefore increasingly hopeful that this will be one of the last elections fought on anything but an environmentally regenerative platform where all parties are arguing about who will do more to build a thriving natural capital economy.

This politically focused opening links seamlessly with time spent at our Leighon Estate this week, where we welcomed the chairman of Natural England and a group of his colleagues.

Leighon Estate

Leighon is a spectacular space, occupying almost 800 acres of East Dartmoor. The East Dartmoor area is bringing forward one of DEFRA's pilot landscape recovery projects – a title some locally find offensive because it suggests the land needs to recover. It does. Most wonderfully, Leighon is home to almost 120 acres of incredible Atlantic rainforest and the most spectacular array of flora, fauna, and funga.

In the eighteen months since we've purchased the property, we've learned a huge amount, listened to a large number of divergent opinions, and made many mistakes. We've also tried to rectify as many as possible of the immediate challenges faced by the landscape:

- We have improved – and continue to invest a significant amount in improving – the infrastructure on the site, including the historic private water supply. As a result of these and other works, we are delighted to have welcomed three new families to our built properties on the estate.

- We have supported a local family business in securing a long-term tenancy on a growing space to provide food to the local community.

- We have started organic transition and experimented with the use of conservation-grazing pigs and ponies.

- Perhaps most impactfully, we've battled against some of the most archaic practices and now ceased all burning on the moor.

All this has been done alongside a wide array of environmental and ecological surveys to better understand the baseline of this outstanding part of Dartmoor.

As we've seen the landscape relax a little, becoming a little scruffier and a little more welcoming to wildlife, one of the most pleasurable things has been welcoming people back to the estate. Leighon and Hound Tor have provided the perfect backdrop for us to begin explaining a little about Oxygen Conservation, and this week we had the pleasure of welcoming Tony Juniper and his colleagues from Natural England to the estate.

Natural England at Leighon

As many of you reading this will know, I'm not overly complimentary of the public sector. I think it is an institution no longer fit for purpose, considers its primary role as stopping anything from happening, is largely devoid of inspiration or ambition, and attracts people that are waiting to retire and consider *hard work* to be an offensive term.

I think it's time we acknowledge, however, that the job the public sector are being asked to do is impossible, and that they are criticised when they come anywhere near doing it. This week has been no exception, with the newspapers attacking noted conservationist and environmentalist Tony Juniper for being... wait for it... an environmentalist!

The combination of government restrictions, risk aversion, and bureaucracy, together with media scrutiny and unreasonable public expectations that none of us can ever meet, has resulted in a situation where the traditional public or charitable environment sector cannot win. There is no opportunity for innovation, and no praise for doing good – just the potential of criticism for having tried and potentially failed, or for not succeeding in the exact right way.

Natural England are forced to try and find consensus in a complicated world, one where we need people to change the way they live and use the land. It's also a world where entrenched, protectionist voices either refuse to accept the presence of a problem or – slightly better – acknowledge the need for change but passionately argue that the solution isn't found through change.

This is where private business needs to step up.

Businesses must be the (electric) vehicle of change. Business can and must succeed to exist, and they can and must make a profit. If they can do that by delivering positive environmental and social impact, we can create a natural capital economy that can herald a bright future for everyone, or at least a future of some kind.

It was a pleasure to walk and talk with Tony, sharing stories of birds, beetles, butterflies, and beavers (the latter now rumoured to be present in the Bovey Valley). I hope the time at Leighon, wandering through the rainforest and picnicking beside the online ponds, provided a little nature-based rest and recovery for Tony. We are very grateful to him and his team for doing what they can to advocate for the environment in the face of ridiculous and often personal attack – largely, for doing exactly what they're employed to do and what more of us should be doing.

For my part, I'm going to encourage the increasing number of businesses appearing in this space, working hard to build a natural capital economy, to raise their voices, to speak louder, and to advocate more for the natural world.

We need this to be the time of the activist founder and business leader. You're supposed to end an article with a call to action, so here's mine: Hold me to this standard!

On reflection

As I reflect on my thoughts following our time at Leighon with Tony and the team, I do so with disappointment.

The state of political discourse has continued to decline, and the country and of course the entire environment sector is severely lacking leadership. While we've achieved much in that time, we haven't done enough. I'm not doing enough.

This is a time when we need more – more passion, more commitment, and more bravery – from everyone. I need to do more and will do more.

Fear. Hope. And Hate.

Written October 2023

In our rapidly changing world, the four-letter word that seems to be echoing louder than ever before is *fear*. Fear permeates our society, particularly within the environment sector, where concerns about shifting government policies, climate change, and the destructive impact of human actions (yes, those of all of us) are on the rise. This fear is not limited to environmentalists alone; even those whose traditional ways of enjoying and exploiting the environment face an uncertain future and are grappling with fear.

Fear, hate, and hope

In this article we consider the powerful emotions of fear, hate, and hope, exploring how they manifest in different groups and individuals. We also examine the roles of those emotions in shaping the very future of the natural world and the future of life on Earth.

Fear and hate

One cannot deny that fear has cast a long shadow over the environment sector, and increasingly beyond that sector, as it occupies public discourse. Those deeply invested in preserving our natural world are especially fearful of the government's increasingly cynical attacks on the environment and of its own net-zero policy.

This fear is compounded by the obvious results of climate change becoming increasingly devastating, with more frequent and severe climate events affecting communities worldwide. At the time of writing, it is 24°C in the UK in October!

Furthermore, there's a growing list of examples illustrating how human actions and – perhaps just as importantly – inactions have led to the death and destruction of wildlife and its precious habitats.

However, fear isn't confined to environmentalists. It also surfaces among those whose lives and livelihoods have long been dependent on the exploitation of nature. A recent encounter in Scotland serves as a poignant example. Two individuals passionately dedicated to pheasant and grouse shooting (ironically from the South West of England) were aggrieved by our decision to halt such activities on land under Oxygen Conservation ownership. It's important to note here that no suggestion or comment was offered about how they choose to manage their own land. The anger and hate came as a result of how we choose to manage our own land, for the benefit of nature. It is important to say that I didn't handle this conversation as well as I hope to in future. I was tired, surprised by the approach, and defensive in my responses. I was perhaps even rude. For that I apologise, and I did so directly to our new friends.

While their feelings were clearly amplified in the moment, I think the real source of their hate was fear. Perhaps it's the fear that the world is evolving beyond their traditional practices. Maybe they're apprehensive about their roles in society, sensing that their time in the limelight has passed. Or it could be the dawning realisation that the entitlement that once propelled them might not suffice in an altered landscape, that landscape marked by evolving societal values and a rapidly changing climate (in every sense of the word).

Fear and change

Interestingly, fear can serve as a catalyst for change, albeit in diverse and sometimes unexpected ways. In contrast to our unexpected discussions, two scheduled meetings this week highlighted different reactions to very similar conversations.

On either side of the above discussion, I felt privileged to be asked to speak to representatives from the Scottish Government on the hillside in Perthshire, and to the European Board of Triodos Bank at their beautiful head office in Bristol.

In our meeting with the pheasant and grouse shooting enthusiasts, as described previously, fear gave rise to anger and hostility. They initiated an uninvited and increasingly unpleasant discussion, followed by a slew of four-letter words.

Conversely, the meetings with the Scottish Government and Triodos bore witness to a very different response. These stakeholders, despite acknowledging the grim state of our environment, were motivated by fear to work harder to find positive change. They recognised the urgency of the situation and were clearly committed to making a difference for people and wildlife.

Their response to a similar conversation was not hate but gratitude. They expressed appreciation for the insights and efforts we've dedicated to environmental conservation, concluding that it offered them a glimmer of hope.

Fear and hope

In a world where fear often seems omnipresent, fostering hope becomes essential. Fear can paralyse us, causing us to cling to outdated practices and beliefs, but hope can empower us to transcend those limitations. Hope is the beacon that guides us through the tumultuous waters of uncertainty and change, and sometimes it is all we have but also all we need.

The Scottish Government and Triodos Bank meetings exemplify the power of hope. They demonstrated that, even in the face of daunting challenges, hope can inspire collaboration and drive meaningful action. While it is the current generation that must act, it is the next generation that will ultimately bear the consequences or reap the benefits of our actions.

Next

The world is undoubtedly facing pressing environmental challenges, and fear is a natural response to these threats. However, as we navigate this increasingly turbulent terrain, we must remember that fear can be a double-edged sword. It can either foster hate and resistance or ignite positive change, collaboration, and – most importantly – hope.

In the environment sector, it is imperative that we choose the path of hope. Hope is the driving force behind innovation, conservation, and the pursuit of a regenerative future. By finding common ground and uniting in our commitment to make a positive impact, we can transcend fear and create a world where hope prevails.

In closing, let us strive to find more hope and less hate in our collective journey towards a healthier, more sustainable planet. For my part, moving forward I will do everything I can to meet the hate with compassion. At least, I hope I will.

On reflection

Much of this chapter has focused on the challenges associated with being agents of change, but that might largely be a reflection on the broken part of my mind that can only focus on the things that need fixing or problems that need solving.

The reality is that our work is almost exclusively met with positivity. We are constantly overwhelmed by kindness, enthusiasm, encouragement, and positivity. We're committed to delivering positive environmental and social impact, and perhaps the biggest impact we've had to date is redefining what's possible in the environment sector. The speed, scale, and sophistication in how we work have been recognised as different, and we hope our approach is helping push the entire sector forward.

One of the best examples of this was a call received recently from a partner at a leading accountancy firm, which had been working hard to make natural capital a feature of their work. Without our knowledge, our work, photography, and videography had formed the basis of the keynote speech at this accountancy firm's recent companywide event. That then inspired superb engagement in how the firm could better contribute to achieving net positive impact on climate and nature. It's amazing to know that our influence is extending into the hearts, minds, and conference rooms far beyond our boundaries.

We can't be everywhere, and we can't reach everyone, but if our work or materials help you in any way, please feel free to share this book and our articles, podcasts, and videos as far and as widely as possible.

Rebranding Conservation – Our Thinking So Far

Written April 2023, in collaboration with Head of Storytelling, Ell Steers

From the first fragments of an idea that became Oxygen Conservation, we have prioritised branding and marketing efforts to create an aspirational, investable brand focused on nature and conservation.

Companies like Patagonia, Tesla, Apple, and Google inspire us, teach us, and shape our approach to marketing, branding, and crafting our business identity and company culture. This has helped us Scale Conservation to deliver positive environmental and social impact and, in the process, to begin mobilising significant investment in an effort to save at least a little of the natural world for the next generation.

This is only the start of our journey.

We continue to look, listen, and learn every way we can, to try and continuously improve the way we present our business, our work, and our world.

In this article we will share our insights on the importance of branding in the environment sector and the lessons we've learned from Oxygen Conservation's adventures to date.

Branding as a barrier to private sector investment

When we founded Oxygen Conservation with Oxygen House, one of the major challenges faced by the environment sector was the lack of private sector investment. We recognised that many companies and investors were hesitant to commit to environmental initiatives. This is perhaps, at least in part, a result of the lack of investment assigned to marketing. That is unsurprising, as many of those organisations in the environment sector have grown from small groups of passionate individuals, motivated to protect and improve the natural environment, often in their own time and without the financial resources or professional support required to present a developed commercial proposition or appearance. We remain eternally grateful to them all for their efforts.

It became clear to our team that branding would play a crucial role in shaping the perception of our industry, influencing investment decisions, and ultimately mobilising the investment we need to give us a chance in saving at least a little of the natural world. If you want to read more on this concept, we recommend picking up a copy of *Alchemy* by Rory Sutherland (Sutherland, 2019).

Raising the bar in marketing and branding

From the very beginning, we understood that our brand needed to convey professionalism, credibility, and a commitment to quality in order to appropriately represent the values and standards of our investors and our team. Furthermore, we knew this would be intrinsically important to attracting private sector investment and support for environmental initiatives. To raise the bar in our marketing and branding, we focused on:

1. Simplicity
2. Natural beauty
3. Beautiful data
4. Wonderful images
5. Quality

1. Simplicity

We recognised that simplicity is so often key to effective branding. Our logo and branding are simple and elegant; primarily in black and white; and borrowing subtle connections to the wider Oxygen House Group, reflecting that this remains a core part of our DNA. This minimalist approach is intended to convey sophistication, aspiration, and professionalism, setting us apart from other organisations in the industry. We wanted our branding to be clean, modern, and easily recognisable, and we believe simplicity is helping us achieve that.

2. Natural beauty

As a company focused on delivering positive environmental and social impact, it is crucial for us to showcase the beauty of the environment and make it a central focus of our brand. To achieve this we hired a brilliant environmental photographer as one of our first team members. This has allowed us to capture stunning images that we use in all our materials, and in the process create aspirational and inspirational roles for future environmental creatives.

Investing in talented creatives and providing them with the right equipment is so important and so rarely done. Sadly, we don't yet have a time machine – if we fail to capture a day, time, event, or season at one of our estates, it's lost forever. Furthermore, we sadly can't invite everyone to the precious environments we own and manage, but through our photography and videography we can share them far and wide without negatively impacting the environment in the process. By highlighting the breathtaking beauty of nature, we aim to inspire others to appreciate, connect with, and protect the natural and built environment.

3. Beautiful data

We understand the importance of making information visually appealing and accessible. We embrace the principle that information is beautiful, and we strive to present information in a way that is visually appealing, meaningful, and engaging to our audience. We're inspired by the mantra first voiced by Scott Belsky when at Adobe: 'Creation must be made accessible for consumption. This is your real job' (Belsky, 2018). We want our work to be powerful enough for professionals but accessible enough for everyone. We use infographics, graphs, charts, and other visual tools in our materials to simplify complex information and make it easy for all audiences to understand. This approach has helped us convey our message more effectively, building interest, momentum, and confidence in our work.

4. Wonderful images

Visuals are a powerful tool that can evoke emotions, create connection, and inspire action. We celebrate and showcase high-quality, captivating images in our marketing materials, website, and social media posts, increasingly preferring video content to take our work to the next level. Where an image is included in our documentation, it owns the page. If it's not good enough to stand alone, it's not included. Far too often in the environment sector, images or tiny photos are included that offer nothing to the experience of those reading the documentation. We've researched extensively into print and digital media to borrow the tools and techniques to make the selection of the right images connect with the audience, in the process helping build interest and engagement in our work. This approach also sits naturally alongside our commitment to simple black-and-white branding, meaning that the audience's focus is completely on the natural world.

5. Quality

At Oxygen Conservation we believe that *How you do anything is how you do everything*. We are therefore committed to excellence in every aspect of our branding efforts. From the quality of our imagery to that of the printing materials we use, we obsess about every detail. That doesn't mean we get everything right – we're making mistakes and learning lessons every day. Over time, though, we're always getting better. We want our branding to convey professionalism and credibility, and we believe that attention to quality is crucial in achieving that. This is achieved by:

- Providing constant, honest feedback to each other
- Seeking ways to improve the quality of our materials
- Involving key creatives, partners, professionals, and decision makers in the process

The power of branding

We are proud of the impact our branding efforts have had on our success in attracting private sector investment and support for our environmental initiatives. The lessons we have learned about the power of branding – simplicity, focus on natural beauty, showcasing wonderful images, making data beautiful, and commitment to quality – can be applied by other organisations in the environment sector to raise the bar and set a new standard for branding and marketing. We urge fellow environmentalists and conservationists to prioritise branding as a strategic tool to convey professionalism, credibility, and quality in order to inspire action, drive positive change, and mobilise investment. Together, let's leverage the power of marketing and branding to protect and improve our environment for future generations.

On reflection

This piece is somewhat overwritten and is the first one I've read back and not enjoyed. Ironically, it could and should have been much simpler – just like our branding!

REBRANDING CONSERVATION – OUR THINKING SO FAR

Branding is essential and the most sustainable way to elevate a concept, idea, and business – adding desirability and a sense of luxury without increasing the underlying environmental footprint.

Over the last twelve months, our marketing materials have become simpler, clearer, more concise, and more creative. We've launched our *Shoot Room Sessions* podcasts; produced our *Field Notes* newsletter; and continue to produce high-quality pieces on videography, photography, and thought leadership. Our reaching is now approaching 100,000 people every month and growing rapidly.

That is absolutely thanks to our wonderful marketing team. They were recently described by a leading finance industry marketing director as the most incredible content creation team he'd ever seen, and I couldn't agree more. Thank you!

FOUR
Oxygen Conservation's Process

Networking Nature: How We Are Pioneering the Natural Capital Economy with Silicon Valley Strategies

Written January 2024

To appreciate the potential of Oxygen Conservation, it's crucial to first understand what a network business is.

Network businesses operate on a model where the value to each participant or aspect of the business increases as more participants or aspects join the network. As examples, this concept is evident in companies such as:

- **Facebook** – where the more users join, the more valuable the network becomes for social connectivity

- **Uber** – where an increase in drivers and riders enhances the utility and efficiency of the service

The success of a network business largely hinges on scaling, data efficiency and utilisation, and creating a community or ecosystem that becomes progressively more valuable and self-sustaining.

In our mission to Scale Conservation and deliver positive environmental and social impact, we're working hard to harness these network effects to help grow the entire natural capital economy. We want to create a self-reinforcing system that scales the level of investment in the protection and restoration of the natural world.

Lesson learned and applied

Let's explore some of the lessons we've learned and how we're seeking to apply them to create a networking effect across the growing natural capital economy:

1. Creating a market-leading landscape portfolio
2. Enjoying first-mover advantage
3. Establishing a team of experts
4. Setting industry standards
5. Increasing value and entry cost with growth
6. Achieving reduced costs and increased demand with scale
7. Viewing environmental challenges as business opportunities
8. Being the greatest hedge against climate change
9. Realising our incredible potential

1. Creating a market-leading landscape portfolio

Just as network businesses like Facebook and Airbnb grew their user bases and listings, we have successfully built the UK's largest natural capital portfolio. This significant landholding provides us with a market-leading position in the UK, with each additional investment adding to that advantage. Further investments in land acquisition not only increase this asset base but also raise the overall value of land designated for natural capital purposes, mirroring how network businesses increase their value as they scale.

In the same way Uber expanded rapidly by increasing its network of drivers and riders, we have moved quickly to acquire ten different estates in seven counties and three countries. Uber's growth strategy – scaling by broadening its service areas and user base – mirrors our expansion in the natural capital sector. We've achieved this by increasing the number and variety of land assets, thereby producing premium natural capital products and services in vastly different geographies.

2. Enjoying first-mover advantage

Thanks to the support of the Oxygen House Group, we have been able to position Oxygen Conservation as one of the first meaningful movers in the natural capital network business.

This advantage is comparable to how companies like eBay or Amazon established themselves as pioneers in their respective online marketplaces. eBay's early establishment in the online marketplace allowed it to capture a significant user base and set market standards.

We are trying to emulate this path in the natural capital sector by building the first conservation-focused natural capital portfolio and by inspiring others to also enter this new asset class.

3. Establishing a team of experts

Establishing a team of experts in a field where specialised knowledge is rare creates a significant barrier to entry, much like how technology companies maintain a competitive edge through their intellectual property and capital. Our award-winning team (giving a shoutout to you all!) not only enhances our commercial advantage and operational efficiency but also has the network effect of increasing our profile and brand awareness, helping attract more and more talented people to join our growing team. We're so grateful talented people want to come and be part of the adventure, and our summer internship programme is launching soon.

Apple's success, driven by its team of experts in technology and design, reflects a similar advantage and inspires our work at Oxygen Conservation. Apple's expertise in creating user-friendly and innovative products has created a high barrier to entry into the tech industry, just as our special team solidifies its standing as the market leader in the growing natural capital economy.

4. Setting industry standards

By committing to delivering the highest-quality natural capital products and services, Oxygen Conservation aims to elevate the performance of the entire industry. Oxygen Conservation is striving to elevate the performance and quality of carbon credits, BNG units, and nature credits (and future products, services, tokens, and derivatives).

This strategy is similar to how Apple set high standards in consumer electronics, allowing the company to charge a premium and lead the market in innovation and quality.

5. Increasing value and entry cost with growth

As we continue to acquire land to Scale Conservation, the cost of entering the natural capital economy will increase, thus elevating the value of our initial investments and developing natural capital products and services. We fully appreciate this will increase the value and therefore cost of land, and we hope this will go some of the way to ensuring we truly value nature moving forward.

This growth pattern is observed in successful network businesses like LinkedIn, where the platform's value increased with its expanding professional network.

6. Achieving reduced costs and increased demand with scale

The infusion of additional investment into the natural capital economy will improve our efficiency in developing and delivering conservation and habitat-creation activities. This will result in a reduction in the overheads required to develop natural capital products and services, thereby increasing profit margins and demand.

Tesla's approach in the electric vehicle market, achieving economies of scale to reduce costs and increase demand, acts as an inspiration for Oxygen Conservation. As Tesla expanded production, it reduced costs and increased demand for electric vehicles, a pattern Oxygen Conservation aims to replicate in creating natural capital products and services.

Before anyone reading this yells about how electric vehicles aren't perfect: of course they aren't; but while you wait for perfect, we will continue making progress towards better.

7. Viewing environmental challenges as business opportunities

Unfortunately, the worsening climate crisis and loss of species increase the demand and urgent need for our work, and in this we find a bittersweet business opportunity. Similar to how renewable energy companies have grown in response to the global energy crisis, the less society does to tackle climate change, the more valuable Oxygen Conservation becomes.

Tesla's growth amidst the global shift towards sustainable energy mirrors how we hope Oxygen Conservation will expand due to the increasing demand for high-quality natural capital solutions.

8. Being the greatest hedge against climate change

In many ways Oxygen Conservation is both a hedge against humanity's climatic and ecological failures and an investment in hope and action to address the planet's greatest challenges. This dual role positions us uniquely, similar to how companies in Silicon Valley (many tech firms) seek to balance profitability with environmental responsibility.

Microsoft stands as a leading example in this, particularly in their fight against climate change. Their ambitious goal to become carbon negative by 2030 is a testament to their commitment. This involves removing more carbon from the atmosphere than they emit, achieved through investments in renewable energy, reforestation, and carbon capture technologies.

9. Realising our incredible potential

We all stand at the cusp of a transformative era in environmental sustainability and economic growth. Our innovative model, combining the principles of successful network businesses like those of Uber, Google, Apple, and Microsoft, is not just a pioneering venture in the realm of natural capital; it's also a blueprint, with multibillion-pound potential, for a sustainable future.

The core strategy of Oxygen Conservation – acquiring and managing land for positive environmental and social impact, creating natural capital as a product of our work – harbours immense global potential. As we expand our footprint, the value of our assets, and the impact of our interventions and initiatives, are poised to escalate dramatically. This will create a network effect that we hope will be felt across the growing natural capital economy and beyond.

This growth trajectory mirrors the expansive reach of companies like Amazon and Facebook, which have shown how scalable models can lead to exponential growth and global influence.

Moreover, our model of increasing the value and entry cost with its growth, similar to Amazon's expansion strategy, indicates a future where our early investments in land and natural capital will appreciate significantly. This appreciation not only promises substantial financial returns but also ensures larger, more impactful environment and social outcomes – our core purpose.

Our Why

In a world grappling with the pressing challenges of climate collapse and environmental crisis, the demand for sustainable and restorative practices is growing exponentially. Oxygen Conservation, with its dual focus – on positive environment and social impact, and on profitable growth – is perfectly positioned to meet this demand. We hope our potential to attract global investments and partnerships, akin to the wide-reaching networks of Facebook and Uber, can turn Oxygen Conservation into the architect of a global natural capital economy.

The model we've developed, borrowing much from the rapid growth of the companies mentioned above, is more than a business strategy. It's an opportunity for action, for corporations, governments, and communities to invest in our planet's future. Our vision aligns economic incentives with ecological stewardship, creating a win-win scenario for investors and the environment alike.

As we seek to Scale Conservation and replicate the Oxygen Conservation model across different regions, we hope to create a global network of natural capital assets. This is with the aim of contributing significantly and at an increasingly more meaningful scale to the fight against climate chaos and the biodiversity collapse.

In essence, Oxygen Conservation is not just restoring land; our aim is to restore hope. We are committed to being a beacon for a future where economic growth and environmental sustainability are not competing interests but are intricately intertwined. The potential of Oxygen Conservation extends beyond financial metrics. We are intent on setting a precedent for how businesses can be a force for good by delivering positive environmental and social impact, providing a profit not as the purpose but as the result of what our business does.

On reflection

The environment sector has to be the most exciting place to be working, and the momentum of regenerative growth in the natural capital sector has continued at an astounding rate, especially in 2024. John Elkington, in his amazing book *Green Swans*, famously talked about creating the exponential 20s. This refers to the second great period of growth, echoing the roaring 1920s, but this time with a focus on environmental and societal regeneration.

We're starting to see the exponential 20s become reality.

In the last few weeks, we've walked away from a potential £250 million capital investment as it wasn't the right deal for Oxygen Conservation. Instead of this being a backwards step, there wasn't even a pause – there was an acceleration!

The inflow of interest in our work, interest in providing additional investment, and interest in forming partnerships have grown almost exponentially. We are in the fortunate position of enjoying exceptional support and funding from the Oxygen House Group. We also have the opportunity to Scale

Conservation to a previously incomprehensible level, through the influx of the billions of pounds of additional investment we all know is required in the environment sector.

The level of support, positivity, and recommendation we've received from across the financial sector has been genuinely humbling. A little over a year ago, this world was completely new to us; but as a result of the openness, transparency, and collaboration we offer, we've been met with the exact same in return.

Building the natural capital economy is difficult, with the almost limitless number of technical and specific details to solve; but just like John, I'm confident we will find a way and together roar into the exponential 20s.

Adventures in Safety

Written September 2023

A large part of what we do at Oxygen Conservation is about adventure.

Our unique blend of environment, impact, and adventure shapes a culture that thrives on inspiration and excitement. This ethos attracts people passionate about embarking on extraordinary experiences. That means we push ourselves out of our comfort zone and experience different things in unique ways. It doesn't mean doing things that are unsafe.

Let's keep things safe

Working as much as we do in the great outdoors can be exhilarating, challenging, and unbelievably changeable. Whether you're an environmentalist, adventure guide, or – perhaps most dangerously – an executive in a business where you are occasionally allowed outside, safety should always be your top priority. Without our unwavering commitment to health, safety, and wellbeing, our way of working and enjoying the natural world wouldn't be possible.

A recent expedition to the Scottish Highlands, where we welcomed two groups of visitors to the wonderful Invergeldie Estate, exemplified our approach. We believe the best way to experience the raw beauty of the estate is either on an e-bike or by traversing its vast expanses on foot. With every visit, the communication, conversation, and fun flow much more freely after time spent on the hill. Fresh air, inspirational landscapes, fabulous wildlife, and physical exertion form a magical combination for bringing a group together. This immersive approach, however, requires meticulous planning and deep consideration for safety, ensuring everyone's wellbeing, health, and happiness.

The vast and unpredictable nature of outdoor environments means that accidents can and sadly do happen. I've learned that adhering to the following five rules can significantly reduce the risks and keep you safe, however you choose to live, work, or play in the great outdoors:

1. Responsible driving
2. Preparation
3. Effective communication
4. Experience (an advantage and a threat)
5. Risk avoidance

1. Responsible driving

Driving – whether on remote dirt roads, on rugged terrain, or on the way to and from an estate – often poses the most significant risk when working outdoors. It's

SCALING CONSERVATION

vital to recognise and manage the risks associated with travel of all kinds, especially driving.

CHOOSE THE RIGHT VEHICLE
The most important aspect of travel in our work is selecting the right vehicle for the journey. Many of our team drive electric vehicles, which, while minimising our impact on the environment, also provides a more comfortable driving experience.

TAKE BREAKS
The need to charge electric vehicles also has the added advantage of mandating breaks and comfort stops. Some might think that charging is disruptive or annoying, but the truth is that it's more of a feature than a bug once you make the change.

It's a lot like making the change from Windows to Mac. It takes a short period of commitment, but you'll be delighted you did – everything is just better. (Our Head of Operations, Dave Keir, does not endorse this perspective, though!)

For the members of the team that most often visit remote and inaccessible sites, there is not yet a practical electric vehicle available to do the job, especially where ground conditions are uneven, wet, and slippery. We therefore always work hard to find the best vehicle for both the journey and the destination.

REMEMBER VEHICLE MAINTENANCE IS ESSENTIAL
Before embarking on any journey, especially into the wilderness, it's important to ensure that your vehicle is in excellent working condition. A flat tyre or engine failure in the wilderness can quickly turn into a life-threatening situation, so preventative measures are essential.

Regular maintenance checks can help prevent breakdowns in remote areas where assistance may be far away.

2. Preparation

The Scout motto, *Be prepared*, is a fundamental principle when working outdoors. Increasingly, the climate can be incredibly unpredictable, especially in remote and inaccessible locations. To stay safe, I like to follow some of the following principles.

PRACTISE THOROUGH PLANNING

Calendar discipline is possibly one of the most impactful things anyone can do to improve their performance in business and in life. Plan your time, know when you're travelling, where you're going, and what you're doing when you get there. Share that information with others who care about you and can help if needed.

We meticulously plan for our visits with consideration of the varying weather conditions. We always advise visitors ahead of time on appropriate attire, preparation, and considerations. We also ask whether they are happy to adventure, since we can welcome visitors with different mobility capabilities and adventure appetites.

PACK SMART

Packing is an absolute skill; it's why the military spend so much time and energy teaching their recruits what to pack and how to pack it. If you carry too much equipment, you'll be slow and burn through energy too quickly. If you don't pack enough, you'll be unprepared for the experience.

As we've travelled more and more, I've enjoyed testing and improving what I pack and how. My list always includes: phone, IT kits, sunglasses, water, food, appropriate clothing, and footwear. I'm working on remembering sunscreen and (ecologically appropriate) insect repellent! All too often, people don't travel with the most basic equipment and supplies. Do you?

KNOW YOUR ESCAPE ROUTE
Always know how you will get yourself and others out of a challenging situation. With our estate tours, a support vehicle is vital in that process. Equipped with essentials like warm clothing and a first aid kit, the support vehicle is always on hand to deliver a rapid response, for example in case of equipment failure or for emergency evacuations. A support vehicle also offers the advantage of allowing our media team to join the trip, giving us the flexibility to share videos and images with visitors to help them remember and share their experiences of adventuring with Oxygen Conservation. This vehicle has proved vital, and I'm sure it will do so again. For instance, on one of our recent tours of the Invergeldie Estate, my bike's battery failed and the chain broke. Swift assistance from the vehicle was invaluable in getting the group up and running again.

3. Effective communication

Communication is your lifeline when working in remote areas. It can mean the difference between a minor inconvenience and a life-threatening situation.

IF YOU'RE GOING FAR (OR WILD), GO TOGETHER
At Oxygen Conservation, it is rare that we travel alone, especially when working remotely. This removes risks associated with lone working and offers many

advantages from a productivity, learning, and culture perspective.

HAVE SPECIFIC BRIEFINGS
Before any trip, we engage with our guests to understand their comfort levels, confidence, and preferences. This proactive dialogue helps tailor a safe and enjoyable experience. This method is noted and recorded as part of our internal processes.

An example of another briefing is during our e-bike tours, where an experienced rider, like our wonderful Head of Environment, Dan, explains the mechanics and safe operation of the bikes. We also select rental bikes from the fantastic neighbouring business at Comrie Croft who always ensures high-quality, well-maintained, and serviced bikes and helmets.

STAY IN TOUCH
Carry a fully charged mobile phone with you at all times. However, keep in mind that mobile phone coverage can be unreliable in remote areas. Where possible, familiarise yourself with areas where you might lose signal, and plan your activities and communication accordingly. I tend to travel with a phone and tablet on different networks to maximise potential coverage.

Check in with your designated contact regularly, especially if you're in a remote location. Let them know when you've safely completed your tasks or returned from an adventure. Establish a communication schedule, and stick to it. Missed check-ins can trigger unnecessary worry and potential rescue efforts – we've trialled this process in a real situation. While it turned out the person was perfectly safe and well, the experience was worrying for all involved, but this trial did show the process worked perfectly.

4. Experience (an advantage and a threat)

Experience can be your greatest asset in the great outdoors, but it can also lead to overconfidence. It's crucial to find a balance between utilising your expertise and respecting the ever-changing nature of outdoor environments.

HAVE AN EXPERIENCED LEADER
Each adventure has a leader. At Invergeldie I often lead the bike tour personally, having done so many times, and I set a pace and a route that are comfortable for our visitors. This also means I am able to bring the group together to brief them ahead of any especially challenging parts of the route, for example where there are particularly slippery areas or steep rises and falls. We always make sure we identify challenging spots and guide participants safely through them. On occasion, we make the decision to change the route or head home, for example if we're losing the light or the weather is turning against us.

KNOW YOUR LIMITS
It is vital to understand your skill level and the conditions you can safely navigate. Don't take unnecessary risks or attempt tasks beyond your capabilities. Overconfidence can lead to poor decision making and increases the likelihood of accidents.

We recently took our team coasteering with fantastic guides in Pembrokeshire. The final set of natural platforms provided a number of options up to a ten-metre final jump. I was so proud to see everyone choose the level that worked for them, pushing themselves safely just outside of their comfort zones.

DON'T ASSUME OTHERS' LIMITS

It's vitally important to recognise the limits of those within your group, and the limitation of your equipment and conditions.

Across the last eighteen months, we've visited more than seventy unique estates, in addition to our own land holdings, many times. On each occasion, we're mindful of the limitations of the members of our groups and especially how the light and weather conditions change in different places.

On one occasion, when visiting an estate offered for sale privately, the owner's vehicle got stuck at the top of a Munro, meaning we had to walk for five hours in the blazing summer heat to get off the hillside. We were the only people in the group that had carried water and were wearing appropriate footwear. This proved essential as we supported our guide down safely in his deck shoes.

BE HUMBLE AND HONEST

As beneficial as experience can be, it can too often lead to complacency. It is important to dynamically assess changing conditions and your varying abilities. Humility and honesty are so important, especially for senior leaders who have spent far longer than they might like to remember in the corner office or coffee shop rather than on the hill in the wet and cold.

It's also important to keep learning – even experienced adventurers can benefit from additional knowledge and training. Attending workshops, courses, and training seminars can provide valuable insights and help you adapt to evolving outdoor challenges. We, for example, are planning on taking the whole team to an advanced off-road driving course in the spring.

5. Risk avoidance

The golden rule of outdoor safety is simple: if it doesn't feel safe, don't do it. Your intuition is your most powerful tool in assessing potential dangers.

TRUST YOUR JUDGEMENT
Our experiences of viewing estates have included every form of vehicle imaginable, with some not as comfortable as you'd hope.

This week was the first time I've had to decline an excursion. We were visiting a large estate in the South West, and on arrival, the selling agent asked us to climb into the back of a gator utility vehicle. The back of the vehicle was full of hay, meaning we would be required to sit atop the bales. We politely shared that we thought this was unsafe and wouldn't be using the vehicle, instead preferring to use our own. It's never comfortable to challenge someone on their own land, but that can be when it's most important to trust your judgement.

If a situation or task feels risky, pause and re-evaluate. Consult with colleagues or experts if needed. It's better to postpone or modify a plan than to push forward when you're uncertain. This experience served as an excellent coaching prompt to share with members of our team and every one of you reading this piece.

BE ADAPTABLE
Our team, especially Estate Managers and Visit Leads, are completely empowered to make tough calls. This includes

cancelling activities due to adverse weather or insufficient light, or if participants are inadequately prepared. Safety always takes precedence, and there will always be another time, as long as we're all safe and well.

WORK AS A TEAM
In group settings, encourage open communication and a culture of safety. If any team member expresses concerns, take them seriously and consider alternative approaches. The collective wisdom of a team can help mitigate risks and ensure everyone's wellbeing.

Adventuring safely

While the natural world offers incredible opportunities for adventure, it also presents unique challenges. By prioritising safety through responsible driving, preparation, effective communication, a balanced approach to experience, and a steadfast commitment to avoiding unnecessary risks, you can enjoy the wonders of nature while keeping yourself and your team safe.

Remember: nature is awe-inspiring, but it demands respect and caution.

Whether you're a business leader overseeing outdoor operations or an adventurer seeking thrills in the wild, these principles can help you navigate the great outdoors safely and successfully.

Finally, it's important to recognise and appreciate those who work tirelessly to ensure not only an enjoyable adventure but also a safe return from these experiences. Sincere thanks go to the wider Oxygen Conservation team for the detailed planning, consideration, and leadership in making everything we do as safe as possible.

Kindness, gratitude, and understanding towards these individuals – especially those who stop and challenge you on your decisions, choices, or actions – are essential. These people play a pivotal role in crafting safe, healthy, and happy adventures.

Please let me know what your principles are for safe adventure, but apologies if I don't reply immediately – I'm going wild swimming!

On reflection

People don't tend to think about health and safety enough until they're forced to. When hazardous situations become real, though, managing the wellbeing of your team becomes the most important thing in your mind.

Ultimately, as with so many things in business, this comes down to leadership and culture. If I don't choose to make health, safety, and wellbeing important and role model that importance through actions and words, no one else will. That's likely not because they think it's unimportant, but because I've told them other things matter more.

It's especially dangerous when a leader has a say–do gap – they say something important but do nothing about it. We've all worked with these people, and I'm sure, like me, you didn't trust them.

I'm delighted to say that, since first writing this piece, we've continued to prioritise our approach to health, safety, and wellbeing at a cultural level, with our brilliant Head of Operations, Dave Keir, taking the leading role. You can tell just how well he has embedded our approach when people reference how Dave would look at a situation or a challenge. One of my favourite of these moments was a trip to meet potential partners in London, when I and my regular travelling companion, the always cheerful Dan Johnson (Head of Environment), ran across the road just as the lights changed. The ever-sensible George Pawley (General Counsel) yelled after us, 'I'm going to tell Dave!'

If you're not lucky enough to have the physical embodiment of a guardian angel figuratively sitting on everyone's shoulders, reminding them of the need to be safe, I highly recommend that you get one. Otherwise – worst-case scenario – you might be chatting to actual angels sooner than you'd like!

Taking the Risk Out of Risk Taking

Written July 2023

Over the last two years, Oxygen Conservation has redefined what's possible in rural land acquisition, in terms of speed and scale and, moreover, purpose. All of this land has been bought principally for conservation. For us conservation means delivering positive environmental and social impact, while making a profit as a result, not as the purpose, of what we achieve.

Throughout this time, people have (very kindly) complimented us by saying that we've disrupted the industry, changed the way land is evaluated and bought, and, in the process, kickstarted the natural capital economy. We've been told we work fast and diligently, and we've even been described as relentless (which I especially enjoyed!).

Others have assumed that our approach brings increased risk and have even playfully (or perhaps not playfully) suggested we must be blind to risk or are reckless in what we do and how we do it.

The truth is that we're committed to Scaling Conservation by demonstrating that long-term capital preservation is best achieved by doing everything we can to protect at least a little of the natural world for people and for wildlife. Moreover, we believe that natural capital will become the world's biggest alternative asset class. We can therefore, by showing that conservation can provide a positive return on investment, showcase a self-perpetuating loop of investment, leading to environmental improvement, restoration of the natural world, and positive change.

This is an intentionally bold and hopefully aspirational ambition. As a result, we're very much conscious of the risks – both real and perceived – in our work, and we invest a large amount of time, energy, and effort in understanding and managing those risks.

Hedging our risks

Here are some of the tools we use to approach risk management in our efforts to Scale Conservation:

1. Diversified portfolio
2. Data-driven decision making
3. Expertise and talent
4. Experience as a risk management tool
5. Relationships and expansive networks
6. Meticulous due diligence

1. Diversified portfolio

Our portfolio currently spans ten estates, in seven counties and three countries. Each estate has unique characteristics in terms of climate, geography, land management challenges, regulatory systems, and community relationships.

By deliberately diversifying our portfolio, we're aiming to demonstrate that positive environmental and social impact can be achieved, regardless of external factors. From a risk management standpoint, this diversified portfolio helps spread and manage risks across multiple geopolitical and thematic variables.

2. Data-driven decision making

Property of any kind is still almost always bought with the heart as opposed to the mind, and in rural economy that is no different. The vast majority of people engaging with or buying rural land are positively motivated to do good on a personal or community level, either through farming, development, or – increasingly – environmental restoration and improvement. While we need everyone to contribute what they can, from an impact perspective, this is a terrible idea!

We have designed an acquisition process that ensures we receive the information and data required to inform our due diligence. This enables us to identify those issues that are material to value, those in respect of which we can take a commercial view, and those which may present an opportunity or an advantage.

Often those working in the environment sector find this a difficult concept. We're regularly pitched a small woodland, meadow, or stream because *It's beautiful and would be a lovely little nature reserve*, or because *It has this really special species*. While a wonderful thing to do philanthropically, these are not natural capital investments. They won't help us in mobilising the significant funding we need to genuinely Scale Conservation and deliver a positive environmental and social impact.

Our commitment to data isn't limited to acquisition. We've developed sophisticated tools and techniques to revolutionise how existing landscape-level changes are measured and monitored. This includes assessment of existing and developing carbon stocks as well as evaluation of biodiversity net gain and future nature credits.

Artificial intelligence and remote sensing will increasingly be a feature of how we work.

3. Expertise and talent

We've worked hard to attract the very best people to help us in our mission to Scale Conservation. This currently consists of a central team of twenty people, supported by brilliant estate teams and a vast array of expert advisers and specialist partners.

Timing is so important in the success of a startup business, and the *unfortunate* reality is we couldn't have picked a better time to begin the Oxygen Conservation adventure. The planet is dying. More and more people are recognising the realities of this, as its impact is beginning to become very real. Fortunately, more and more people are therefore wanting to do something that matters – something that will help in the fight against climate change and biodiversity loss – and we offer that opportunity.

This includes opportunities for environmentalists, ecologists, data scientists, economists, data visualisation experts, financial services professionals, commercial lawyers, land managers, and – most importantly – leaders in every aspect of what we do.

Oxygen Conservation is not a normal place to work. We are committed to impact, the environment, and adventure. We expect the world from everyone who works with us, because it's the world we're trying to save. This necessitates a high-performance culture that attracts the best and pushes everyone further, faster, and harder to achieve more. For my part, I am increasingly spending time helping people manage energy levels and longevity, as the longer they are with us, the more they want to work. That's because what we do matters.

4. Experience as a risk management tool

We have a lot of experience in identifying, measuring, and managing risk, especially in relation to environment and land management.

Traditionally, risk is not well understood, especially in the environment sector. Within public and charitable organisations, the culture and operating environment are often such that any form of risk is considered an immediate red flag to any type of project or investment. For example, many organisations wanting to acquire land at scale cannot do so if that land includes certain undesirable assets or features. This means those organisations either miss out on excellent acquisition opportunities or immediately have to dispose of potentially lucrative assets at below market value.

From our perspective, the identification and management of risk have allowed us to secure some excellent assets at below what we consider to be their true market value and natural capital potential. This includes:

- Taking on large-scale site clearance of potentially contaminated materials

- Assessing historic land use challenges, including mining and mineral extraction
- Mitigating risks associated with access issues, legacy sporting rights, private water supplies, and every conceivable legal wrangling associated with historic land ownership and management

We see risk as an opportunity. It provides incredibly important information to make a more informed decision, and our ability to manage risk has helped us redefine what was thought to be impossible in conservation.

We've spent a lot of time learning to be comfortable with being uncomfortable. As a result, where for others the identification of risk means *Stop!*, for us it means *Go, with caution.*

5. Relationships and expansive networks

One of our guiding principles when we began Oxygen Conservation was to be wonderfully easy to work with. This extends to professional partners, the public sector agents, and sellers themselves.

Buying and selling land can be difficult and often stressful for all involved. We've always tried and thankfully often succeeded in making this easier. As a result, we have developed positive relationships with everyone from whom we've purchased land. This includes establishing a farming partnership with one family; buying multiple properties from another; and remaining in regular correspondence with many others, who subsequently return to visit the estate they have sold, after they have moved on to new adventures.

As well as being the right thing to do, this is crucial in the management of historic risk. It ensures we retain access to valuable information often held only by the families that have loved these places for many generations.

Similarly, the relationships and networks we have built with professional partners and experts not only mean we're offered unique opportunities that others don't have the chance to see, but also that, when we encounter a unique risk or opportunity, we can quickly and easily access the information we need to quantify and manage that risk. This includes but certainly isn't limited to:

- Legal and tax advice
- Ground risk
- Building surveys
- Utilities (electricity, gas, and water)
- Independent assessment of property valuations

An important way of working with these experts and advisers is our commitment to radical transparency. We're open about our data, information, and questions, such that the advice we receive is fully informed and therefore immediately applicable to our dynamic risk assessments, measurements, and mitigations.

If you're thinking about large-scale land acquisition, especially for environmental improvement and restoration, you will need a wide network of amazing people.

6. Meticulous due diligence

People only see times we say *Yes*, and the celebration of wonderful new acquisitions that add to our portfolio of estates.

We also say *No, thank you* to many sites, at any stage of the process. We've declined sites before a visit, after a visit, after an offer, and – fortunately on one occasion only – during the due diligence processes. If a site's impact or economic viability falls below our measure of success, we go no further.

We invest in detailed due diligence at speed. Consequently, declining or exiting an acquisition process at any stage can come with significant cost, but we never progress an acquisition chasing sunk costs. Instead, we will always happily celebrate the abortive costs associated with successful due diligence if this means we avoid what would in the long run be a bad investment. Capital preservation is a key principle of our approach, and is absolutely vital to mobilising the investment needed to grow the natural capital economy.

The biggest risk

Without a doubt, our biggest risk is inactivity. We're very much aware of the real and perceived risk in our work, and we and invest a lot of time, energy, and effort in understanding and managing that risk. We all recognise, however, that inactivity is the risk that we must manage above all others. If humans continue exploiting the natural world in the way we do currently, there will be no future life on Earth.

On reflection

The way we talk about risk is changing dramatically over time. Having worked hard to develop tools and techniques to manage risks associated with the screening and acquisition of land, our focus now, when it comes to developing and enhancing natural capital, is increasingly on delivery risk.

The biggest risk we now face comes from government bureaucracy, a systematic lack of investment, and the level and quality of resourcing provided to those organisations tasked with encouraging and regulating environmental recovery and improvement.

When government bodies across the UK consistently fail to meet their targets for woodland creation and wider nature restoration, you have to ask if they have ever really intended to meet them at all.

When the documents required to seek approval for the positive change specified in government targets sit unread, for years in some cases, it forces us to consider new and increasingly innovative ways of influencing these failing processes and institutions.

Didn't someone say there was a climate emergency?

How We Buy Land

Written July 2023, proudly written in partnership with General Counsel, George Pawley

We've recently exchanged contracts for Oxygen Conservation's tenth land acquisition in under two years. With this new site, our portfolio will span just shy of 30,000 acres, across eight counties and in three countries – England, Scotland, and Wales. Our sites range from 304 acres in Ceredigion to over 12,000 acres in Perthshire, with purchase prices from just £90,000 to over £20 million. We've had the privilege of working with some fantastic sellers, talented agents, and skilled lawyers, and each transaction has presented its own particular (and occasionally unusual) challenges. Our brilliant operations team has successfully overcome many of these challenges, but some are still being actively managed as we embrace our role as the new custodians of these incredible landscapes.

The Oxygen Conservation approach to buying land

Reflecting on our progress and learnings across these deals, in this article we describe what has become the Oxygen Conservation model for buying land at a revolutionary pace to Scale Conservation. The impetus of this model comes from the following principles:

1. We are not afraid of complexity.
2. We are decisive.
3. We are honest.
4. We work at pace and meet our commitments.
5. We expect sellers to be ready to sell.
6. We invest heavily in every transaction.
7. We focus on what's important.
8. We welcome the opportunity to engage early with key stakeholders.
9. We don't always get it right.

1. We are not afraid of complexity

Buying land in rural areas can be unbelievably difficult. Many estates have not changed hands for years, so the legal title may be unregistered, meaning we need to untangle a web of historic title deeds to understand what we are taking on. In our perspective, this can be a feature of the site rather than an insurmountable concern.

Investing time and resources to unlock a complicated yet environmentally significant estate is something we are especially well geared up to achieve, and it is something we have found to be incredibly rewarding. We also intend to own our conservation sites for multiple generations, so we are happy to respect things that are uniquely important to the current owners, even where this means the deal structure is unconventional or we are asked to approach certain matters with extra sensitivity or care.

2. We are decisive

We are urgently working to Scale Conservation, so we make quick decisions about whether we wish to acquire a site. We can screen an opportunity within minutes and will almost certainly make a decision on an estate on our first visit. (This is of course before our meticulous due diligence.) On one occasion, a site had such special conservation value that we shook hands on a deal with the seller over a cup of tea in his kitchen, at the end of a beautiful afternoon exploring his unique property.

3. We are honest

We explain our observations and concerns openly and without delay, and we try to work with sellers and agents to find solutions. Our approach has always been to strike and stick to a deal that both parties are equally delighted with, and we aim to build strong relationships with our sellers.

In one instance, while we did not ultimately proceed with the acquisition, we developed such a positive rapport, based on our mutual love for nature, that the seller in question decided to take their estate off the market and start to implement their own significant environmental restoration projects. If we don't remain honest, we have found that problems that can be difficult to resolve arise in the course of the transaction.

Of course, honesty works both ways, and we will reconsider the site's value to us or even walk away if we haven't been given full disclosure of material issues upfront, regardless of the associated abortive costs. It may be a great site, but others will come along, and we won't buy a site if we can't maintain open and positive relationships with everyone involved. It's not the way we do business.

4. We work at pace and meet our commitments

We know that some deals must be done quickly, and keeping up momentum is crucial. With the largest site we have acquired, the deal was closed in just four weeks. However, complex transactions can take time, and our rule is now to commit only to deliver against a specified timeline if we are confident we can do so.

We've learned that agreeing to a *best-endeavours* approach in the pursuit of unrealistic timelines leads to unnecessary and avoidable angst and tension later. With the site that gave us this learning, issues were fortunately positively resolved, but this is not a situation we wish to put ourselves in again.

5. We expect sellers to be ready to sell

Having a fully populated, well-ordered data room, and a draft contract pack proactively prepared by engaged agents and lawyers, helps get the legal process up and running quickly and gives us confidence that the seller is committed to proceed. The more work that can be done before our offer is accepted, the smoother, quicker, and cheaper the transaction is likely to be. It is frustrating when we have to deal with issues that could (and often should) have been dealt with or tidied up before the site came to market.

The vast majority of sellers want to go at an astounding pace but aren't often actually ready to do so. In our view, this is an area where professional advisers can do more to help their clients and make everyone's lives a bit easier.

6. We invest heavily in every transaction

We're fortunate to work with an excellent team of external specialists, advisers, and partners (not least Ross Simpson and his team at Burges Salmon), who go above and beyond to help us Scale Conservation. We resource each deal suitably – from both funding and personnel perspectives – to ensure that our due diligence (including a wide range of traditional and environmental surveys) is thorough and we meet agreed deadlines.

Our approach is to take the keys confident that we know our priorities and challenges for the first twelve months of ownership.

7. We focus on what's important

When we embark on a transaction, we are clear about the reasons we wish to acquire the site, and about the risks it brings that we need to mitigate, manage, and resolve. We endeavour not to battle over details that do not matter and will never let ego or emotion derail the deal.

Bankability is critical for us as we strive to demonstrate the benefits of deploying private capital into nature and scale the entire natural capital economy. This approach was a key feature of our recent landmark conservation-focused debt facility with Triodos Bank UK (Stockdale, 2023).

8. We welcome the opportunity to engage early with key stakeholders

We appreciate engaging early with key stakeholders is not always possible for a range of reasons. However, we have found that being able to talk to tenants, employees, and community members about our intentions as soon as possible leads to positive outcomes for all involved.

Where this has not been permitted, our experience is that the unknown (the intentions of a mystery buyer) or the unforeseen (for example, the key stakeholders not hearing of our purchase until after we have exchanged contracts) can result in concern, upset, and resistance. Indeed, we have not pursued some wonderful sites where immediate engagement with the local community – which we deemed vital to a successful transition – was not supported.

9. We don't always get it right

We're extremely proud of the relationships we've built with many sellers over the past two years. We do, however, realise that our approach will not suit every seller. The normal ebbs and flows of a transaction can result in (unintended) stress and frustration, most commonly because sellers are quite understandably emotionally invested in the site they are parting with. We urge sellers to tell us if this is the case; we always welcome direct conversations and will listen and adapt to mitigate their concerns as best as we can.

We've had so much fun buying land in the past two years. The excitement of the following points energises us to keep Scaling Conservation as quickly as possible:

- Seeing a special new site
- Envisioning its potential for positive environmental and social impact
- Bringing it into our ownership, giving us the opportunity to deliver that positive environmental and social impact

Our next ten acquisitions will no doubt bring new experiences and challenges, and our model will inevitably evolve further. That is all part of the adventure, though, as we seek to deliver positive impact for people and the environment.

On reflection

I'm sitting writing this reflection in a coffee shop in Edinburgh, the Bastard Barista. It is so cool that it would almost certainly make our brilliant Head of Environment, Dan Johnson, feel rather unwell – he hates cool places!

We're in Edinburgh ahead of a second visit to one of the most wonderful estates we've seen to date. It's more than 15,000 acres in the Cairngorms and one of our most exceptional opportunities yet. Our relationship with this estate highlights how our process of buying land has changed already over the past year.

Our first visit was an absolute joy – it is the most beautiful, well-maintained, and ecologically diverse sporting estate we've visited. The estate is currently managed well, by an agent that we respect and have worked with previously, meaning it is offered with far more information and with better-developed systems and processes than we often encounter.

This return visit is focused on the built property elements of the estate, which have a significant bearing on value, and on the potential returns from residential rentals and amazing ecotourism potential. As our approach has become more informed and more sophisticated, we can better establish the immediate and future return potential from all three interconnected lenses: environmental, social, and economic.

It would be great if we could add this estate to the portfolio, but when it comes to landscape-level acquisitions, they're never done until they're done. Every estate and many owners offer surprises along the way.

If we don't manage to make this deal work now, we may well in the future... it's not like the sky is going to fall...

Embracing Change

Written February 2024

We draw inspiration from across the business, sporting, and technological worlds and work hard to apply their lessons to our work in Scaling Conservation. Despite the innovations of those worlds, the path to advancements is so often littered with resistance, scepticism, and sometimes even outright hostility.

Innovation is inherently disruptive

The inertia of the status quo creates an environment where groundbreaking ideas are initially met with resistance, only for them to be embraced as the new norm once their success is undeniable. This phenomenon is vividly illustrated almost everywhere we've looked, and we've outlined some of our favourite examples below.

Football: From traditional to tactical revolutions

Football has seen a significant evolution in its tactical approach. In the past, particularly during the 1980s, the game was dominated by a straightforward, physically aggressive style of play, often characterised by the *long-ball strategy*. This approach prioritised physical strength and direct play, valuing long passes aimed at quickly moving the ball up field. The introduction of more nuanced tactics such as *passing football* or the *false nine* marked a stark contrast to this traditional style. Initially, these innovative strategies were met with scepticism, criticism, and even ridicule. They emphasised skill, precise positioning, and intelligent movement, offering a more refined and tactical approach to the game.

The transformation in football strategy became more pronounced with the rise of teams like FC Barcelona, particularly under the guidance of Pep Guardiola (Perarnau, 2014). Guardiola, ironically drawing inspiration from historical tactics such as the false nine used by the 1930s Austrian National Team, reinvented these approaches for the modern era. His philosophy centred around ball control, positional flexibility, and intelligent off-the-ball movement, challenging the conventional wisdom of the time. The success of Barcelona, culminating in numerous major victories and a distinctive, attractive style of play, played a pivotal role in changing perceptions around these tactics (Kuper, 2021). What once was revolutionary gradually became a new standard in football strategy, influencing teams and coaches worldwide. This shift highlighted a broader trend in sports and other fields, where revisiting and adapting historical concepts can lead to groundbreaking innovations and a redefinition of what is considered the norm.

Cricket: Embracing the aggressive batting paradigm

In cricket the traditional approach once centred around patience and conservative batting. This was perhaps best exemplified by players like Geoffrey Boycott of Yorkshire, who was known for his meticulously slow scoring rate, including an instance of facing thirty-eight balls before scoring his first run in a match.

The introduction of Twenty20 cricket marked a shift towards an ultra-aggressive batting style. Initially met with scepticism and viewed as a crude deviation from the sport's spirit, it was feared this approach might negatively alter the game. Despite resistance, including campaigns against the advent of Twenty20, this explosive form of play has not only gained acceptance but also contributed to cricket's rise as the world's second most popular sport, adding dynamism and making the game more diverse and inclusive (Hayter and Miller, 2019; Szymanski and Wigmore, 2023).

This transformation in playing style is now extending beyond limited-overs cricket to the traditional Test format, particularly evident in the England Test team's recent approach. Under the leadership of Brendon 'Baz' McCullum, and with players like Ben Stokes and Jos Buttler, the team has adopted an aggressive, high-risk strategy, termed *Bazball*. This new approach, emphasising rapid scoring and bold decision making, is seen as a potential saviour for the future of Test cricket, keeping it relevant and exciting in an era dominated by shorter attention spans and a wider range of viewing options for fans across the globe. The evolution from conservative to aggressive playstyles in cricket reflects a broader trend of innovation and adaptability in sports. It is challenging norms and reshaping the game for modern audiences.

The NFL: The evolution of the passing game

The evolution of the passing game in the NFL represents a significant shift in the league's strategic approach, moving away from a traditional, run-dominated game to one that emphasises passing efficiency and innovation in the aerial offence. This transformation can be traced back to 1980s visionaries like Bill Walsh, whose *West Coast offense* revolutionised offensive play (Long, no date). Walsh's strategy focused on short, horizontal passing routes, designed to control the ball and time of possession, while methodically advancing down the field. This approach was in complete contrast to the then prevalent strategy of relying on the running game to establish offensive dominance. The approach made the game more open, more entertaining, more diverse, and more inclusive, both as a spectacle and in terms of those who could play professionally.

In recent years this evolution in the NFL's passing game has continued to develop. Teams are now integrating elements of the college-style spread offence, which emphasises spreading out the defence and using the quarterback's mobility as a key component – something previously thought too high-risk and not in the spirit of football (Associated Press, no date). This has led to a new generation of mobile and versatile quarterbacks like Patrick Mahomes, Lamar Jackson, and Josh Allen, who are as adept at running with the ball as they are at throwing it.

Additionally, the rise of analytics in football has further influenced passing strategies. Teams are increasingly relying on data to make decisions such as for the increased use of fourth-down conversions, and for passing in traditionally run-heavy situations (Bechtold, 2021). These developments represent continued innovation in the NFL's offensive strategy, showing that the league is not just about adopting new tactics but also about continuously evolving them. As the game progresses, these current evolutions in the passing game are setting new standards and redefining what is considered an effective, entertaining, and championship-winning strategy in the NFL.

Elite cycling: Team Sky's methodical approach

In elite cycling the British Team Sky (now known as INEOS Grenadiers) represents a paradigm shift in how the sport is approached (Walsh, 2014). Their philosophy, often described as the *marginal-gains* approach, focused on optimising every conceivable element that could affect a cyclist's performance. This method, championed by Sir Dave Brailsford, involved meticulous attention to detail – from the most aerodynamic equipment and the most effective training regimes to optimising nutrition and recovery strategies. This comprehensive approach was initially met with scepticism, as it moved away from traditional focuses targeting training and endurance. However, Team Sky's dominant performances in events like the Tour de France, where they secured numerous victories, effectively validated their strategies. These successes illustrated how a systematic, data-driven approach could provide a competitive edge in a sport where victory can often depend on mere seconds.

Team Sky's influence extended beyond their own victories, setting new standards in professional cycling. Their focus on marginal gains inspired other teams to adopt similar approaches, leading to a broader transformation in the sport's competitive landscape. Technology played a significant role in this transformation, with advancements in bike design, aerodynamics, and wearable technology contributing to enhanced performance. For example, the development of more aerodynamic cycling suits and the use of wind tunnels for testing became standard practices in the peloton. Furthermore, Team Sky's legacy is not limited to technical innovations; they also influenced the strategic aspects of racing. Their emphasis on team dynamics and the role of domestiques (support riders) in controlling the race pace and protecting the team leader has been widely emulated – another idea proudly borrowed from historic tour teams. As a result, professional cycling has seen a shift towards a more team-oriented approach, contrasting with the previous focus on individual stars.

This evolution, driven by Team Sky's methodical and innovative strategies, underscores the impact that a single team's philosophy can have on an entire sport.

The double-edged sword – unsuccessful innovations in sports and business

While successful innovations become norms, failed ones are often vilified, if not forgotten. Early failures in experimental sports tactics are used to reinforce the safety of conventional methods, hindering progress and providing keyboard critics with plentiful ammunition to attack those trying to change the business or sporting world.

In recent times, sports especially have witnessed several innovative ideas that have failed to become game changers. In football the much-hyped *libero* or *sweeper* role, which saw a revival attempt in modern football, failed to integrate successfully into contemporary tactics dominated by fast-paced and high-pressing styles (Kuper and Szymanski, 2012). Similarly, in cricket, the introduction of the *powerplay* rules in One Day Internationals underwent several modifications (Szymanski and Wigmore, 2023). Some of these variations, like the batting powerplay chosen by the batting team, were eventually discarded due to strategic imbalances they introduced in the game.

This can be equally true in business. An example is the automotive industry, which, particularly in its pursuit of sustainable alternatives, has seen its share of unsuccessful ventures. For instance, the early models of solar-powered cars, while innovative, struggled with practical viability due to limitations in solar technology and efficiency. They failed to gain mainstream traction as a reliable alternative to traditional or electric vehicles. In another case, some of the early autonomous vehicle technologies, which promised a revolution in personal transportation, faced setbacks due to safety and regulatory concerns, delaying their widespread adoption. These examples underscore the inherent uncertainty in the process of innovation. While some ideas hold the potential to change the game, others falter, often providing valuable lessons and paving the way for future advancements.

Learning from the past, looking to the future

Innovation, while often met with initial resistance, holds the key to transformative change and the redefinition of norms. Embracing both the successes and failures of innovative endeavours is crucial, as it embodies a commitment to progress and improvement. The essence of living is to strive for advancement; stagnation is not an option, especially in our quest for Scaling Conservation. Our mission to generate positive environmental and social impact is intrinsically linked with the need for constant innovation and change. While the path is fraught with mistakes, criticism, and opposition, the alternative – to uphold a deteriorating world marked by the climate crisis, biodiversity collapse, and decline of local communities – ultimately means accepting the end of life on Earth.

The pursuit of innovation in our work often wonderfully draws inspiration from historic concepts reimagined for the modern world. Wind turbines, for example, are in many ways a contemporary take on traditional windmills. Similarly, regenerative agriculture, is rooted in age-old farming practices, re-envisioned to meet today's ecological challenges.

We aspire for our innovations to mirror the transformative impacts seen in sports, technology, and in industry. By making environmental and rural communities more vibrant, diverse, and inclusive, we aim to contribute positively to the world, environmentally and socially. The changes we advocate, though controversial to some today, could well become the standard practices of tomorrow. This vision underscores the importance of challenging the status quo for the sake of our planet and for future generations.

On reflection

Innovation is inherently disruptive, and the environment sector is one in need of positive disruption if we're going to address the aligned challenges of climate change, the biodiversity crisis, and the combined impact they're having on people and wildlife.

I'm excited to see the innovations and ideas that will come next.

Green Is the New Black

Written April 2024

In the words of the late football legend Gianluca Vialli, embracing a new identity as a brand, rather than as just a player, is a significant learning curve, but it is one professional footballers and athletes faced in the late 1990s and early 2000s. This concept, although rooted in the world of sports, highlights the future that is beginning to develop in the environment sector. As we all increasingly grapple with the escalating challenges of climate change and biodiversity loss, environmentalists and conservationists will be viewed more and more not just as advocates for the Earth, but also as brands and commodities in a critical market of ideas and solutions.

In every industry, there are far too few genuinely talented people, ie those who can genuinely make a positive impact. This is of course also true in the environment sector, where the race to attract the most talented people is gathering increasing momentum. This foreshadows a future where environmentalists and conservationists will be the predominant role models, celebrities, and brands. Here are the factors and roles that are driving this change (spoiler alert: we might just have several people in these roles at the very start of their careers within Oxygen Conservation):

1. The emergence of environmental brands
2. The commodification of sustainability
3. The media's role in green branding
4. The first superstar environmentalist
5. Professional support for environmental superstars
6. Agents and managers
7. Performance coaches
8. The role of strategic public relations
9. Tailored financial advice
10. Legal support

1. The emergence of environmental brands

The environment is no longer just a backdrop for human activity or a place to be extracted and abused. It has become a central player in the global economy.

As the impacts of climate change become more evident and immediate, the entities involved in environmental restoration and conservation are shifting from being seen merely as non-profits or advocacy groups to becoming (renewable) powerhouse brands. These brands – whether they represent natural capital investment funds, renewable energy companies, electric vehicle manufacturers, or sustainable fashion lines – market not only goods and services but also ideals of a sustainable future.

2. The commodification of sustainability

Sustainability is becoming a commodity – a valuable and tradable aspect of modern business practices.

This commodification reflects a profound change in how we value nature and natural resources. For instance, carbon credits and green bonds are now increasingly common financial instruments, framing the health of our environment as a bankable alternative asset. This shift not only makes environmental concerns more relatable to the business-minded community; it also opens new avenues for funding and investment for 'green' brands.

3. The media's role in green branding

Just as professional athletes came to understand their potential as media products, environmentalists and conservationists are increasingly harnessing the power of the media to amplify their message.

Social media campaigns, viral videos, and influencer partnerships are all tactics that have been adopted to elevate the visibility and impact of environmental messaging. This strategic use of media helps transform abstract or global concerns like climate change into tangible and immediate calls to action that resonate on a personal level.

4. The first superstar environmentalist

The most prominent environmentalist of our time and the first global environmental superstar is Greta Thunberg. She has been so impactful that multiple academic papers have analysed the 'Greta Effect' (Ballew et al, 2021).

A measure of Greta's reach includes millions of followers across her social media platforms, including over

5 million on X and more than 13 million on Instagram. She has also made countless appearances in print media, on television, and at significant global events, including at the 2019 United Nations Climate Action Summit and the World Economic Forum in Davos in 2019 and 2020. Thunberg's impact and recognition are also reflected in the awards and honours she has received. She was named *Time Magazine*'s Person of the Year in 2019 – a significant indicator of her global influence – as well as being nominated multiple times for the Nobel Peace Prize, highlighting her standing on the international stage.

5. Professional support for environmental superstars

As environmentalists and conservationists transition into the role of global influencers, brand ambassadors, and brands themselves, a new support industry will emerge, akin to that which transformed sports stars into media icons.

This burgeoning sector includes agents, managers, and performance coaches, all geared towards maximising the potential of environmental superstars.

6. Agents and managers

Just as agents and managers negotiate contracts and endorsements for sportspeople, we will soon begin to see similar roles develop for environmental figures. These professionals are tasked with managing the complex demands placed on high-profile environmentalists, from managing image rights and negotiating speaking engagements and book deals, to handling media rights and partnerships with eco-conscious companies.

The expertise of agents and managers helps navigate the intricate landscape of global advocacy, ensuring that their clients can focus on their missions while also maximising their public impact and revenue streams.

7. Performance coaches

Performance coaches, traditionally associated with sports, will find a new niche in the environmental movement. These coaches are not focused on physical training but rather on helping activists manage stress, public speaking, and the relentless pressure of being under the public eye.

Coaches will provide guidance on effective communication strategies, helping environmentalists articulate complex scientific concepts in impactful ways to the public and policymakers.

8. The role of strategic public relations

As environmental activists become akin to brands, the need for sophisticated public relations strategies becomes crucial. PR professionals specialising in environmental advocacy work to shape public perception, manage crises, and build narratives that resonate with both the general public and key stakeholders.

This strategic communication will be absolutely vital in a world where public opinion can significantly influence policy and corporate behaviour.

9. Tailored financial advice

Financial advisers with expertise in sustainable investments are crucial in this new landscape. They will guide environmental superstars in managing their earnings ethically, and investing in ventures that align with their values and contribute to global sustainability goals.

This financial guidance ensures that the personal brands of environmental activists not only generate income but also foster a broader positive impact, helping influence the flow of investment into regenerative and sustainable impact investments.

10. Legal support

Legal support will become indispensable as environmental activists navigate complex international laws and regulations related to environmental advocacy and public speaking.

Lawyers specialising in environmental law, intellectual property, and contract law will ensure that activists' work remains protected and compliant with global standards.

As the environment sector continues to evolve and its importance grows, the professionalisation of its leading figures will likely expand, mirroring trends seen in sports, entertainment, and other high-profile fields. This professional ecosystem not only supports the individuals at the forefront of the movement but also enhances their effectiveness and sustainability as they champion critical causes.

Green is the new black

The journey of environmentalism, from grassroots advocacy to powerhouse of influence and change, reflects a profound shift in our global priorities and perspectives.

As we begin to witness the birth of environmental superstars and the rise of 'green' leaders and brands, it's not just making environmentalism marketable that is key. It's also vital to embed sustainable practices into the core of societal values. This evolution offers a beacon of hope, illustrating that environmental consciousness is becoming integrated into the fabric of global business, policy, and individual actions.

A future that sees the increased professionalisation of environmental advocates – complete with agents, managers, and strategic advisers – underscores a better, more optimistic narrative: that the fight for our planet is gaining the sophistication and support traditionally reserved for top-tier celebrities and athletes. This isn't about merely adapting to a trend. It's about leading it, ensuring that those at the forefront of environmental advocacy are empowered to inspire, influence, and instigate real change.

With each step forward, we are redefining what it means to be an environmentalist in the twenty-first century. We are shifting our work from the periphery to the very heart of global discourse and action. Let us embrace these changes with the hope and commitment they deserve, driving towards a future where living green isn't just considered fashionable. It's fundamental.

If you want to know where the next environmental superstars are coming from, you might want to take a look at Oxygen Conservation's early-career professionals!

On reflection

Since first writing this article in April 2024, the future I imagined isn't just on the horizon – it's already here. Our most competitive intern programme to date attracted nearly 2,000 applications ahead of 2025, and the calibre of talent was staggering. Among them: Oxbridge firsts, international athletes, gifted artists and performers, social media influencers, and global environmental activists. These aren't just the rising stars of conservation; they are the future superstars of the natural capital economy.

I am incredibly fortunate to be leading a team filled with the brightest minds and the best people in the environment sector. And I know this: in the years and decades to come, the leaders of several companies shaping the future of the natural capital economy will all have one thing in common – Oxygen Conservation on their career path.

I've always admired everything about Silicon Valley, so perhaps it was inevitable that Oxygen Conservation would become our very own Oxygen Incubator – not just a company, but a launchpad for the next generation of impact-driven businesses. That's not an idea; it's a spoiler.

FIVE
Peak Performance

The Untold Truth of High-Performance Environments

Written May 2024

Being in a high-performance environment, whether in sports, the corporate world, or any other arena, is not for everyone. The reality is it's often unpleasant and it's sometimes painful.

The pros and cons

A high-performance environment is a place where the best of the best come to compete, and where the stakes are high. The rewards for those who succeed can be great, but the price of entry is equally steep. I'm fortunate to have played and worked in some high-performance environments, and I've experienced the discomfort, the pain, the sacrifices, and the failures. I've also learned many lessons about life and myself along the way.

So often, when the concept of a high-performance environment is discussed it is misunderstood, with focus placed only on the celebration that comes with success or victory. Little attention is placed on the realities of what it takes to live and work in such an environment.

In this article I'll explore the untold truth of high-performance environments and begin to consider what it takes to succeed:

1. It's worth it!
2. It's hard.
3. You'll be asked to make sacrifices.
4. You're *always* competing.
5. You'll get constant feedback (that will often feel like criticism).
6. You'll be pushed to your limits (and beyond).
7. The performance bar keeps rising.
8. People won't understand.
9. You need to grasp the opportunity.
10. Winning might not feel like you expected it to.

1. It's worth it!

Despite the challenges, being in a high-performance environment is worth it, especially if you're the type of person who doesn't know how not to compete, or if you strive for constant personal and professional improvement. In fact, if you're a driven person, not finding a high-performance environment is mentally and emotionally almost certainly worse. Looking back on your life and career with regret, thinking you could have achieved more, will hurt way more than the pain of knowing and realising your limits along the way.

A high-performance environment provides an opportunity to be part of something bigger than yourself, to work with the best and learn from them, and to push yourself to new limits. The rewards can be significant, in terms of personal growth and achievement, and in the recognition and respect that come with success. It isn't for everyone, though.

2. It's hard

One of the hardest aspects of a high-performance environment is the intense pressure that comes with it – pressure that is constant and hard. You need to constantly ask yourself:

- *Will it make the boat go faster?*
- *Will what I'm about to do positively or negatively improve my performance?*
- *What aren't I doing that I should be?*

Throughout my time in high-level sport, with much of the time spent training alone, I would imagine a perfect athlete competing for my place in the team. I would then always try and beat them, ignoring the fact that in reality I never could.

Whether it's the pressure to win, to achieve a goal, or to meet a deadline, the stakes are high. For the most driven people, the pressure you place on yourself will be greater than the pressure from anyone else. That pressure can be all-consuming, and it can take a toll on anyone's mental health. It's not uncommon for athletes or business leaders in high-performance environments to experience anxiety, depression, or burnout.

Lots of high performers will tell you that the success doesn't bring euphoria or even happiness. It just numbs the pain for a moment, and then they ask what's next.

THE UNTOLD TRUTH OF HIGH-PERFORMANCE ENVIRONMENTS

3. You'll be asked to make sacrifices

Success in a high-performance environment requires a significant amount of sacrifice – not just from you but also from your family and your friends. Athletes (in sport or business) must dedicate themselves fully, often sacrificing time with family and friends and missing out on other life experiences. In the corporate world, it will mean working long hours, sacrificing vacations, and missing important family events. These sacrifices can be challenging, and they can lead to feelings of isolation and loneliness.

Before you start, ask yourself, *Do I really want this enough to make the sacrifices needed to succeed?* Then consider that often they won't always be your sacrifices; you'll often be asking somebody close to you to pay the bill for your dreams.

4. You're *always* competing

In a high-performance environment, you're always competing with yourself and others. The competition is intense, and it can create a cut-throat environment. This level of competition will push you forward and give you an opportunity to achieve your full potential, but the journey will be painful, both physically and emotionally. For many people it can lead to feelings of bitterness and resentment. Sometimes the successes and wins wash away this feeling, but ultimately the stress catches up with even the most competitive people.

You will also be facing a marathon, not a sprint – think about an Olympic cycle of four years. You will be competing constantly, with yourself and with others, to find that next level of performance, and that tiny advantage that can make the difference between winning and losing. It's constant – 24/7, 365 – you're never off the clock. Of course you don't *have* to work that hard, but if you don't, someone else will.

5. You'll get constant feedback (that will often feel like criticism)

In a high-performance environment, feedback is constant, and I mean truly constant. That feedback can feel like criticism; and when you're hurt or tired, it might feel personal and painful. Athletes and business leaders are continually evaluated and critiqued, often unfairly by people not qualified to judge, and their performance is analysed in great detail. This level of scrutiny can be hard to handle, and it can lead to self-doubt and anxiety.

In the best high-performance environments, including in some forward-thinking businesses, performance psychologists and mindset coaches are increasingly available to provide support. In much the same way sports teams have had strength and conditioning coaches and physiotherapists to prepare athletes and help in the process of recovery, businesses are now investing in mental health training, preparation, and support. For avoidance of doubt: I don't mean mental health first aiders. I mean exceptional high-performance professionals able to coach and support people to be the best they can be.

6. You'll be pushed to your limits (and beyond)

In a high-performance environment, you'll be pushed to your limits and often beyond. You'll find out what you're capable of and what you're not. You'll get knocked down and have to decide if you're willing to get back up. You'll be pushed to the breaking point, but it's in those moments that you'll learn the most. I know that has applied to my own experience – in sport, in business, and in life.

You'll need to adapt and improve continually to stay ahead of the competition. If this is the environment for you, you'll love the process of immediate impactful feedback as a powerful tool for learning and development.

You'll also learn some often harsh truths. One of those truths is that there are levels to everything in life. Everyone thinks they work hard… until they meet someone who works harder. You'll need to put in the time and effort to reach the next level, and you'll need to be willing to make the necessary sacrifices to get there, so hard work is often the answer, regardless of the question.

7. The performance bar keeps rising

As you reach new levels of success, the bar is raised higher, and the pressure to maintain that level of performance increases. It is a never-ending cycle of striving for excellence and constantly pushing yourself to new limits. The expectations can come from yourself, your coaches or team leaders, your colleagues, and even friends and family (or demons from your past – people who didn't believe in you before).

The challenge with increasing expectations is that it can lead to a sense of never being satisfied with your performance, however well you do. You'll feel there's always something more you could have done or something you could have done better. Some people suggest it's essential to find a balance between striving for excellence and acknowledging your accomplishments and progress. Others use the dissatisfaction as motivation, but that can be an explosive fuel.

8. People won't understand

Living and working in a high-performance environment isn't normal, and most people won't understand why you make the decisions you make. They may challenge, criticise, and even ridicule your sacrifices, but remember they're *your* sacrifices. If you want to achieve what others haven't, you have to do what others won't.

Being in a high-performance environment can be isolating, and it can be challenging to find support from people outside the high-performance environment (and sometimes from those within it, especially in individual sport). The environment can feel lonely, and it can be tough to find people who truly understand what you're going through, but I'd encourage you to try. Find people who have achieved great things, treat them with absolute respect, and listen and learn from their experiences. Then, when you can, share your experiences to help the next generation.

9. You need to grasp the opportunity

There is a finite window of opportunity for high performance, and it's essential to make the most of it while you can. Whether you're an athlete, an entrepreneur, or a business leader, there will come a time when your physical or mental abilities start to decline or circumstances change, and your opportunity disappears.

It's easy to get caught up in the day-to-day demands of a high-performance environment and forget that time is always ticking. It's crucial to be mindful of this reality and take advantage of every opportunity to grow, learn, and excel while you can. Don't take your health, time, or resources for granted, and be proactive in pursuing your goals and aspirations.

Take care of your physical and mental health, surround yourself with a supportive team, and be willing to adapt and evolve as circumstances change. This will enable you to maximise your potential and make the most of the time you have to achieve high performance.

10. Winning might not feel like you expected it to

As you progress in a high-performance environment, the wins don't move the needle as much as they used to. You become used to winning and achieving success – it becomes an addiction, where you need the wins (and the endorphins) to feel normal. However, that means the mistakes, losses, and failures hurt more. They can be a setback to progress, and they can lead to self-doubt and erode confidence.

When you achieve a significant victory in a high-performance environment, everyone will celebrate with you. They'll tell you that they were with you on the journey and that they're proud of you. However, once the celebrations are over, you may feel at your lowest.

Many gold medal athletes have talked about crying alone in their hotel rooms, feeling a sense of loss as their purpose and sole focus for so many years has been achieved but now taken away. If you're a high performer, you might recognise the absence of celebration, failing to recognise successes, and instead often find yourself asking, *What's next?*

Is it really worth it?

Being in a high-performance environment is not easy, and it takes a significant amount of sacrifice and dedication to succeed, and not just from you. You'll be pushed to your limits and beyond, and you'll need to be willing to continuously adapt and improve.

Despite the challenges, though, being in a high-performance environment is worth it if you want to achieve incredible things. It's an opportunity to be part of something bigger than yourself, to work with the best, and to push yourself to new limits. The rewards can be significant, both in terms of personal growth and achievement, and in the recognition and respect that come with success.

If you're considering entering a high-performance environment, be prepared for the challenges ahead. Seek out support from others who have been through similar experiences, and be willing to make the necessary sacrifices to succeed.

On reflection

I'm proud that Oxygen Conservation is a high-performance environment where we've continued to attract and develop the most talented people, working to build the natural capital economy.

The challenges of working in a high-performance environment remain very real. We continue to push people into their red zones, where genuine improvement and development really happen.

As a result, virtually everyone within the team has been pushed to the point of having to take a break and reset. This reset often takes the form of learning new systems or processes, making more purposeful choices about rest and recovery, or just being more open to help and support from the wider team and beyond.

THE UNTOLD TRUTH OF HIGH-PERFORMANCE ENVIRONMENTS

This can be a remarkably challenging process for high performers who have always been able to outwork everything they've done in the past, but that's just not possible at Oxygen Conservation. We collectively move too fast and too much. We have to; the planet needs us to.

The other thing with talented and driven people is that the help they need is rarely confined to practical solutions to technical or logistical challenges. They can easily solve those. It's about life and relationships, and it's always about nuance and complexity. So often we talk about decision making and the thoughts, feelings, and consequences of those decisions.

I'm truly blessed to work with the most talented group of people, and it's my job to help them achieve everything they want and more, and to help them develop the tools and techniques to do just that.

Radical Transparency

Written June 2023

So much of the genesis of Oxygen Conservation has been stolen from the way businesses and business leadership have developed in Silicon Valley. Thank you Google, Apple, LinkedIn, Tesla, and so many more! One of the key concepts directly borrowed from Google – specifically, from the work of Laszlo Bock (Bock, 2015) – has been a commitment to *radical transparency*.

Why transparency is vital

Radical transparency is a concept that promotes openness, honesty, and disclosure to an extreme degree within a business or team. We apply a simple test to determine whether we're being true to our commitment to radical transparency, asking ourselves, *Are we sharing everything we're comfortable sharing with the team?* Then we share just a little more.

If you want people to genuinely feel ownership of the business and the decisions that are made, you have to give them all the information they need and involve them in the decision-making process. We also believe that radical transparency is a key tool in creating a culture of trust, accountability, and collaboration, by ensuring that everyone involved has access to the same information.

Radical transparency in Oxygen Conservation includes the sharing of virtually all information, short of individuals' personal information such as salaries. We draw the line there for many reasons, including the fact that we've seen first-hand the toxic effect of openly shared salaries, especially salary bandings in the public sector. Openly shared and often discussed salary bands enforce hierarchy, leading to people asking *What grade are you?* (shorthand for *What do you earn?*) before deciding whether to take a meeting, share data and information, or consider you for a promotion. It also results in endless comparisons, frustration, and complaints about performance with respect to grade. Instead, we craft unique reward packages, working arrangements, and benefits that make everyone delighted to be part of the team.

We have built structures and processes that force radical transparency to be a feature of what we do. An example of this is us bookending our week with meetings. We start with a team meeting (named after its inspiration: the Blackstone meeting), with our entire central team, including interns, where we discuss key strategic issues and operational challenges. We then end the week by producing a long-form update report for the board, which is also shared with the entire team.

We believe that radical transparency creates many important competitive advantages for a business:

1. Improved decision making
2. Continuous improvement
3. Enhanced collaboration

4. Engagement and empowerment
5. Trust

1. Improved decision making

If you want people to make fantastic decisions, you have to give them all the information they need. In a complex world with many interconnected factors, the more information that is shared, the better. We include as many of the team as possible in all key decisions, from potential landscape acquisitions to the hiring of new members of the team. Before anyone says this isn't the most efficient way to make decisions, they'd be absolutely right! It isn't, but we believe it is the best if you want to create an excellent culture for amazing people.

Radical transparency allows for a better understanding of situations, enabling individuals to evaluate options and consequences more accurately. If you're not prepared to share enough information to allow people to make decisions with full understanding and context, is it fair to ask their views?

2. Continuous improvement

Radical transparency creates a learning culture where mistakes and failures are openly discussed and celebrated as opportunities. By sharing successes and failures, everyone can learn from past experiences and continuously improve.

This approach exposes everyone to new ways of working, experiences, and opportunities. If you're committed to recruiting only people better than you (and the rest of the team) in a meaningful way, surely you want to create as many opportunities as possible for teams to share experiences and learn from each other.

3. Enhanced collaboration

Openly sharing information encourages collaboration and teamwork. At our weekly Blackstone meeting, for example, heads of departments share updates with the team, where anyone is free to ask for more information and for additional context. Most importantly, they can ask for and offer help, as long as we keep moving at pace.

When people have access to relevant information, they can contribute their insights, ideas, and expertise to projects and discussions. Assuming you've got your recruitment right, this leads to more inclusive and diverse perspectives, ultimately fostering innovation and creativity, and creating more opportunities for serendipitous moments of magic

4. Engagement and empowerment

If you want people to work for you, all you can expect is for them to do as they're told. If you want a team of talented people to work with you, then you have to welcome them into the decision-making process as equals, and that means giving them the information they need to make fantastic decisions.

This doesn't mean we're frozen by debate or stuck with the mediocracy that so often comes with democracy, where everyone gets to have an opinion but the decision is made by the person best placed to decide. Put simply, radical transparency is one of our best tools for creating a team that works together to help Scale Conservation.

5. Trust

One of the most powerful tools I've ever acquired in creating trusting relationships isn't just to give people something, nor only to ask them for something, but to do both simultaneously. With every new team member, we quickly give them access to a huge amount of information, alongside creating a role they're delighted to take. In exchange, we ask them to be considerate and respectful with what we've shared. As long as they are, we continue to give them access to anything and everything that will help them be incredible in their role. I always begin from a point of trust. If you can't do that, then it's your fault as a business leader for hiring poorly or for keeping someone you can't trust within your team.

Not so radical transparency

I started this article thinking I was going to talk about radical transparency and end it thinking that it's not radical at all. Being more transparent than you're initially comfortable with is really the only option if you want to work with talented people and together recruit, build, and continue to develop a high-performing team.

On reflection

If you're not being more transparent than you're comfortable with, you're leaving a competitive advantage unrealised. Within almost three years I've been very open and transparent with the team and never once regretted it.

If you can't trust your people with information, then you've hired the wrong people. Solve that problem rather than restricting the information you give to the brilliant people you do trust.

Business Athletes: Learning from the track, the road, and the hillside

Written December 2023

In the realm of high performance, whether in business or sports, the parallels are striking and the principles of success remarkably similar. My experience in demanding environments such as international sports, academia, and high-pressure business contexts has shaped my perspective. The more I learn and think about high performance, the more I realise that the best business performers are essentially performance athletes, just of a different kind.

This is especially true at Oxygen Conservation, where we're committed to redefining what's possible from a conservation company and from the environment sector, and to building a whole new economic system: the natural capital economy.

The guiding principles of this approach are informed by many of the most successful sports teams, but our approach finds the most alignment and similarities with the work of Sir Dave Brailsford with the GB cycling team, Team Sky, and now INEOS Grenadiers.

The Brailsford approach: A paradigm for success

Sir Dave Brailsford's philosophy in building the GB cycling team and Team Sky revolved around the concept of *marginal gains* (Clear, 2018). This is the concept that small, incremental improvements (evolutions) in any process will cumulatively lead to significant performance improvements and, in the process, produce success. In cycling, that success translates to medals and yellow jerseys.

I have always found this philosophy to be equally applicable in the business world, especially in environments that demand high levels of performance and innovation.

One of the ways we directly translate this approach is in the identification of talent. We're in the fortunate position of having a remarkable number of people wanting to be part of the Oxygen Conservation journey, such that we can select the top 1%. In our most recent internship recruitment campaign we made offers to only four candidates from 455 applicants. Here's an outline of how we make our recruitment decisions, linked below to examples from Sir Dave's world to help illustrate the alignment of our respective thinking:

1. Talent
2. Coachability
3. Work ethic
4. Character
5. Decision making
6. Delivery

1. Talent

In both business and sports, the raw talent, ability, and intelligence of individuals are paramount. Like Brailsford's approach in scouting cyclists with innate potential, businesses must identify individuals who possess unique talents (Moore, 2011).

Chris Froome, four-time winner of the Tour de France, is a testament to this approach. He was first scouted in 2006, seven years before his first Tour de France win in 2013. His incredible power-to-weight output and climbing endurance, despite little or no professional coaching or support, highlighted genuinely raw talent and potential. While talent and potential are the most important aspect when selecting people to join elite teams, it is only the first gateway. Without the key attributes in the following points, a person is likely to become yet another failed talent that didn't reach anywhere near their full potential.

In 2011, after a disastrous campaign at the Tour de France (in the previous season), Team Sky considered firing Sir Bradley Wiggins – this outstanding talent finished outside of the top twenty riders because of failing to commit to coaching and simply not working hard enough ahead of the tour (The Cycling Channel, 2019; Walsh, 2014). Embarrassment, together with the prospect of missing out on a once-in-a-lifetime opportunity of competing at a home Olympics, helped Sir Bradley make the decision to truly commit to realising his potential, and the rest is history. In 2012 he became the first-ever British winner of the Tour de France, and he won Olympic gold shortly after.

2. Coachability

The willingness to learn, adapt, and continuously improve is critical. In Brailsford's team, this is perhaps best exemplified by the career of Geraint Thomas.

Geraint Thomas's ascent, from a promising track cyclist to a Tour de France champion, is a remarkable narrative of development within the British cycling system (Thomas, 2018). His journey began with GB Cycling's Olympic Development Programme, where he cultivated the skills that propelled him to gold in the 2008 Beijing Games. Geraint transitioned to road cycling with Team Sky, where his role initially was that of a domestique (working hard, feeding and watering the team's stars). His unwavering work ethic and versatility contributed significantly to the team's Grand Tour successes, laying the groundwork for his evolution as a rider.

Geraint's transformation into a Grand Tour contender was gradual and marked by resilience in the face of adversity, including numerous crashes and injuries. Under Team Sky (later named INEOS Grenadiers), he honed his climbing, time-trialling, and endurance skills. This culminated in his triumphant 2018 Tour de France victory, where he emerged not only as a race leader but also as the first Welshman to win the prestigious event. His consistent performances and leadership qualities continue to make him an integral member of the team, embodying their ethos of continuous improvement.

We are already seeing this same exceptional progress at Oxygen Conservation, with early-career professionals learning and developing at pace, as a result of their coachability, among other key characteristics. We have former interns now playing leading roles in estate management, natural capital, engagement, and ecology, and we know that we have future heads of department and directors (our Grand Tour champions) in the team. It's also great motivation for our existing senior leaders to continue pushing, learning, and developing ourselves.

3. Work ethic

Commitment in sports is often visible and tangible. Elite-level cyclists face an array of physical and mental pressures that are both rigorous and relentless. Physically, they endure extreme training loads, often cycling hundreds of kilometres per week, with sessions that push their endurance, speed, and strength to the limits. The wear and tear on the body can lead to overuse injuries, and the constant demand for peak physical condition means that recovery and nutrition are as critical as the training itself. In competition they face the pain barrier of long climbs, the danger of high-speed descents, and the fatigue of multi-stage races like the Tour de France.

Mentally, the pressures are equally challenging. Cyclists must maintain unwavering focus, discipline, and motivation to train and compete at the highest levels. The expectation to perform consistently, handle setbacks, and manage the stress of competition, while being away from family and support systems for long periods, can be psychologically taxing. Moreover, the need to stay mentally resilient in the face of injuries, weather conditions, and the inherent risks of the sport adds to the mental strain.

Many of these pressures present, albeit in different ways, in our work at Oxygen Conservation. The pace and workload are remarkable, and – despite how much we share with potential new hires – people always seem surprised by how much everybody works and the quality of work that is produced. Physical discomfort is a factor too as many of us travel extensively, spending a lot of time away from home, friends, and family. Working as part of Oxygen Conservation can therefore be physically, emotionally, and mentally taxing. Those of us that have been here to see the growth of the company, though, will all tell you it's worth it, even if it's not for everyone.

When Sir Dave Brailsford set out to change the fortunes of the GB cycling team in the early 2000s, with the team having won only one Olympic gold medal (in 1992), he recognised that to achieve success they would have to commit in a way that no one had done previously. As a result, the GB cycling team and Team Sky have become one of the most successful sporting dynasties of all time, achieving sixteen Olympic gold medals and six Tour de France victories.

We recognise that we are going to need to make the same complete commitment at Oxygen Conservation if we're going to deliver world-changing positive impact for people and wildlife.

4. Character

Character is paramount in high-pressure situations. Sir Dave Brailsford emphasised the importance of a culture of collective responsibility and strong character in his teams. A focus on character development was evident in the dynamics of Team Sky, where riders like Sir Bradley Wiggins and Chris Froome not only excelled individually but also supported their teammates. At the 2012 Tour de France, Chris sacrificed his own ambitions to pull Sir Bradley up several demanding climbs, which were vital in the success of Team Sky's first Tour de France success. Fast-forward only days, and Sir Bradley became a support rider to help propel Mark Cavendish to glory on the Champs-Élysées, taking the most iconic sprint finish in cycling.

At Oxygen Conservation we have that same emphasis on character, expecting everyone to be willing and able to help anyone else in the team. Often you will see directors (including me) picking up processes, documentation, and even admin tasks to help others in the team when they need it most. We have also rejected talented candidates based on character concerns, entitlement, or an unwillingness to work hard to help others in the team.

In a similar way to the carers working as a key part of Team Sky – travelling ahead of the team, changing mattresses, pillows, and bedding and ensuring the team are fed, watered, and fully supported – we are blessed with some especially kind and caring team members. These people always ensure we're looked after when we travel and make sure we have wonderful experiences together as a team. These are key parts of building our team culture, which is based on environment, impact, and adventure.

5. Decision making

In sport split-second decisions can make or break a race. Sir Dave's teams were known for their strategic acumen, often adopting bold race tactics that led to some of cycling's most iconic stage wins.

2012 TOUR DE FRANCE, STAGE 19 – SIR BRADLEY WIGGINS'S TIME TRIAL VICTORY

This stage was pivotal for Sir Bradley Wiggins to cement his overall lead in the Tour de France. He delivered a masterful performance in the individual time trial, a discipline where Team Sky's emphasis on aerodynamics and precision paid off. Sir Bradley won the stage by a significant margin, which all but assured his place as the overall winner of the Tour, marking the first time a British rider would take the title.

2013 TOUR DE FRANCE, STAGE 8 – CHRIS FROOME'S ATTACK ON AX 3 DOMAINES

In what would be his first Tour de France victory, Chris Froome's attack on the first mountain stage of the 2013 Tour de France at Ax 3 Domaines was a display of sheer power and team support. Team Sky controlled the peloton throughout the day, and Froome's devastating acceleration in the final kilometres distanced him from all his rivals, earning him the stage win and the yellow jersey.

2015 TOUR DE FRANCE, STAGE 10 – FROOME'S DOMINANCE ON LA PIERRE-SAINT-MARTIN

Chris Froome again demonstrated his and Team Sky's superiority on the first mountain finish of the 2015 Tour de France. The 'Sky Train' set a punishing pace on the climb to La Pierre Saint-Martin, and Froome's subsequent attack saw him take the stage win and extend his lead in the general classification – a lead he would not relinquish.

2016 TOUR DE FRANCE, STAGE 8 – FROOME'S DARING DESCENT TO BAGNÈRES-DE-LUCHON

Chris Froome took an unexpected stage win with a daring descent on the Col de Peyresourde. After attacking over the summit, he used an unconventional and aggressive aero tuck position to solo to the finish in Bagnères-de-Luchon, catching his rivals off guard and gaining time on the descent – a rare feat in professional cycling.

2018 TOUR DE FRANCE, STAGE 11 – GERAINT THOMAS'S VICTORY ON LA ROSIÈRE

Geraint Thomas showed his strength in the Alps with an impressive win on La Rosière during the 2018 Tour de France. After bridging to the leading group, he launched a powerful sprint to take the stage victory, which put him in the yellow jersey – a lead he would defend all the way to Paris.

2018 TOUR DE FRANCE, STAGE 12 – GERAINT WINS ON ALPE D'HUEZ

The very next day, Geraint further solidified his overall lead by winning on the legendary Alpe d'Huez. This back-to-back victory in the Alps was a rare and impressive feat and marked him as the clear frontrunner for the overall victory.

The Oxygen Conservation approach

In both sport and business, leaders often face decisions with incomplete information. Throughout my career, I've seen so many opportunities missed through people failing to make a decision – not even making the wrong one, just failing to act in time at all.

At Oxygen Conservation we excel at making decisions and doing so quickly, often with incomplete information. We communicate at pace, openly, and widely, which is made possible by a commitment to radical transparency, ensuring everyone has as much information as possible to make a decision. This speed of execution has allowed us to revolutionise the way landscapes are bought and sold across the UK. This same decision-making expertise is vital throughout the organisation and something we look for in every potential new addition. When we're recruiting, if the answer isn't *Hell, yes!*, it's a *No, thank you* from us.

6. Delivery

Ultimately, key is delivering results when it matters most. Sir Dave Brailsford's teams were celebrated for their peak performances on the biggest stages. This includes the 2012 London Olympics, where the team – with iconic performance from Sir Chris Hoy, Victoria Pendleton, Laura Kenny (Trott) and Jason Kenny – equalled their 2008 performance by claiming eight gold medals. For many of these athletes, this meant decades of work towards delivering the performance of a lifetime at the exact moment when it matters most.

Unlike professional athletes, in business we don't always know when the biggest moments will arrive. At Oxygen Conservation we know that we're fortunate to have the opportunity to be part of some excellent deals and transcendent moments in the environment sector. To that end, we ensure we're always ready to perform when it matters most.

Oxygen Conservation: Developing elite performers

The principles that led to the success of Brailsford's cycling teams are a blueprint for excellence in any high-performance environment. At Oxygen Conservation we embody the same principles in our talent selection and development process. We seek individuals who not only possess exceptional talent but also demonstrate coachability, a strong work ethic, exemplary character, astute decision-making abilities, and the capacity to perform under pressure.

The synergy between high performers in business and among professional athletes is undeniable but still underexplored. Both realms demand all the winning qualities described above. At Oxygen Conservation we are committed to fostering these qualities, as we strive to redefine the environment sector and build the natural capital economy.

On reflection

This article, written over the Christmas period in 2023, is a love letter to performance cycling, Sir Dave Brailsford, and everything Team Sky onwards. Having previously found Christmas periods challenging, with an enforced break from adventuring every day with the team, in that year I decided to deep dive into the detail of elite cycling to borrow what we could and apply it to our work at Oxygen Conservation.

I've always loved the idea of conceptual collisions (an unfortunate term when talking about cycling), taking ideas from one world and applying them to another, as we've done here.

Who knows where we will go next; recommendations are always appreciated.

There Are Five Quarters of Performance

Written January 2023

I generally reject convention in business. Instead, I seek to borrow ideas from the best across sport, business, finance, and nature, and then try to apply them to our work in new and creative ways. I'm therefore embarrassed to admit that, for too long, I've clung to the traditional approach of four quarterly performance reviews for the teams I have managed, albeit treating these as opportunities to share learning and celebrate performance and growth.

Typical review processes

I've always believed what the great All Blacks rugby team teach: give feedback as soon as possible, kindly (my addition), and if you've held it for too long, you've lost the right to share it (Kerr, 2013).

That aside, up until 2022 I fell in line with the conventional wisdom of holding a Q4 or end-of-year review, which I'd like to apologise for. When delivered in the conventional way, as taught by so many public sector or large corporate organisations, they're a terrible idea!

Our business year aligns with the calendar year, so our Q4 ends in December. This is the time of the year when people are tired and often slightly unwell, have worked hard all year, and are thinking about Christmas. We're often told to use this time to:

- Reflect on the year that has passed (good)
- Celebrate successes (good)
- Reflect on our learning and development (mostly good)
- Talk about reward and recognition for the following year (terrible idea)
- Set ambitious, impactful, and inspirational goals for the following year (madness!)

Imagine replicating this in the world of sport. You're the head coach, and with five minutes to go before the end of the last game of the season, you take the team off the field and ask them to review performance across the whole game and season. At the same time, you ask them to set goals for the following year, make their case for how they should be rewarded next season, and then tell them get back out there and finish the game!

Our new review process

This year we did things differently at Oxygen Conservation. Our Q4 reviews were celebrations of achievement, growth, and improvements made in 2022, and they encouraged everyone to take the time and space they needed to rest and recover ready for 2023. We didn't talk about reward and recognition. This is (and absolutely should be) dealt with in a separate conversation, between Q3 and Q4. In our case this also aligns with our budget cycles.

Note: You must absolutely be transparent about this process – ensure people know when and how this conversation will happen, who the decision makers are, and (please!) separate it from conversations about development. Otherwise, people won't hear anything until you talk about the numbers, and this will be the overriding takeaway from the session.

We then started 2023 with our Q0. We brought everyone together in the same place and space (vital, especially for remote teams) and began by celebrating the excellent successes of the previous year (again) and thanking everyone (again) for their hard work in the previous year.

Next it was time to look to the future. We set a small number of clear, measurable goals that will allow us to Scale Conservation and fight climate change and the biodiversity crisis we're all facing.

We then talked about the strategies and tactics that would allow us to achieve those goals – providing a framework for everyone to draw a straight line from their individual contributions to our principal goal of Scaling Conservation. Everyone then met with their business groups and line managers to set individual objectives with all objectives openly shared (with the team's full support in doing so) to help make collaboration and support a practical reality.

We will continue to have four quarterly reviews and use these to realign, celebrate, and develop throughout the year. These are also great opportunities to understand people's long-term ambitions and to discuss creative approaches to experiential development and ideas to radically change our business for the better.

Here's an overview of how this works in practice:

- **Q0 – January.** Start with purpose. Start the year strong by setting ambitious objectives.

- **Q1 – end of March.** Foundations and fundamentals. Focus on key fundamentals of the business and individual performance. Are we doing the work we need to do to set us up for an excellent year? If we haven't got our systems and processes set by the end of Q1, we will pay for it later in the year.

- **Q2 – end of June.** Build momentum. Reflect on the first half of the year. Celebrate achievements. Reward the team with experiential learning, inspirational visits, and engagement with the environment. Focus on rest, recovery, and rejuvenation to ensure we're able to maximise opportunities throughout the second half of the year.

- **Q3 – end of September.** Finish strong. Provide continued support on health, wellbeing, and happiness to ensure we finish strong when others are slowing down, easing up, and relaxing by the end of the year. We will keep getting better when others are already thinking about next year.

- **Reward and recognition meeting.** You've now got eleven months of performance data for the business, and often for the individual, to have an informed conversation about performance to date, future potential, and how this impacts rewards and recognition for the following year. If you don't have this discussion before your budget-setting process, you're not giving a person the opportunity to make their case, because the decision has already been made. Remember this isn't just about money. Everyone should get more creative about the ways in which we can better recognise high performers and help to create opportunities where they can be even more awesome in their roles.

- **Q4 – December.** Reflect. Reset. Recovery. In the sporting context, this is your season review or debrief, ice bath, and recovery work, all required to ensure you come back after the break ready to be even more phenomenal.

We will continue to evolve our performance cadence alongside our company culture as we work hard to create a high-performance environment, where everyone can have positive impact, great learning experiences, and incredible adventures along the way.

How do you manage your performance year?

On reflection

As is the Oxygen Conservation way, we've continued to evolve our processes. In 2024 our Q0 meeting was a two-day performance preparation event at our Mornacott Estate. We know we push people hard, so we wanted to give them the tools and techniques to make that possible, and the world of performance cycling from my Christmas deep dive provided the backdrop to the event.

THERE ARE FIVE QUARTERS OF PERFORMANCE

We learned about the planning, preparations, and logistics associated with travel, nutrition, and timing of performance, as well as about rest and recovery. Two of my favourite parts of the event were:

1. The team together being led in pairs through ice bath sessions to demonstrate the positive impacts on mental and physical rest and recovery. This was such a brilliant team-building activity and one that continues to benefit people today.
2. Viewing a documentary from the Jumbo Visma Tour de France team (van der Zon, 2023) that demonstrated the individual choices, changes, and sacrifices the team made for performance. This was followed by an impromptu discussion, when I watched as the team spent almost an hour highlighting learnings they could apply. I was so proud of every single person in that room for identifying and learning, and for what we all do and could do to find that next level of performance.

As I sit writing this reflection, we've just had our first set of performance data from Q1. We've outperformed our commitment to work every month this quarter. Not just that, but we've also increased that level of outperformance month on month.

Have we helped people learn, develop, and adapt? The data seems to think so.

Unsung Heroes: Recognising the Domestiques of Business

Written July 2023

Since the time of Team Sky and Sir Dave Brailsford's doctrine of marginal gains, I've loved the Tour de France. As with so many sports, the more you recognise and appreciate the nuance, the more the sacrifices, the stories, and the sport itself become meaningful.

Unsung heroes

One thing unique in the Tour de France, and in professional cycling in general, is the role of the domestique. A domestique's primary role is to assist and aid their team leader (protected rider) in achieving the best possible results. Domestiques perform tasks such as setting the pace, protecting the leader from wind, fetching supplies, chasing breakaways, and assisting with mechanical issues. All domestiques are elite cyclists in their own right, and they sacrifice themselves completely for the greater good, for one goal: a Grand Tour victory. This sacrifice is very real physically, mentally, and emotionally – literally fetching, carrying, feeding, and sheltering the team leader to bring them within touching distance of the finish line when they are ready to strike.

While the concept of domestiques is specific to sport, I can't help but see a number of similarities in many of the incredible people we work with every day in high-performing teams in business. These team members so rarely get the praise and thanks they deserve, though.

In the Tour de France, an athlete called Wout van Aert is changing this dynamic by becoming a global superstar and an iconic domestique. By producing hero-like performances, propelling his team and his time leader, Jonas Vingegaard, to back-to-back Tour wins, Wout has transformed the role of the domestique.

I think it's time we made the domestiques (team members) of the business world the superstars they deserve to be! Here are just some of the benefits they bring to our business:

Sacrificing for the team

Domestiques sacrifice their personal ambitions and success in races to ensure that their team leader has the best chance of winning. Similarly, key team members may need to sacrifice personal time and preferences to meet company goals and deadlines – this needs to be recognised, appreciated, and better rewarded.

Here are some of the factors that make sacrificing beneficial to teams, both in cycling and in business:

1. Making sacrifices for the team
2. Supporting the greater goal

3. Ensuring delivery

4. Promoting team culture

5. Providing adaptability and flexibility

6. Boosting team morale

1. Making sacrifices for the team

Domestiques sacrifice their personal ambitions and success in races to ensure that their team leader has the best chance of winning.

Key team members may need to sacrifice personal time and preferences to meet company goals and deadlines. This needs to be recognised, appreciated, and better rewarded.

2. Supporting the greater goal

Domestiques in cycling work extremely hard for the benefit of their team leader, recognising that their success comes from that of the team leader.

Team members in business support executives and senior managers by handling more routine tasks and assisting in various aspects of the company's operations.

3. Ensuring delivery

In cycling, domestiques form the backbone of a team, providing the necessary support, protection, and strategic assistance during races – they carry food and drink for the team leader and make his ride easier by shielding him from the oncoming wind.

In business, key team members form the backbone of an organisation, as they perform essential day-to-day functions that keep the company running smoothly, thereby often protecting the senior leaders in many ways.

4. Promoting team culture

Both roles require strong team culture and communication skills. Domestiques must work together seamlessly, communicating effectively to optimise their team's performance in races.

Business team members need to collaborate with their colleagues and senior leaders to ensure the efficient functioning of the company, controlling the pace and the direction of leadership team.

5. Providing adaptability and flexibility

Domestiques in cycling must be adaptable and ready to respond to changing race conditions, unexpected events, and occasionally, diva superstar team leaders!

Key team members in business also need to be flexible, as they will often be required to change priorities and shift direction, and in a scaling startup, deal with endless chaos.

6. Boosting team morale

Domestiques play a crucial role in maintaining team morale and motivation during races, offering encouragement and support to their fellow riders.

Key team members in business are the architects of a team culture and can impact team morale by fostering a positive work environment and supporting their colleagues, even when they're making personal sacrifices for others for the bigger goal.

Opportunity

There are also some benefits for the domestique and their equivalent role in business.

Domestiques often learn from experienced team leaders and improve their skills over time, with the potential to become superstar team leaders themselves in the future. Similarly, key team members in business can use their experiences to grow and advance within the company, potentially moving into higher-level positions or starting their own businesses.

The price is a high one to pay in terms of time, energy, and effort, but the rewards – whatever that means to a specific person – can be great.

Recognition and appreciation

While the achievements of team leaders in cycling and those of high-level executives in business may receive more attention, those people need to remember that the victories are not theirs alone – they belong to the team. It is therefore time to make sure we thank the hard-working individuals who do a fantastic job, often quietly and without the same overt recognition that those traditionally considered superstars enjoy.

The world of elite sport and business are of course different, and this in part explains the reasons domestiques – certainly the best domestiques – are increasingly recognised and richly rewarded. The impact of domestiques, and the hero narratives that can be found in such obvious and often painful sacrifice, are recognised by more people as a result of the global coverage of the Tour de France. Sport also attracts a glamour that is rarely

UNSUNG HEROES: RECOGNISING THE DOMESTIQUES OF BUSINESS

afforded to most businesses, albeit we're trying hard to make the environment sector a more aspirational place to work.

This is a call to everyone out there: reach out to the domestique in your business that has made it possible for you to succeed, to develop, or to just do your job, and say thank you. Share with them how much you appreciate what they do, and make them feel like the superstar they are – make them Wout van Aert!

PS My ambition is that, by 2030, Oxygen Conservation will be the first environmental business to sponsor a Tour de France team, challenging the dominance of fossil fuel companies that use this iconic bike race as part of their greenwashing efforts.

On reflection

Watching Oxygen Conservation grow from an idea into one of the most significant natural capital portfolios in the world has been a wild ride. One thing that's remained clear throughout is that success isn't a solo pursuit – it's all about the team.

We have been and continue to be blessed with some incredible domestiques, and some people we previously thought of as domestiques are now leading their own departments and estates with great success.

In some ways, we all start as domestiques. Dan and I did nearly everything in year one (appreciating Dave Keir's help from the sidelines). Then, as we scaled, we brought in superstars who took their turn at the front, making us stronger, faster, and most importantly, much better.

Now, as we wrap up the second chapter of this adventure, I find myself more often than not back in role of a

SCALING CONSERVATION

domestique – helping an insanely talented team find their own rhythm. Leadership isn't about being the smartest person in the room; it's about orchestrating the idiosyncrasies, obsessions, and brilliance that make high performers great. It's about building a culture.

You don't always need to lead from the front, but you do always need to remember it's your job to serve your team. That's why whenever we eat together – especially with new starters – I clear the plates. Small things matter. If you get too used to others doing things for you, it goes to your head.

To those taking the wind, carrying the load, and setting the pace: thank you.

The real win isn't crossing the line first; it's making sure the whole team gets there together.

Calendar Defence

Written January 2024

I take every opportunity to learn from the best and the brightest in their individual fields and love trying to apply this to our context. While not a football fan, one of the most useful concepts I've borrowed from the books of Pep Guardiola and Jürgen Klopp is that everything starts with defence.

In Jürgen Klopp's biography (Neveling, 2020) he talks about how his famed *Gegenpress* philosophy is a defensive strategy that seeks to create immediate opportunities to attack, based on organisation, immediacy, commitment, and effort.

Pep Guardiola, recognised for his outstanding attacking football, prefers to talk about defence. He's quoted as saying, 'Defensive organisation is the cornerstone of everything else I want to achieve in my football' (Perarnau, 2014).

Both these managers, albeit in different ways, describe that the most immediate and long-lasting impact you can have on any team is to put in a well-organised and practised defensive system. Again, they both recognise that you can do this quickly and easily, but it takes discipline and teamwork.

Calendar management

Adapting and applying this concept to our work has led me to focus on the value of developing an effective calendar management (defence) system. While your calendar of course allows you to prioritise your time and schedule key events, and it helps you to know when and where you need to be, it can do so much more. In the same way defensive organisation on the football pitch allows a player to tackle, to press, or to attack because they know where their support is, your calendar can allow you to do the same in business.

I love to apply concepts from other environments to business, and I try and identify the key principles. This approach gives a sense of direction without being prescriptive, helping us all to borrow from the best but leaving room for continued evolution. If your entire team commits to adopting some key calendar management principles, this will provide a fantastic foundation for communication and collaboration, and it will even help you respect each other's priorities, commitments, and ambitions.

Here are my principles for organising my calendar, my time, and ultimately my life:

1. Make your calendar visible.
2. Recognise your time is an investment.
3. Create the conditions for success.
4. Remember that details matter (let the calendar do the work).

5. Be flexible, and say no more.

1. Make your calendar visible

At Oxygen Conservation everyone's calendar is visible to everyone else. That doesn't mean we don't have private appointments and events, but it means that we can see when others are busy (or free), are visiting one of our estates, might have an opportunity to collaborate, or might just need some help.

Visibility is especially important for remote teams, with increasingly many of us working remotely for at least some of the time. The health, safety, and happiness of your colleagues will always be better if people know where you are and what you're doing.

There are so many simple advantages too, including – but not limited to – not inviting people to meetings when they're double-booked, being aware of those on annual leave, respecting people's boundaries when they have a personal appointment, and not giving deadlines to people just before they go on leave or the day they return.

If anyone is worried about others in the team knowing what they're working on – or not working on – then perhaps there needs to be a conversation about culture fit, and this may lead to you inviting them to be successful elsewhere.

2. Recognise your time is an investment

Commit fully to using your calendar as an expression of what's important to you, and recognise that it's an investment of your most precious and limited asset: your time.

Unless you've managed to conquer time travel, your time is limited. No matter how efficient and effective you are, what you choose to do with your time should be an investment and a conscious, purposeful choice. Your time should be spent on things that help achieve your goals and ambitions. If that isn't the case, challenge your investment decision. I appreciate that not everyone has full control of their calendar, but you almost certainly have more autonomy than you're currently taking.

Within your calendar, make sure you invest in the things that are most important to you, and do them first. Invest time in your health and wellbeing, and prioritise your friends, family, and fun. If you don't make space for these things first, they will never get in the calendar. If you do make space for them, you can move or adjust the time slot, but you've still committed to those things happening.

3. Create the conditions for success

At Oxygen Conservation we want to be the world-first conservation-focused unicorn company. We know that if you want to achieve something no one has ever done, you have to be prepared to do the things no one has ever done. To make this possible, we constantly talk about performance and personal development, recognising that this is about much more than training courses and traditional learning.

This is about creating the conditions for success. For me this means managing several weeks at a time (I schedule over seven days a week) and ensuring I prioritise time for family, exercise, travel, and opportunities for environmental adventures. I know I need to spend time surrounded by the team, and by people better than me whom I can learn from. I also need to have enough time at home so that I look forward to the travel. Oh, and cool coffee shops – they have to feature too!

We all need different factors and conditions to ensure we can be the best versions of ourselves, so start by writing an honest list of what you need, share it with friends and family, and ask them to challenge you on it. When you know the things you (and they) need to be successful – whatever success means to you – build it into your calendar for the future.

4. Remember that details matter
(let the calendar do the work)

When planning, details matter. When an event or appointment goes in the calendar, put it in as early as possible, and include all the information you need to get there and be successful. Make sure you know where you're going and when you need to be there, then allow your calendar and your appointments to do the hard work and free up a little more of your time for more creative, better-quality thinking, or just for fun.

5. Be flexible, and say no more

Make sure everything that's important to you gets in the diary as soon as possible, but recognise that things will move, and likely a lot. Be comfortable flexing and adjusting. Sometimes the challenges of life get in the way, or exciting new opportunities appear, meaning you need to adjust priorities. By having everything set in the calendar, you can make informed decisions about what to change, move, or cancel. How to make these decisions is something I'm still working on, so I would love to hear about your decision models for how you prioritise and consider new opportunities and invitations; and yes, I think instinct is a legitimate decision model and the one most of us use most of the time.

Your time is a limited resource

I'll say it again for the people in the back: your time is a limited resource. Increasingly throughout my career, I've learned that I'll have to politely say *No, thank you* to a meeting or an event. This applies even to fun stuff I yearn to do, because other things take priority. By having visibility of your whole team's calendar, you have the opportunity to offer opportunities (fun or not) to others, who themselves then have the ability to make an informed decision about accepting your invitation.

Just because Pep, Jürgen, and I think a well-organised defence is super-important in creating the conditions to be successful and attack your future ambitions, it doesn't mean we're right. There are always other philosophies, styles, and ways of working. I do, however, hope the above calendar rules help some of you achieve an improved level of organisation for you and your team, in the process creating the conditions you need to do wonderful things and have incredible experiences along the way.

I'm constantly trying to improve the way I invest and manage my time and would love to hear from you about how you work and what I could learn from your systems and processes. The coffee's on me!

On reflection

Having an organised calendar defence system remains the most important technique I think most of us can learn to be more effective – in work and in life. If you've got this far in the book, you'll know that I am fortunate enough to work with the most incredible group of people, but virtually all of those people have needed help and support in making difficult decisions and choices. Your calendar is a big part of that process.

Having a weekly family planning meeting – usually on Friday evening if I'm not travelling, or on Sunday evening if I am – where we look at the next at least two weeks has helped ensure the most important things get the priority they deserve.

For the line managers and leaders out there: it's important to remember that you cannot push coaching tools and techniques that you haven't yourself embraced. I think the reason the team accept my constant push for calendar management (and electronic to-do lists) is because I live each of these rules myself and continue to iterate and improve how I work. That involves borrowing different calendar approaches, trialling them, and then deciding which to adopt or discard.

Open your calendar now. Does it really represent what's important to you? If not, change it!

Oxygenating Your Time

Written October 2023

In our fast-paced world, mastering time management has become paramount for personal and professional success, and let's be honest, it's not something you can ever complete. It's a constantly evolving work in progress. While many of us grapple with the overwhelming demands of daily life, a potentially transformative solution lies within our grasp: controlling our time domain.

A guide to productivity and sustainable time management

Through the implementation of a structured calendar and a searchable electronic to-do list, you can stop trying to manage, sort, and search an increasingly complex workload in your mind in the minutes, hours, and days immediately in front of you. This approach, inspired by our personal experiences, many mistakes, and years of practice, is endorsed by leading thinkers in business and sustainability. In this article we offer a powerful strategy to reclaim your time, boost creativity, and foster a sustainable mindset in the way you approach work and life, especially if – like me – you think they're one and the same.

The overwhelming time domain: My experience

The journey begins with a stark realisation: we all struggle to organise our time effectively. Without a structured calendar, we find ourselves adrift in the vast sea of days and weeks, losing sight of the time and space available.

We all too often try and complete everything in the amount of time we can comfortably perceive or hold in our mind – likely days and weeks. Moreover, the absence of a digital to-do list means we attempt to hold a multitude of tasks and ideas in our heads, with this leading to mental fatigue and a stressful, disorganised existence. If you have never felt this way, you haven't been challenged to the point of being unable to complete everything required of you. At Oxygen Conservation everyone is challenged to that point.

At the time of writing, since founding Oxygen Conservation, I have 3,415 items in my to-do list; 798 items remain incomplete, but I have no more than eight items scheduled for a single day, and planning for some of those actions extends into the early 2030s. By adopting the following tools and techniques, you can consider your time domain in a completely different way.

This observation mirrors the sentiments of productivity guru David Allen, whose 'getting things done' methodology (Allen, 2015) emphasises the importance of decluttering the mind. Allen's system promotes the capture, categorisation, and organisation of tasks and ideas, akin to the concept of a searchable electronic to-do list. By adopting this approach, individuals can regain control over their mental space, freeing it up for creative thinking and strategic planning.

The key to effective time management, however, goes beyond the mere implementation of these tools. It also involves a shift in mindset – a recognition that time is both a finite and precious resource, and that how we use it greatly impacts our personal and professional lives.

Reducing mental fatigue: Sustaining the marathon of sprints

It's crucial to recognise that our mental energy and capacity – like time – are finite resources. Just as athletes pace themselves for a marathon, professionals must also adopt a strategic approach to managing their cognitive resources. The tools and techniques outlined here not only enhance productivity but also serve as an antidote against the mental fatigue that comes from trying to remember everything.

In the modern business landscape, it often feels like we're engaged in a marathon of sprints. The demands are relentless, and the pace is unrelenting. However, sustaining this level of intensity without proper time management can quickly lead to burnout and decreased effectiveness.

This concept resonates deeply with the wisdom offered by Arianna Huffington. In her book *Thrive* (Huffington, 2015), Arianna emphasises the importance of wellbeing and the detrimental effects of burnout on individuals and organisations. She advocates for a holistic approach to success – one that values not just the quantity of work but also the quality of life.

THE PENSIEVE APPROACH: A PAGE FROM HARRY POTTER

Imagine a tool akin to the Pensieve – a magical repository for thoughts and actions from the wizarding world of Harry Potter. Such a tool would create space for innovation, enabling you to offload mental clutter and to focus on the most important tasks. That tool exists, in the form of an electronic to-do list. This echoes the philosophy of sustainability leaders like Paul Polman, former CEO of Unilever, who championed sustainable business practices (Polman and Winston, 2021). Polman's ability to steer a multinational corporation towards sustainability goals required not only visionary thinking but also the capacity to manage complex agendas and choose what to dedicate time to and when. An organised calendar and a digital to-do list were undoubtedly valuable tools in his arsenal.

Paul Polman's legacy exemplifies the idea that sustainability is not merely an abstract concept but also a strategic imperative for businesses in the modern world. His leadership at Unilever demonstrated that aligning sustainability with business goals not only benefits the planet but also boosts profitability. Polman's success underscores the importance of carving out time for strategic thinking – a task made significantly easier through effective time management tools.

In essence, the Pensieve approach, inspired by Harry Potter's world, encourages us to externalise our thoughts and tasks, creating a mental space free from clutter. By doing so, we not only improve our productivity but also create room for innovative ideas and sustainable strategies.

Prioritisation: Quality over quantity

Much like Tim Ferriss's emphasis on prioritisation in his four-hour-workweek philosophy (Ferriss, 2011), our approach recognises the importance of quality over quantity (and for the avoidance of doubt: I'm not comfortable with a forty-hour workweek, never mind a four-hour one!). Setting a limit of no more than eight tasks per day ensures efficient spacing and prevents the overwhelming feeling that comes with an overburdened schedule. Ferriss himself advocates for identifying the most critical tasks and focusing efforts there, aligning with our philosophy of mindful prioritisation.

Tim Ferriss's approach to time management emphasises a profound shift in how we view work and productivity. His work challenges the conventional notion that busyness equals productivity. Instead, Ferriss encourages us to focus on the most impactful tasks, optimise our workflow, and create more time for adventure, fun, and creativity.

In a world that often glorifies busyness, Ferriss's approach is a testament to the power of deliberate prioritisation. It serves as a reminder that productivity should not be measured solely by the number of tasks completed, but also by the significance of those tasks and the quality of the results achieved.

Harnessing the power of reminders

Leading figures like Richard Branson, founder of Virgin Group, emphasise setting reminders for regular reflection and goal assessment. This practice mirrors our approach of setting reminders for thoughts and ideas, effectively turning them into self-coaching points for personal and professional growth. Branson's belief in the power of reflection underscores the importance of maintaining a clear and structured mental space (Branson, 2014).

Richard Branson's entrepreneurial journey is a testament to the importance of continuous learning and reflection. His ability to adapt to new challenges and industries, while maintaining a playful and adventurous spirit, has made him a global icon. Central to Branson's success is his commitment to self-improvement and self-coaching, a practice facilitated by regular reminders.

By incorporating reminders into our time management strategy, we create a mechanism for ongoing self-assessment and growth. These reminders serve as guideposts, nudging us to revisit our goals, re-evaluate our priorities, and make necessary adjustments. In doing so, we not only enhance our personal development but also cultivate a sustainable mindset that values continuous improvement.

I have the same group of reminders I see every Sunday; and then a range of different ideas, on concepts borrowed from the books I've read, that appear throughout the year to help remind me of key concepts guiding the way.

Simplifying complex tasks:
A design thinking perspective

In the realm of design thinking, simplicity is a core principle. Experts like Tim Brown of IDEO advocate distilling complex challenges into manageable components, aligning with our approach to capturing the essence of tasks without overwhelming ourselves with excessive details (Brown, 2009). This approach creates a user-friendly mental interface, akin to a contents page for the mind, making it easier to navigate our goals and ideas.

By adopting a design thinking perspective within our time management strategy, we can approach our tasks with a structured and systematic mindset. We can deconstruct complex projects into actionable steps, making them more approachable and less daunting.

The journey of effective time management

Effective time management is not a solitary endeavour but a journey that combines personal insights with the wisdom of leading thinkers. Through the integration of structured calendars, searchable electronic to-do lists, mindful prioritisation, reminders, and simplified task management, you can transform your approach to time management, unlocking the doors to enhanced productivity, creativity, and sustainability.

In the fast-paced symphony of life, orchestrating our time is an art form, and this article offers us the baton. This journey has shown us the cacophony of demands that can disorient our existence when left unmanaged, but it's also illuminated a path towards harmony and empowerment. With structured calendars and digital to-do lists as our instruments, we've composed a melody that liberates our minds from chaos, allowing creativity to soar. We've learned that the true treasure of time management is not in the mere ticking-off of tasks; it is in sculpting a life with purpose, capacity, creativity, and sustainability. As we take a final bow, exhaling the chaos and inhaling success, we know that our journey is a symphony that continues to evolve, each note more melodious than the last. Now to compose our sheet music for 2024!

On reflection

A well-organised calendar and an electronic to-do list are two of the most important tools in improving your health, happiness, and performance, whether you're in business or in any other high-level environment.

You need to:

- Be clear on your schedule and capacity for activity (work, rest, and play)
- Know the activities you need to complete (again, work, rest, and play)

In the absence of this information, you're just guessing or – more accurately – hoping something good will happen.

Over the last three years, coaching and reinforcing the importance of calendar management and electronic to-do lists have been the simplest and most impactful improvements I've been able to provide the team, from interns through to heads of departments and directors.

If you're not working in this way, then I can only assume you're not working in an environment that is pushing you to learn and develop anywhere near your potential, but you tell me.

SIX
Green Finance

The Business of Conservation: Why Conservation for Profit Is a Sustainable Approach for the Planet's Future

Written April 2023

Conservation has long been associated with non-profit organisations and government agencies trying to protect our planet's precious habitats, biodiversity, and natural resources. This is changing.

Let's talk business

In the face of absolute climate collapse and a worsening biodiversity crisis, the time for action is now, and the need for positive environmental and social impact has never been greater. A strategic, business-like approach allows us to mobilise the investment required to make an impact at scale and pace, giving future generations the chance of life on Earth. Conservation for profit provides a sustainable approach for our planet's future. Here are some of the key factors involved:

1. Leveraging market forces for conservation
2. Creating economic opportunities for local communities
3. Promoting innovation and technology-driven solutions
4. Addressing the concerns of critics
5. The importance of engagement
6. Making more land more accessible
7. Exploring profit-sharing solutions

1. Leveraging market forces for conservation

Our approach recognises the economic value of nature and seeks to harness market forces to drive conservation efforts. While we appreciate it may seem counterintuitive to some, conservation for profit has the potential to provide positive impact for people and the environment, creating a win-win situation for all stakeholders (including the planet).

In a capitalist economy and society, profit is a powerful motivator that drives innovation, investment, and resource allocation. By attaching economic value to conservation, we can leverage market forces to incentivise regenerative and sustainable practices. For example, organic regenerative agriculture can generate income from food production, while also protecting biodiversity and ensuring long-term food security (all while improving soil health). This creates a financial incentive for landowners, farmers, and growers to manage their land sustainably, leading to better conservation outcomes.

2. Creating economic opportunities for local communities

Conservation for profit can provide tangible benefits to local communities, particularly in rural areas where many of our most precious habitats are located.

An example is ecotourism, which promotes responsible tourism in natural areas and can generate revenue for local communities through visitor fees, accommodation, and other services. This not only creates jobs and improves livelihoods, helping visitors connect with and understand nature; it also fosters a sense of ownership and stewardship among local communities, emotionally (and economically) incentivising them to protect their natural heritage.

3. Promoting innovation and technology-driven solutions

Conservation for profit can also promote innovation and technology-driven solutions to environmental challenges. With the potential for financial gains, businesses and entrepreneurs are incentivised to develop new technologies and practices that can help conserve natural resources and protect the environment.

An example is renewable energy sources such as solar or wind (though never hydropower schemes, as they destroy river systems). These energy sources are sustainable, do not produce harmful greenhouse gas emissions, and can contribute to mitigating climate change. Renewable energy projects can generate income through the production of clean energy, while also promoting environmental conservation. This could be wind over a growing woodland canopy, or integrated regenerative farming alongside renewable energy projects, reducing dependence on fossil fuels and minimising environmental pollution.

4. Addressing the concerns of critics

Critics of conservation for profit argue that putting a price tag on nature commodifies it and undermines its intrinsic value. They argue that conservation efforts should be driven only by ethical and moral considerations rather than by profit motives.

While it's important to acknowledge the moral and ethical aspects of conservation, we recognise the reality that without mobilising the investment required to protect and improve the natural world, there won't be a planet left to conserve. By attaching economic value to nature, we can ensure that it is taken into account in economic calculations and decision-making processes, rather than being ignored or undervalued.

Another concern raised by critics is that conservation for profit may exacerbate inequality and lead to the privatisation of natural resources, potentially leading to the displacement of local communities and the loss of access to traditional lands. Commerce-based conservation must therefore include safeguards to prevent such negative impacts. For example, partnerships between conservation organisations, local communities, and businesses can ensure that benefits are shared and that local people have the opportunity to be involved in these changing landscapes.

5. The importance of engagement

Our approach when acquiring land is to engage with the local community to watch, listen, and learn.

Soon after acquisition of any new landscape, we welcome local people to visit. For example, we've invited local communities and key stakeholders to afternoon tea on Dartmoor, for mulled wine and mince pies at Christmas in Perthshire, and to lunch at Hartsgarth Farm in the Scottish Borders. We've welcomed the Rivers Trust, the Wildlife Trusts, individual National Parks, the National Trust, Natural England, MPs, local community groups, local councils, students, and former owners and tenants (old and new) to our different land holdings.

6. Making more land more accessible

We are committed to making the landscape we manage more accessible (where the environment makes it appropriate to do so) to those who live, work, and play within these truly outstanding landscapes.

We prioritise investment locally, at every opportunity, when selecting consultants or contractors, recognising that money spent locally is more beneficial to the local economy. Where we have built property on an estate, we invite local tenancies (with more people living and working on our estates than before our ownership). We also plan on developing unique ecotourism opportunities that can create new employment opportunities and bring additional revenues to local communities.

7. Exploring profit-sharing solutions

We hope that in the future we can develop commercially viable ways of helping local communities benefit financially more directly from our work. This might include:

- Profit-share arrangements where we can develop renewable energy

- Helping local business access natural capital products and services at a reduced rate
- Returning areas of land, where possible, to the local community as mature woodlands, nature reserves, or other areas for public access

Aligning human nature and market forces

We believe that conservation for profit is a sustainable approach that recognises the economic value of nature and leverages market forces to drive conservation efforts. By attaching economic incentives to conservation, we can align human nature and market forces to promote sustainable practices, provide tangible benefits for people and the environment, foster innovation, and ensure that nature is considered in economic decision making. While we recognise there are concerns that need to be addressed, conservation for profit has the potential to create a sustainable and scalable model for protecting our planet's natural resources and biodiversity, offering future generations the chance of life on Earth.

On reflection

I am surer every day that our collective failure to appropriately value the natural world and everything it provides for us all is the principal cause of climate change and biodiversity collapse. When something is free to use, we're conditioned to assume it's limitless and therefore can be easily wasted, disregarded, and replaced without consequence.

Our failure to put a price on emitting carbon into the atmosphere, allowing sewage into our rivers, and dumping plastic into our oceans are big, horrible, smelly examples of the way our current economic system incentivises these behaviours.

We've taken far too much from the world for too long and run up debt that my generation are expecting the future to pay. If they can't, which seems increasingly likely, instead they will have to default on the future of this planet and life on Earth.

For anyone reading this and still being offended by the concept of putting a price on nature: I choose to be more offended by the systematic collapse of our climate and the fact we're wilfully overseeing the next mass extinction.

The New Paradigm of Natural Capital Investment

Written November 2023

In the world of financial services, there is a growing buzz surrounding an unconventional but increasingly important asset class: natural capital. This term encompasses the Earth's ecosystems, biodiversity, clean air, soil, and fresh water, which form the bedrock of our existence on this planet. Despite its critical role, the concept of natural capital as an investment class is still in its infancy. Nevertheless, it's becoming increasingly apparent that natural capital is the ultimate 'alternative asset class'. Without it, all other investments become completely irrelevant.

As the impact of the climate collapse and biodiversity crisis becomes increasingly real, both across the globe and much closer to home – seen most recently in the form of increasingly familiar unprecedented amounts of rain leading to widespread flooding – the imperative for change has never been greater.

A hedge against our collective future

At this point in time the very existence of natural capital holds a dual role:

- It is a potential solution to provide for the future of life on Earth.
- It is a hedge against society's potential failure to act quickly enough.

In this article we will explore the two equally powerful but different natural capital investment theses.

1. Investing in natural capital: A moral imperative

Our planet's ecosystems, biodiversity, clean air, soil, and fresh water are not mere commodities. They are the essence of life itself. The preservation of these resources is fundamental to our survival. By investing in natural capital, we can actively participate in safeguarding the environment for future generations.

The degradation of natural capital has far-reaching consequences, from the loss of species and habitats to the deterioration of air and water quality. The moral argument for investing in natural capital is rooted in our shared responsibility to protect the Earth's ecological treasures. This is not only about doing well financially but also about doing good for the planet. As conscientious global citizens, we must recognise our duty to act in the best interests of the planet and all its inhabitants.

You should invest in natural capital if you want to help save at least a little of the world.

2. Investing in natural capital: As a financial hedge

Beyond the moral imperative, the financial case for natural capital investment presents a compelling rationale. Many investors are sceptical about society's willingness and capacity to address environmental challenges with the urgency they demand. This scepticism offers a great opportunity, effectively short-selling the planet and investing in natural capital as a unique hedge against societal inaction.

It is a depressing thought, but as our world grapples with environmental crises, those who invest in natural capital may witness their wealth appreciate as the planet's ecosystems deteriorate. This is a harsh reality: environmental degradation can lead to scarcity, driving up the value of natural resources. This is a paradox we recognise and carry heavily. Those who foresaw the crisis, acted, and invested in natural capital could potentially profit as the planet and its ecosystems continue to deteriorate.

You should invest in natural capital even if you don't believe society will act quickly enough to save the world, because you will make a (literal) killing as the planet and everything on it dies.

The path forward: Balancing profit and purpose

As the climate rapidly crumbles and we prepare to live through the next mass extinction, the idea of investing in natural capital transcends traditional financial motives, offering a solution, no matter what the question. It becomes a statement of purpose – a testament to our commitment to securing a better future for the planet and for future generations.

The interplay between morality and finance in the realm of natural capital investment is complex. It will almost certainly require us to endure contradictions and make compromises. It underscores a new paradigm that demands consideration, though. As investors, we've long been told we must weigh potential short-term financial gains against the imperative to protect the environment and profit in the long term. Natural capital investment, through the forward sale of credits, provides a solution to the perceived problem of illiquidity and long-term capital commitment.

Striking a balance between profit and purpose is now not only feasible but also essential for the wellbeing of our planet, for future generations, and for the performance of all our investments.

In a world where the UN recently declared that our society has opened the gates to hell and welcomed the time of global boiling, I'm not sure the net present value of our oil and gas investment is going to help in the firefight. Natural capital is not merely a buzzword; it represents the single biggest investment opportunity the world has ever seen, where moral responsibility and great financial returns converge. Our choices today will determine whether we are on the right side of history, safeguarding our planet and the prosperity of future generations. Embracing natural capital as a legitimate investment class is not just a decision – it's a commitment to a sustainable and thriving future for all.

The question isn't whether you should invest in natural capital; it's at what point you will choose to invest in the ultimate alternative asset class that could shape the destiny of our planet.

THE NEW PARADIGM OF NATURAL CAPITAL INVESTMENT

Whether we can do enough to save the planet, I don't know. I do know, though, that when my time comes to an end, I'll know that I tried.

On reflection

Recognition of the incredible opportunity offered by natural capital has continued to gather momentum, almost as fast as the realities of climate change aggressively reveal themselves across the globe.

Increasingly frequent, unprecedented events are happening on a now daily basis. Yesterday the desert region of Dubai experienced 25 centimetres of rain in twenty-four hours, with a whole year's worth of rain falling in twelve hours alone (Ebrahim, 2024). Absolute chaos ensued, with the famed international airport rapidly resembling an ocean, as planes struggled to land and other vehicles were abandoned.

Returning to this piece written almost eighteen months ago, it's an increasingly depressing thought that for natural capital investors, the worsening effect of climate change and the biodiversity crisis is great for business. This is a paradox that sits uncomfortably and unpleasantly, but without it, we have no hope of mobilising the investment needed to start changing our way of life and the world for the better.

Over the last year we've met with a large number of institutional investors, asset managers, banks, and businesses with the ability and intention to invest significant sums into natural capital. More so than ever, I am sure that natural capital represents the single biggest investment opportunity the world has ever seen, where moral responsibility and great financial returns converge.

Creating Pathways for Private Finance

Written April 2023

Scaling Conservation has become a global imperative as the world faces increasing threats from climate change, pollution, habitat destruction, and the loss of biodiversity. The need for restoration and conservation has never been more urgent, and the stakes have never been higher. Amidst the challenges, though, there is also hope. Conservation is not just about preserving the natural world. It's also about harnessing the power of humanity to protect our planet for future generations and – perhaps above all – give the next generations a chance of life on Earth.

Oxygen Conservation and Triodos Bank

If you want to go fast, go alone. If you want to go far, go together.

We are delighted to share that we have agreed a fantastic partnership with the country's leading sustainable bank, Triodos Bank, to help us further Scale Conservation. With the backing of a £20.55 million loan facility from Triodos, we have acquired 23,000 acres in Scotland. This consists of 11,407 acres of Langholm Moor, known as Blackburn and Hartsgarth; and a 11,626-acre estate at Invergeldie, near Comrie in Perthshire. Together, they mark a landmark, conservation-focused commercial debt package. The additional investment from Triodos will allow us to deliver real change on the ground at these two spectacular sites and to continue purchasing land at an unprecedented pace and scale.

In the same way that Oxygen Conservation is changing conservation, Triodos is changing what it means to be a bank. That's why, when we were looking for someone to partner with to put together a significant, conservation-focused debt package, there was only one answer. It's only by us creating these types of funding packages and frameworks with respected financial institutions that people can have the confidence to allow private finance to flow into natural capital at scale, thereby funding the protection of the natural world. We'd like to say a huge thank you to everyone at Triodos for their passion, vision, and commitment in making this possible.

Creating the pathways for private finance

In the same way that we have redefined what was once thought possible in terms of the speed and scale of land acquisition for conservation, we are committed to growing the entire natural capital economy. We recognise the importance of both financial products and services in this process, and the transparency, auditability, and credibility these demand.

We're delighted that Triodos have the desire and trust to structure an innovative lending package linked to natural capital development. In partnership with Triodos and our investors, we will develop several of the key instruments and metrics that future conservation projects will need to demonstrate when seeking private investment, creating a framework that we intend to share publicly to help others Scale Conservation. This framework includes:

1. Enhanced risk management
2. Transparent reporting
3. Investor confidence
4. Mobilising more capital
5. Impact measurement and reporting

1. Enhanced risk management

Conservation projects often involve inherent risk such as regulatory changes, ecosystem uncertainties, and social impact. We need to create a shared understanding and language to allow environmental and financial professionals to jointly consider, understand, and evaluate these risks.

2. Transparent reporting

Ensuring the transparency of project risks, financial performance, and outcomes allows investors to assess the risks accurately. Traditional approaches to reporting used in the environment sector do not have the detail, timeliness, or level of quantification required to inform decision making in the financial sector. We're working with excellent operational professionals, data scientists, economists, and environmental experts to radically improve risk management and reporting.

3. Investor confidence

Private investors, including financial institutions, require confidence in the scale and credibility of conservation projects. There is a growing interest in investing in the environment sector through natural capital, but few financial institutions want to move first. Being the first comes with increased risk, whereas there is safety and security in numbers. Creating a track record of successful delivery and performance brings credibility and is fundamental to attracting private finance. This is because investors seek projects that align with their sustainability goals and generate positive environmental, social, and financial outcomes.

4. Mobilising more capital

Transparent and credible conservation projects can act as a catalyst for attracting more private capital and we need to work together to build momentum. Successful projects with transparent reporting create positive examples and best practices that inspire other investors to follow suit. This can lead to increased mobilisation of private finance for conservation, unlocking additional capital to address the significant financial requirements of conservation projects worldwide.

5. Impact measurement and reporting

Private investors are increasingly seeking to invest in projects that generate measurable and meaningful environmental and social impact. The transparent and quantitative impact measurement and reporting frameworks we will design and develop with Triodos Bank and our other partners will enable investors to assess the effectiveness of conservation projects. They will also help conservation organisations demonstrate the positive outcomes of their projects, which can further attract additional private finance and support future fundraising.

Committing to Scaling Conservation

When we founded Oxygen Conservation with Oxygen House, we committed to Scaling Conservation, not just our own business. We need to grow the entire conservation sector and grow natural capital markets. It is only by doing this that we can hope to mobilise the significant private sector investment we need, to give us a chance at fighting against climate change and the biodiversity crisis. The planet needs all the help it can get, and we're delighted to have Triodos Bank as a key delivery partner in our journey.

On reflection

We feel privileged to be among a small but rapidly growing group of founders of the natural capital economy and the ecosystem that this economy needs to thrive. Part of the responsibility, on all of us working in this space, is to:

- Provide solutions to an almost infinite number of unknowns
- Provide confidence where there is doubt
- Collectively build the systems and processes we need to create the world's most important asset class

Our collaboration with Triodos Bank is repeatedly described to us as one of the most impactful things that has happened in the natural capital economy in recent times, as it made carbon credits a bankable investment.

The future of the natural capital economy is about collaboration and partnership. In working with Triodos, we found the perfect partner – culturally, technically, and reputationally – to help raise the profile and increase confidence around natural capital and the role it will play in the future of our financial system.

This deal wouldn't have been possible without the support and hard work of Simon Crichton, Mavric Webbstock, Phillip Bate, and Bevis Watts from Triodos Bank; and of course our brilliant FD, Elly Adams, and equally brilliant General Counsel, George Pawley.

Navigating the State of UK Environmental Data

Written November 2023, in partnership with our Data Visualisation Lead, Lara Salam, and Terrain Detective, Tom Bloom

In the landscape of environmental data in the UK, notable strides have been made, marked by the establishment of the Geospatial Commission and the proliferation of open-data initiatives. Technologies like satellites and drones and movements like citizen science have significantly expanded our ability to collect and analyse environmental data. However, challenges persist, including data gaps, issues with standardisation, and privacy concerns. This article explores the current state of environmental data in the UK, highlighting both progress and existing hurdles in our journey towards a more comprehensive and sustainable understanding of our ecosystems. This is an understanding we all need in the fight against climate collapse and the biodiversity crisis.

The good

Let's think first about the positives – the factors that work to our advantage in navigating UK environmental data:

1. The golden age for open data
2. Remote data collection revolution
3. Big data and AI
4. Citizen science and crowdsourcing
5. Interdisciplinary collaboration
6. Data visualisation tools

1. The golden age for open data

In the realm of environmental data, the UK finds itself in a relative golden age. The establishment of the Geospatial Commission in 2018 marked a turning point, ushering in a strategy to unleash the treasure trove of spatial data held by public bodies. Entities like the Ordnance Survey, Defra, and the Met Office have paved the way, offering online portals and APIs (application processing interfaces) for businesses and individuals to tap into a vast array of open environmental data. The Defra data services platform alone boasts over 12,000 datasets, providing a rich source for analytical endeavours.

2. Remote data collection revolution

Advancements in satellite technology, drone capabilities, and the Internet of Things (IoT) have revolutionised data collection. Satellites and drones (armed with multi-spectral imaging) and IoT sensors capture an unprecedented volume of data without physical presence. The data encompasses everything from Earth's surface imagery to digital elevation models, real-time river flow, and water-quality monitoring. As emerging technologies like low-Earth orbit satellites and autonomous drones take the stage, the scale and resolution of environmental data are poised for exponential growth before we even mention the impact of the next point.

3. Big data and AI

In a landscape inundated with data, the rise of machine learning offers an exciting next chapter in our understanding of the natural world. Data-driven algorithms are now deployed to analyse and classify remotely sensed data on a scale previously deemed impossible. Projects like Living England showcase the power of this synergy, where satellite imagery and field data – combined with machine learning – create national-scale environmental datasets, continuously evolving and improving with each iteration.

4. Citizen science and crowdsourcing

Beyond institutional channels, citizen science and crowdsourcing initiatives are contributing to the richness of environmental data. Engaging the public in data collection, platforms like iNaturalist and citizen weather stations enable a decentralised approach to monitoring, fostering a more comprehensive understanding of local ecosystems.

5. Interdisciplinary collaboration

The synergy of diverse disciplines, from ecology to technology, is fostering a holistic approach to data analysis. Cross-disciplinary collaboration ensures that environmental data is not just a numbers game but also a nuanced representation of complex ecological interactions. This interdisciplinary approach enriches datasets with qualitative insights often overlooked in purely quantitative analyses.

6. Data visualisation tools

The rise of sophisticated data visualisation tools has empowered researchers, policymakers, and the public to interact with and comprehend complex datasets in new and increasingly interesting ways. From GIS platforms to interactive dashboards and mobile applications, these tools make environmental data more accessible, fostering a broader understanding and engagement with the information.

The bad and the ugly

There are a few aspects to data that don't work in our favour, and areas where we need to overcome challenges, including:

1. Darker shades of data
2. Boundaries as barriers
3. Standardisation
4. Data privacy concerns
5. Data silos and accessibility gaps
6. Ethical considerations in AI

1. Darker shades of data

Amidst the data abundance, shadows and gaps persist. The condition of half of Wales's protected sites remains unknown, and the last comprehensive, high-resolution habitat survey dates back to 1991. Ageing or absent data poses challenges in identifying areas that need restoration, establishing ecological baselines, and comprehending temporal changes within sites.

2. Boundaries as barriers

Political boundaries prove to be formidable obstacles to seamless data collection and analysis. With sites spanning England, Scotland, and Wales, the UK's environmental datasets sometimes come in triplicate, each tailored to its respective nation. Differences in collection methods or structures further complicate cross-portfolio comparisons. Nature doesn't care about politics or political borders; neither should the data we collect in seeking to understand it.

3. Standardisation

It's extremely hard to quantify nature. Assigning ones and zeros to the natural world can be a divisive topic (although we find the challenge fascinating), but without standardised measuring and reporting, it's impossible to quantify environmental loss (or gain) or to easily compare one location with another. We've experienced this first-hand through our use of ecological consultants for our baselining work at each site. While we use first-rate consultants, it's often the case that each has a unique way of recording environmental information, and it has been challenging to collate that information into a single portfolio-level dataset. As a result, we've now created our own standard for data collection and monitoring in this space. In the future, we intend to share these standards wider to help improve those across the sector.*

4. Data privacy concerns

As data collection expands, so do concerns about privacy. In the pursuit of detailed environmental information, personal data may inadvertently be collected or exposed. Balancing the need for comprehensive datasets with the imperative to protect individual privacy poses a significant challenge that demands careful consideration and robust safeguards.

5. Data silos and accessibility gaps

While there is a wealth of data, accessibility is not uniform. Data silos – where information is compartmentalised and not easily shared – hinder the collective understanding of environmental issues (and opportunities). Bridging these silos and ensuring equitable access to data is crucial for a comprehensive and inclusive approach to environmental planning and management.

6. Ethical considerations in AI

As machine learning takes centre stage in data analysis, ethical considerations come to the fore. The algorithms

---

* If we don't ultimately share these standards, we're just making the process worse for everyone, and we're here to scale the entire natural capital economy. In the words of our Head of Environment, Dan Johnson: 'We aspire to view partnerships as the default.'

shaping our environmental datasets must be transparent, unbiased, and ethically sound – I appreciate some would ask whether human-led approaches are up to this standard. Ensuring that AI does not inadvertently perpetuate or exacerbate environmental injustices is a challenge that demands ongoing scrutiny and refinement.

The complex path ahead

The sustainability of long-term datasets is a pressing concern. Ensuring that environmental data collection is not just a short-term endeavour requires continued commitment, in terms of both funding and technological advancements. A robust, sustained effort is necessary to monitor changes over extended periods, providing invaluable insights into the evolving state of the environment. I'm left wondering if this is perhaps a problem ultimately better solved by the private sector in the same way that large-scale data collection and analysis has transformed sporting analytics in recent years.

Environmental challenges transcend borders, making global collaboration imperative. Harmonising data collection methodologies and fostering international standards would enable seamless (or at least improved) collaboration, ensuring a more comprehensive and accurate understanding of global environmental trends.

How we can improve data, and how you can help

The following points outline areas where we need help, and where you might well be able to play your part in assisting Oxygen Conservation.

Enhanced data quality

Our wish: We need to strive for continuous improvement in data quality and ensure regular monitoring and resurveying to understand change over time.

How you can help: Report inaccuracies, support initiatives that promote data quality and regularity of monitoring, and engage with platforms providing feedback mechanisms.

Cross-border data integration

Our wish: Standardised data collection methods are needed across political boundaries.

How you can help: Encourage policymakers to adopt unified data standards, participate in cross-border environmental initiatives, and promote awareness of the need for seamless data integration.

Community-led data initiatives

Our wish: Community-led data collection projects need to be fostered, to complement institutional efforts.

How you can help: Participate in citizen science projects, share local knowledge, and support initiatives that empower communities to contribute to environmental data.

Transparent AI algorithms

Our wish: Transparency and ethical considerations are vital in the development and deployment of AI algorithms for data analysis.

How you can help: Stay informed about the ethical implications of AI, engage in discussions, and advocate for responsible AI practices.

Breaking down data silos

Our wish: Open data sharing and collaboration need to be promoted.

How you can help: Advocate for open-data policies, participate in open-data platforms, and support organisations working towards breaking down data silos.

Happy data exploring!

As we wrap up this data-driven expedition through the UK's environmental landscape, it's clear that, while we've donned our high-tech gear and trekked through the digital wilderness, there's still a wild frontier waiting to be explored. Our satellite-guided compass may be accurate, but the terrain of environmental data is as unpredictable as the British weather.

Let's keep our data binoculars polished, our citizen science hats on, and our collective enthusiasm high. The future of understanding and protecting our environment may just be a data point, a drone flight, and hopefully a community project away.

Happy data exploring!

NAVIGATING THE STATE OF UK ENVIRONMENTAL DATA

On reflection

Our approach to data analysis, our brilliant team of people, and the amazing financial backing provided by the Oxygen House Group are the reasons we've been able to achieve so much so quickly for people and wildlife since founding Oxygen Conservation.

We've seen data change the world, and that continues at an increasing rate. In recent times we've seen data capture and analysis become vital in media and in sport, yet in the environment sector, data is still not truly recognised as an asset.

Reflecting on this piece, written at the end of 2023, I didn't articulate as passionately and as importantly as I should that environmental data is itself one of the key natural capital assets. As a result, if they ever hope to capitalise on the true value of our underlying natural capital asset base, the government need to better recognise environmental data as an asset.

Of course, the government won't do this. Even if they try, they won't do it quickly or effectively; therefore, businesses will. Businesses like Oxygen Conservation and the amazing number of startups, environmental data providers, and platforms that reach out to us every week will begin to capitalise on the remarkable value this data offers.

If you're the next amazing startup in the environmental data space, please reach out – I want to hear from you!

Crediting Nature

Written October 2023

In an era marked by absolute climate collapse, growing water scarcity, and increasing biodiversity destruction, the need for innovative and scalable solutions has never been more urgent. As businesses and some governments (not ours) grapple with the growing realities of these impacts, a new economic system has emerged: the natural capital economy.

Natural capital credits

Natural capital credits allow organisations to fund measurable positive environmental efforts such as:

- Removing carbon from the atmosphere or stopping it from being released (carbon credits)
- Improving biodiversity habitat or species diversity and abundance (biodiversity credits)
- Improving water quality and quantity (water credits)

The purchase of these credits allows organisations to offset the damage they have done elsewhere. Alternatively, they can use some of their profits to provide wider benefits to society through investing in the protection and restoration of natural capital.

These market-based instruments offer a unique opportunity to drive investment into conservation while delivering positive economic benefits. The protection of the environment is made more profitable than its destruction, with the potential of transforming the way we restore and protect the planet. However, alongside this great potential comes significant risk. If we have learned anything from the current market system, it is that people will always try to manipulate or cheat the system for personal priorities and, most often, financial gain.

In this article we explore at a high level:

- The imperative for natural capital credits
- The risks of natural capital credits
- The Oxygen Conservation approach

The imperative for natural capital credits

Natural capital credits are needed for:

1. Mobilising funding for conservation
2. Preserving biodiversity
3. Mitigating climate change

1. MOBILISING FUNDING FOR CONSERVATION
Natural capital credits provide financial incentives for individuals, organisations, and governments to engage

in conservation and restoration efforts. These incentives can help drive investment to deliver positive environmental improvement, while fostering economic development and stimulating a natural capital-based economy.

2. PRESERVING BIODIVERSITY
Biodiversity and ecological abundance are essential for ecosystem stability, resilience, and human wellbeing. Natural capital credits place a value on the services ecosystems provide, incentivising their preservation, restoration, and creation.

3. MITIGATING CLIMATE CHANGE
There is a wonderful relationship between the natural world and our planet's carbon cycle. Since natural capital credits can sequester significant amounts of carbon dioxide, protecting, restoring, and creating habitats – particularly woodlands, peatlands, and salt marshes – plays an essential role in mitigating climate change.[*]

The risks of natural capital credits

While the promise of natural capital credits is undeniable, they come with inherent risks that must be carefully managed:

---

[*] I appreciate some, including me, would argue that our pursuit of uncontrolled economic growth is both inane and, ultimately, self-destructive. Sadly, at least for the foreseeable future, I don't see that changing. As a result, a move towards a natural capital economy can at least focus that obsession or addiction onto something far more positive. I have an addictive personality, but I choose to focus that on coffee, business, and weightlifting – hopefully far more positive diversions.

1. Commodification of nature
2. Greenwashing
3. Ecosystem simplification
4. Short-term focus
5. Market volatility

1. COMMODIFICATION OF NATURE
There's a concern held by some that nature capital credits could reduce nature to a tradable commodity, prioritising profit over conservation goals. While that is a legitimate moral or emotional argument, the economic reality is that nature is a tradable commodity and profit is already being prioritised over conservation. In the absence of a framework that is actively valuing nature, its destruction and exploitation will sadly continue.

2. GREENWASHING
The risk of companies or governments appearing environmentally responsible without implementing effective conservation measures is a valid concern. Natural capital credits can create opportunities for organisations to see the purchase of credits as a licence to carry on with their destructive practices. For credits to be effective, they need to be used simply as part of a larger mitigation hierarchy that puts avoidance and reduction of harm first, and compensation for unavoidable damage second.

3. ECOSYSTEM SIMPLIFICATION
Natural capital credits often focus on specific ecosystem services, which is a legitimate challenge frequently levied at carbon credits. This can incentivise the development of monocultures or simplified ecosystems optimised for credit generation rather than the creation of diverse, resilient natural ecosystems.

4. SHORT-TERM FOCUS

Market-driven approaches may prioritise short-term gains over long-term ecological health. Conservation efforts often require sustained, multigenerational commitments, which can be undermined by market pressures.

5. MARKET VOLATILITY

Just like financial markets, natural capital credit markets can experience volatility, with that being especially likely in the immediate future. The value of such credits can fluctuate, potentially leading to unexpected economic outcomes or disincentivising long-term conservation efforts. Then again, two tech bubbles have previously (incorrectly) signalled the end of Silicon Valley; if you don't remember these, you can google them!

The Oxygen Conservation approach

Amidst these challenges, we are committed to offering a high-quality, genuinely impactful range of natural capital products, services, and credits to allow nature to pay to protect and restore itself.

Here are some of the ways we're approaching this:

1. Holistic approach
2. Community engagement
3. Integrity of sale
4. Commitment to transparency
5. Multigeneration longevity
6. Sustainable funding

1. Holistic approach

We recognise that conservation means delivering positive environmental and social impact. This approach takes into account the ecological and social aspects of sustainability and ensures that natural capital products, services, and credits are produced as a result – not as the purpose – of conservation initiatives. For each of our projects we set a series of environmental, social, and economic targets that contribute to the UN Sustainable Development Goals (SDGs) (UN, no date), allowing all our credits to provide wide-ranging sustainability impacts.

2. Community engagement

We actively involve local communities in our conservation plans and projects, ensuring that the benefits are shared and that traditional knowledge is respected. This begins immediately following the acquisition of a new site, when we welcome people to the estate to listen, learn, and collaborate. It is important to note that engagement doesn't mean everyone will be happy with landscape restoration or change, and some will never accept the landscape needs to (or in fact should) change. We are at all times respectful of those views, always listening, even when we may not agree.

3. Integrity of sale

We believe in creating partnerships, not transactions, and are incredibly selective in who we choose to work with. We recognise that if we sell natural capital credits to a business or organisation, we become their business partner, as does anyone else who holds an Oxygen

Conservation natural capital product. As a result, we intend to sell only to high-integrity, purpose-driven organisations that have science-backed targets and demonstrate a genuine and meaningful commitment to making a positive environmental and social impact. We do recognise the argument that the best way to help influence those industries and businesses not doing enough on climate change is to work with them and help them move forward, but at this time it just doesn't feel authentic to our purpose.

4. Commitment to transparency

We have made transparency a cornerstone of our approach – not only in our approach to the development of natural capital credits, but also in the very way we do business. When you purchase a credit from Oxygen Conservation, you are encouraged to visit the estate where your credits are based, to walk the hills; to swim in the rivers, lochs, and lakes; and to listen to the increasingly diverse wildlife that calls that estate home.

5. Multigeneration longevity

Our conservation work is delivered exclusively on land we own and manage, ensuring the security and multigenerational integrity of our natural capital credits. With each of our projects we establish long-term partnerships with local communities, businesses, and organisations to deliver lasting positive impact.

6. Sustainable funding

Revenue generated from our natural capital credit projects is intended to be reinvested into further conservation efforts, creating a self-sustaining funding source for ongoing environmental protection, thereby allowing us to continue Scaling Conservation.

Oxygen Conservation natural capital

As we work hard to pioneer the creation of market-leading natural capital products, services, and credits, we hope to provide a model for responsible and effective environmental conservation and investment. With the right approach – by sequestering carbon and restoring biodiversity – natural capital credits can drive large-scale positive change, creating a regenerative future for us all.

In a world that desperately needs scalable solutions to combat environmental damage and destruction, natural capital credits offer another tool that we all need to help fix the damage we've done to the planet.

On reflection

Our thinking around the development and sale of our natural capital products has continued to evolve but remains based on the core principles described above.

In April 2024 we published an updated article, outlining what we believe to be the world's first *premium carbon credits*. Our first carbon credits, the 2024 edition, will be available from late 2024 from Leighon on Dartmoor, Swineley in the Yorkshire Dales, and Esgair Arth in West Wales.

You can read all about the approach in the next article.

We had the pleasure of welcoming the super-cool Andrew Shirley, who at the time of recording was Head of Rural and Luxury Research at Knight Frank, to the *Shoot Room Sessions* podcast (Stockdale, 2024b). Andrew was also the editor-in-chief and architect of the Knight Frank *Wealth Report*, which provides the market-leading review of unique, luxury physical assets such as vintage cars, works of arts, and rare whisky and wines. Combining decades of experience working in the rural and luxury sectors, Andrew is uniquely placed to opine on the future of the natural capital economy.

During our podcast session, Andrew spoke passionately about the environment and concluded by describing how natural capital is fast becoming the new luxury asset class. This aligns perfectly with our views on the future direction of the natural capital economy

The Best Carbon Credits (Quality Matters)

Written spring 2024

Increasingly, I'm sure the overriding cause of climate change is our collective failure to value the atmosphere and, by extension, the natural world. By failing to recognise its true value, we have all continued to consume carbon-intensive goods and services without the checks and balances that would be afforded by the cost of that carbon being taken into account. What is free we take, and continue to take to the extreme, without thought of the consequences.

The emergence of carbon credits serves two vital purposes:

1. Carbon credits impose a definitive value for each unit of carbon dioxide equivalent (tCO2e) removed from the atmosphere, simultaneously recognising the cost of emitting or polluting the atmosphere.

2. Where removal credits are concerned, carbon credits ensure that tCO2e is removed from the

atmosphere, directly helping in the battle to push back against the damage we've all done.

Pollution is (tragically) good for economic growth

The impact of failing to appropriately price the environment is perhaps best demonstrated by considering how we account for environmental disasters.

Consider the damage inflicted on our rivers by the water companies actively pumping sewage into our river systems. In our current measure of GDP, there is no recognition of the loss of fish, invertebrates, and other wildlife; of the loss of amenity opportunities; or of the costs of increased rates of illness in those living close by these environments. By contrast, the cost of the cleanup – including the associated equipment, salaries, and legal bills – all appear as productive expenditure in GDP and therefore present as economic growth.

Let that sink in for a second. Polluting the environment and destroying the natural world is good for economic growth. How broken can a system be?

Despite the importance of correctly pricing for our carbon impacts, this idea has faced public criticism, with some arguing that carbon credits allow people to wilfully pollute more. Increasingly, though, this has proven not to be the case, with the biggest purchasers of carbon credits also demonstrating the biggest reductions in their carbon footprints. As anyone who has sat in a boardroom will know, businesses have done and always will do everything they can to minimise their costs. The easiest way to do this when carbon is properly priced is to reduce emissions and thereby seek to reduce the costs of the carbon credits that need to be acquired. The higher and more realistic the price for the impact of carbon emissions, the faster this transition occurs.

Transformative carbon credits

Carbon markets are developing rapidly, but they still provide only a fraction of the reach and scale needed for us to see a meaningful impact on climate change and biodiversity collapse. To help these markets scale, and to create an effective global carbon price, we need a giant leap in the quality of products available. In the same way that the Tesla Model S transformed our perception of what's possible from an electric vehicle, and the way the iPhone introduced the world to the possibilities of a smartphone, we need a new suite of natural capital products and services that completely change our perception of and relationship with paid ecosystem services.

By introducing premium carbon credits that address the most prominent challenges and criticisms facing existing carbon credits, we can build the integrity, confidence, and desirability of these products and investments, helping to mobilise the incredible levels of investment desperately needed to make a positive impact on the natural world.

Premium carbon credits

The premium nature of Oxygen Conservation's carbon credits comes down to these commitments:

1. UK-based credits generated on land we own

2. Independent, advanced verification

3. Credit insurance
4. Regular impact reports
5. Bespoke biodiversity plans
6. Geo-location tagging
7. Opportunities to visit the site
8. Exclusive content
9. Social value commitment

1. UK-based credits generated on land we own

All of our natural capital products and services, including our carbon credits, are developed on land owned and managed by Oxygen Conservation. This ensures the permanence of projects and provides buyers with absolute confidence in the underlying security of the land associated with their carbon-based investments.

2. Independent, advanced verification

All of our carbon credits are validated and verified by independent experts. Every aspect of our work, from baseline environment surveys through to project design, delivery, registration, and verification is delivered in partnership with independent experts. This builds trust that every carbon credit removes one tonne of carbon from the atmosphere or prevents it from being released through the restoration of peatland.

This external validation process is supplemented by our own extensive monitoring, reporting, and verification process, which utilises advanced drone- and lidar-based technology to measure every centimetre of the land we own. This allows us to know everything that happens across our portfolio, thanks to our brilliant team of ecologists, economists, and data scientists, with expertise in data acquisition, analysis, and assessment.

3. Credit insurance

We are working with market leaders in the development of carbon-based insurance to make our credits an insurable investment. This means that buyers of our credits can be confident in the delivery of any carbon they buy, even in the face of increasing risk of natural disasters, political change, and extreme weather events.

4. Regular impact reports

Every one of our projects is part of a large-scale landscape restoration project that delivers environmental and social impact first, and carbon credits as a result of our work, to protect and improve the natural world for people and wildlife.

For each of our projects we set targets for making a meaningful contribution towards nine of the UN SDGs, from providing clean water to generating renewable energy and producing organic food.

Each year we produce an impact report quantifying and measuring our progress towards each of these targets. This demonstrates the wider environmental and social impact of each credit we generate. It also places carbon credits at the heart of a wider environmental, social, and governance (ESG) strategy that delivers impact for people and wildlife beyond carbon.

5. Bespoke biodiversity plans

Each of our carbon credits is generated through nature-based conservation projects, and the finance used from the sale of credits is used to Scale Conservation. All of our credits are currently developed through native woodland creation and peatland restoration. In the future, they will also be produced through blue carbon projects focused on the restoration of seagrass meadows and the creation of wetlands and salt marshes.

For each project we create a long-term biodiversity restoration plan that sets out how we are aiming to restore natural capital assets, allowing natural processes to function and bringing back the wildlife that has been lost.

We measure the impacts on biodiversity through a data-led natural capital accounting framework, which provides an evidence-based approach to quantifying and demonstrating the biodiversity impact of each of our projects.

6. Geo-location tagging

Given the challenges that some schemes have faced in terms of demonstrating that carbon has actually been removed from the atmosphere, transparency and evidence of delivery are essential when investing in carbon credits.

At all of our projects we undertake detailed surveys of the landscape, digitally mapping areas where trees are planted and peatland is restored. This allows us to provide geo-location tagging of our carbon credits so that buyers can identify the specific assets they are purchasing, obtain high-resolution remote sensing imagery of their credits, and access detailed drone footage of specific areas where their individual carbon credits are created. This provides unparalleled transparency and evidence of impact.

7. Opportunities to visit the site

We believe that a premium carbon product goes beyond a digital record on a spreadsheet, providing something that you can touch, see, and feel. We make all of our projects accessible and visitable to credit buyers, through guided walks around the sites and opportunities to stay at our unique and sustainable ecotourism experiences.

This means that the organisations we partner with can take their teams to see their trees in person, connect to the wider restoration of the site, and swim in the rivers they are helping to restore. Experiencing nature in this way allows buyers of our credits to see first-hand how they have positively impacted the environment for people and wildlife. It also provides unrivalled confidence and integrity, and accessibility to where credits have been created and remain.

8. Exclusive content

We see the natural capital economy as key to our shared future on Earth, and we are committed to elevating carbon markets as a sector. We want the buyers of our carbon credits to be proud of the impact their investments are making.

We provide a unique set of digital images and videography with each vintage of our carbon credits, allowing buyers to share the stories of these charismatic carbon credits and of the people, places, and wildlife they are protecting and enhancing. By working together to share these wonderful stories, we're committed to making premium carbon credits aspirational and inspirational, helping to build the world's most important alternative asset class.

9. Social value commitment

We're committed to positive environmental and social impact at each of our projects, and we use the revenues generated from our carbon credit sales to help Scale Conservation for people and wildlife. This includes a specific set of targets that work to allow people to be a part of nature through:

- Providing homes and employment in rural communities
- Supporting educational and learning opportunities around nature conservation
- Encouraging people to access and enjoy the natural world through ecotourism opportunities

These opportunities range from luxury holiday cottages to glamping enterprises, and they even incorporate our partnership with CampWild, the UK's leading wild camping platform.

Reassuringly expensive carbon

As the demand for high-quality carbon credits grows, buyers are becoming more sophisticated and are rightly demanding increased visibility, transparency, and confidence in their purchases and investments. One highly respected private bank recently approached us to discuss carbon credits. They described how they intended to purchase 'reassuringly expensive' carbon so they could be confident of every aspect of the product and the project from which it came.

Launching 2024 vintage

In 2024 we will bring our first vintage of premium carbon credits to the market, totalling around 50,000 tonnes, at a minimum price point of £75 tCO2e. We will be engaging a single partnership for the sale of this vintage. The partner we choose will be able to demonstrate their commitment to net zero through a clear climate transition plan as well as evidencing the changes they've made to their business already. In forming a partnership, we will help to elevate and amplify premium carbon credits in the UK and internationally.

The choice of our language is specific and purposeful. We're talking in terms of vintages, as in French champagne or Scottish whisky, because we seek to elevate carbon credits in the same way as other premium, geographically unique products. Each vintage of single malt has its own unique origins, story, and environmental conditions, and each vintage of our carbon credits will have the same. It is only by creating that same sense of appreciation and reverence that we will be able to achieve the price point we need to grow the natural capital economy and create the world's most important asset class.

Pricing the priceless

The single biggest cause of climate change is our failure to recognise the unique and remarkable value provided to us all by the atmosphere and the wider natural environment. In failing to price the priceless, we've made our environment free to exploit and abuse.

Carbon credits offer the most practical tool at our disposal to change our relationship with the environment and to begin to repay the debt we owe.

In a nascent market filled with doubt, scepticism, and criticism, we need a transformative product that can inspire people to believe that the impossible is possible. In the same way the Tesla Model S was a quantum leap in electric vehicles and redefined our perception of the car, we will do the same for carbon credits, offering a premium product that completely resets our expectations of natural capital products. In the process, we will begin to build a sustainable foundation for the world's most important asset class, and maybe even the UK's next greatest export.

Didn't someone talk about the world's first unicorn conservation company?

On reflection

The best ideas don't scream for attention; they reshape reality so completely that we forget how things were before. Carbon credits have the potential to be just that: a financial instrument so well integrated into our economic fabric that, one day, we'll wonder how we ever ignored the value of clean air – but only if we build them right. Not as an excuse to pollute, not as an abstract ledger entry, but as something tangible, traceable, and irrefutably real.

Forget compliance. The future belongs to those who want to own carbon credits, not because they must, but because they reflect a deeper alignment with value, ambition, and legacy. The companies that lead this transition won't be the ones ticking boxes; they'll be the ones setting new rules entirely. Carbon credits shouldn't be a reluctant purchase – they should be an investment in the physical, social, and economic landscapes of tomorrow.

Every great market shift has its tipping point, the moment when an old paradigm crumbles, and a new one emerges, fully formed. This isn't about offsets anymore; it's about assets. A tonne of carbon stored isn't just a metric – it's a stake in a more resilient future. When the best carbon credits carry the weight of certainty, provenance, and impact, they will no longer be seen as a cost, but as currency.

The question isn't whether the market will evolve. It's whether we'll be the ones shaping it, or whether we'll look back and realise we left the door open for someone else. The best carbon credits will belong to those who make them undeniable, invaluable, and, perhaps most importantly, inevitable.

SEVEN
Breaking Barriers, Shifting The Paradigm

Tearing Down the Red Book: Growing a Greener Valuation Standard

Written April 2024

Don't be scared – we're here to help you realise this is the best opportunity to be a part of building the future nature-connected economy, where we all value what matters most.

Over the past three years, we have built the UK's first genuine natural capital portfolio, and in the process, we have changed how land is bought and sold. We have challenged the status quo and found new and innovative ways to accelerate the land-buying process, making it more transparent, more inclusive, and more enjoyable for those involved.

One of the most challenging, problematic, archaic legacies that remains, though, is the concept of the Red Book valuation, ie a formal, evidence-based property valuation by a member of the Royal Institution of Chartered Surveyors. As we face the realities of climate and biodiversity collapse, Red Book valuations are increasingly dangerous and limited, due to their failure to adapt to the emerging environmental and market actualities. Rooted in traditional metrics, adhering to a global 'standard', the methodology often overlooks critical factors such as climate change risks, ecological sustainability, and the potential for properties to become stranded assets in a rapidly evolving economic landscape. This myopia can lead to significant financial misjudgements, as it:

- Undervalues properties with environmental benefits

- Overvalues properties at risk of changing regulations and shifting societal values towards sustainability

Consequently, stakeholders relying on these valuations face heightened risks in making investment decisions that are not only financially precarious but also environmentally detrimental, undermining the urgent global shift towards sustainability and climate resilience.

In this piece we offer a critical examination focusing on the urgent need to reformulate property valuation standards in the UK. We need less red and more green!

The shortcomings of Red Book

Red Book valuations have a number of flaws, especially regarding:

1. Climate change risks
2. Overlooking natural capital
3. Stranded assets and market myopia

1. Climate change risks

Current shortcomings: The Red Book's traditional methodologies are alarmingly silent on climate change risks, basing current valuations on past and present data points, rather than looking forward to future trends. This glaring omission renders these valuations dangerously short-sighted and potentially misleading. For example, insufficient consideration is given to the increasing frequency of severe weather events such as droughts and floods and their effects on property and land. In the long term, all assets will be worthless if we are unable to manage the climate and biodiversity crisis.

Strategic failures: This lack of future proofing exposes stakeholders to significant financial risks and undermines the long-term sustainability of investments, in an era where environmental factors are crucial. For example, climate change is significantly increasing wildfire risk, especially to monocultures such as commercial forestry or grouse moors, which are largely absent of natural moisture.

2. Overlooking natural capital

Methodological blind spots: The Red Book methodology is markedly deficient in recognising the value and implications of natural capital, leading to an outdated and incomplete approach to asset valuation that is not keeping pace with changes in the market. By definition, it is a valuation framework built on historic market comparables. In a world where we're breaking (restoring) new ground, how can this approach possibly account for the future value of an emerging asset class?

Blind spots can also lead to the overvaluation of environmentally damaging assets, and to the undervaluation of more sustainably managed land and properties. Take, for example, an intensively managed commercial farm with a business model underpinned by the widespread use of fertiliser, insecticides, and intensive stocking. The very act of farming conventionally (in a non-regenerative way) significantly reduces the land's future potential through soil and water degradation. The land is more at risk to climatic events and contributes significant greenhouse gas emissions, the reduction of which will need substantial investment, meaning conventional farming is unlikely to be a sustainable model. By contrast, a regeneratively managed farm, combining conservation grazing, agroforestry, and organic arable production with the sale of carbon and biodiversity credits, is actively improving the condition of the asset, opening up significant new revenue streams in the process, and building long-term sustainable value. Sadly, under Red Book methodology, we have been told by valuers that this approach makes the land 'untidy' and therefore lowers value for potential future investors.

Business consequences: This oversight fails to equip investors with the complete picture, potentially skewing investment decisions and risk assessments in sectors heavily reliant on land and property. For example, the widespread loss of soils from our fields is a clear demonstration of how we treat the natural world and presents a terrible risk to food production and, therefore, the underlying value of agricultural land. The current approach is based on subjective, historic land classifications, and assumptions on quality with no consideration of fertility, biodiversity, or bioabundance. I'm left wondering how comfortable the owners of Grade 1 arable land should be when they've lost vast volumes of soil and seen its fertility literally washed away, often with downstream impacts for nearby communities.

3. Stranded assets and market myopia

Inadequate foresight: The current valuation framework is ill-prepared to identify and appraise stranded assets such as lands adversely affected by evolving environmental regulations and by shifting societal norms. Take, for example, grouse moors and sporting estates, which are decreasing in numbers every year as social acceptance of and demand for traditional sporting pursuits collapses.

Wilful ignorance: This lack of foresight in the Red Book approach could lead to significant misallocations of capital and missed opportunities for positive impact and profit, especially for those not actively involved in the rural economy. If you are seeking investment diversification, the traditional focus would be targeted at farmland, with farming clearly now an industry experiencing significant challenges. This is hardly offering the safe, secure, long-term diversification one might seek. The dogged determination of a dying industry to cling to the Red Book will almost certainly be remembered in the same way as the videotapes we borrowed from Blockbuster and the hours spent playing Snake on our Nokias. Instead, natural capital presents the very hedge we need against society's climate inaction. Sadly, every significant portfolio now requires – or will soon realise it requires – natural capital investment.

Envisioning a future-forward valuation model

One of the rules we have at Oxygen Conservation is that you can only criticise something if you offer an alternative or try to help find a solution. We have therefore begun the process of considering how we might inform, develop, and begin to build a future approach to rural property valuation. To help in this process we are working with some of the country's leading land agents, law firms, and professional services consultancies.

We have drawn inspiration from across the developing natural capital economy, together with the many incredible minds of the people we have the pleasure of calling friends and colleagues. We have integrated elements of the Treasury's Green Book (HM Treasury, 2024), the Dasgupta Review (HM Treasury, 2021), and guidance from the Natural Capital Committee (GOV.UK, no date). Elements of our new rural property valuation will include:

1. Advanced environmental risk analysis
2. Natural capital valuation framework
3. The greatest hedge against human inaction

1. Advanced environmental risk analysis

Cutting-edge climate risk tools: Employing innovative tools to assess land and built properties' vulnerabilities, with respect to climate change scenarios, is essential for forward-looking investment decisions. For example, developing digital twins will allow a wider range of climate scenarios to be explored to consider impacts and their necessary mitigations to better inform value potential.

Ecosystem valuation: Recognising natural capital as a key valuation approach provides a more rounded and future-proofed assessment of land and property values. Take for example the potential offered by an estate with unique or rare habitat that must be protected. Currently, the Red Book system would consider this a liability and, as a result, seek to reduce the value of the underlying asset. Let that settle in for a second: the more precious the nature asset, the lower the Red Book valuation. The Red Book system is broken and is at least partly to blame for the ongoing degradation of the natural world. A natural capital-based approach would fully recognise the value of natural assets and the restoration of degraded assets to a functioning state, based on the value generated through the sale of biodiversity units.

2. Natural capital valuation framework

Integrating Green Book insights: By embedding Green Book principles into valuation practices, a more environmentally accountable and financially sound framework, with nature at its heart, can be established, building on environmental, social, and economic foundations. For example, estimating the true value of natural capital assets such as through recognising and measuring the carbon stored within natural habitats as well as the unique value that access to nature offers to people and wildlife, can transform how we look at and value different properties.

Green Book insights also allow investors, lenders, accountants, legal, regulators, and all of us to see and account for the financial value created from positive environmental and social impact. When we have built the nature-connected economy, we will realise what we value most has, as yet, not been fully valued.

Risk assessment reimagined: Incorporating comprehensive environmental risk assessments is crucial to reflect the true value and future viability of land and properties in today's market. An example is recognising the value for money offered by providing improved environmental performance of built properties, making them sustainable in future climate change scenarios.

3. The greatest hedge against human inaction

Nature-based carbon sequestration: Nature-based solutions leverage the natural ability of ecosystems to absorb and store carbon. By valuing estates based on their carbon sequestration potential, we incentivise the conservation and restoration of vital ecosystems like forests, wetlands, and grasslands. For instance, a property with extensive woodland potential (and future mature woodlands) should be appraised more highly due to its significant carbon capture and storage capabilities, which play a critical role in mitigating climate change. This method not only reflects a property's environmental contribution but also aligns real estate valuation with global carbon reduction goals.

Natural capital credits as a hedge to human inaction: Incorporating the concept of carbon credits into land and built property valuation addresses the urgency of climate action. Properties that generate carbon credits through sustainable practices should be valued more highly, recognising their contribution to reducing the global carbon footprint. This model transforms individual estates into active players in the fight against climate change, offering a tangible financial incentive for reducing greenhouse gas emissions – the greatest challenge of our time. By doing so, it provides a direct economic response to human inaction in environmental preservation, turning rural real estates into proactive agents for ecological sustainability. As markets continue to develop, the inclusion of biodiversity-based credits into valuation estimates also provides an economic response to biodiversity loss, generating a financial incentive to protect and restore natural habitats for their biodiversity as well as their carbon value.

Leveraging technology for dynamic valuation

Embracing technological innovation is key to driving a more accurate and holistic approach to land and property valuation.

When analysed effectively, the increasingly rich pool of data now available can illuminate a property's true environmental potential. This moves us away from subjective judgements and towards quantitative assessments of environmental value.

From the experience of our in-house drone survey team, which has scanned ten individual estates in millimetre-level detail, we have found that utilising remote sensing for environmental data collection offers a transformative insight into the speed, detail, and accuracy of property valuation.

Charting a sustainable course in property valuation

The transformation of land and property valuation methodologies is not only a strategic necessity but also a significant opportunity for innovation. By integrating sustainability-focused principles and embracing cutting-edge technologies, the real estate sector can align itself with the environmental imperatives of the twenty-first century. This pivot is essential for maintaining asset relevance, ensuring long-term profitability, and contributing meaningfully to global sustainability efforts.

The future of property valuation lies in its adaptability and commitment to encompassing both financial robustness and environmental stewardship.

On reflection

I'm especially interested in the views of those that rely so heavily on the existing Red Book methodologies. Will they recognise that its time has been and is now long gone, or will they cling on to the tool they know is no longer fit for purpose, providing the wrong answer but in a reassuringly familiar way?

Like so many aspects of our lives with respect to climate change, we have the choice of whether or not we evolve and change. Change is happening anyway, though, whether we like it or not.

Why Rainforests Are Worthless

Written March 2024

We are fortunate to be the custodians of one of the largest areas of unspoilt temperate rainforest in the entire UK. The Leighon Estate on Dartmoor – Oxygen Conservation's first-ever acquisition and one of our most ecologically precious landscapes – highlights one of the many limitations of the emerging natural capital economy.

The current natural capital valuation system is predicated on proving additionality – ie the development of the new – and almost completely neglects the preservation of the old, the mature, and the rare. From a natural capital perspective, rainforests are therefore worthless.

From a carbon credit perspective, a newly planted tree (plastic tree guard included) is considered to be more valuable in our fight against climate change and biodiversity loss than the incredibly rare landscapes that risk extinction if we don't consider the environment and the natural capital economy in a more complete and interconnected way.

Let's explore this further.

What is temperate rainforest?

Located in the South West of England, Dartmoor is renowned for its open moorlands and for its precious patches of temperate rainforest, often nestled in steep river valleys or cleaves. These areas receive a significant amount of rainfall, creating a moist and humid environment that supports a lush and vibrant ecosystem, characterised by a rich tapestry of bryophytes, lichens, ferns, and ancient woodland.

Temperate rainforests are biodiversity hotspots, teeming with a variety of species that thrive in cool, damp conditions. Towering trees such as oak, ash, and birch species dominate the canopy, while in the understorey lies a lush layer of ferns; scrub like rowan, holly, and hazel; and magnificently diverse fungi, some of which are almost unique to this environment. The forests are alive with the sounds of wildlife, including a range of bird species and insects; and mammals like the elusive otter, the pine marten, and even (it is rumoured) beavers. These ecosystems are not only crucial for the wildlife they support; they also serve as important carbon banks, storing carbon within their vegetation and soils, as well as playing a key role in (both the quality and quantity of) water regulation.

Despite their significance, temperate rainforests are extremely rare and fragile. They face significant threats from human activities and climate change, making their conservation vital for our country's ecological health and cultural heritage.

An underappreciated carbon bank

Despite their majestic beauty and ecological significance, the temperate rainforests on Dartmoor are undervalued, especially concerning their role in carbon sequestration. These forests, dense with ancient trees and rich undergrowth, are veritable carbon vaults, locking away hundreds of years' worth of carbon within their biomass. From a carbon perspective, current regulations failing to recognise their worth present a grave oversight. Those regulations have erroneously branded them as worthless, due to the absence of additionality when considered through a purely carbon lens.

On the path to net zero, of course, it's imperative that we plant millions of new trees. We also need, though, to protect our existing woodlands, recognising and respecting the work they are currently doing and have been doing for hundreds of thousands of years. Our woodlands had been locking carbon away long before we realised that as an ecosystem service our existence depends on.

A haven for wildlife

The temperate rainforests of Dartmoor are a biodiversity hotspot, and their complexity and richness have built up over many thousands of years. As a result, they offer refuge and sustenance to a plethora of species found nowhere else. These forests are home to a myriad of wildlife, ranging from the elusive European otter to a variety of bird species such as the majestic buzzards and the enigmatic wood warblers. The damp, richly organic environment also provides a fertile haven for an array of plant species, including the iconic English oak; and a diverse assembly of ferns, mosses, and fungi. Each of these plays a crucial role in the forest's ecological balance. These exceptional habitats form one of the most biodiverse habitats on Earth and can be home to more than 400 species of lichen and bryophytes, some of which are of international conservation importance, being found nowhere else in the world. The UK's temperate rainforests not only help to tackle climate change through storing significant volumes of carbon; they also help to tackle the biodiversity crisis by protecting some of the rarest and most important species.

The need for conservation credits

Given the multifaceted benefits these rainforests provide, from carbon storage to biodiversity and bioabundance, it is imperative to establish a system that recognises and truly values their contribution to the natural world. The concept of conservation credits offers a promising solution – one that recognises value in a holistic way, not through oversimplified, arbitrary lenses. A system that attributed a tangible value to the ecosystem services rendered by these temperate rainforests would ensure that they are more valuable protected than destroyed.

Conservation credits could incentivise the preservation of these habitats, allowing natural capital investors to generate revenue from maintaining and enhancing the ecological integrity of these areas. This financial mechanism could catalyse conservation efforts, ensuring that temperate rainforests are preserved for future generations to admire and benefit from.

The Leighon Estate and the other temperate rainforests of Dartmoor are not just scenic marvels; they are vital components of our natural world, offering lessons in resilience, symbiosis, and sustainability. In an age where natural habitats are increasingly under threat, recognising and compensating for the true value of these rainforests is not only beneficial – it is essential. By implementing conservation credits, we can safeguard these treasures, ensuring that they continue to thrive and support the intricate web of life they harbour.

Why rainforests are priceless

The temperate rainforests on Dartmoor, exemplified by the Leighon Estate, embody the profound contradiction within our current natural capital valuation systems, highlighting a need for a paradigm shift. These ecosystems, teeming with life and ancient wisdom, stand as a testament to nature's intricate complexity and resilience. They challenge us to broaden our perspective, to see beyond immediate, tangible benefits and recognise the intrinsic value of nature's multifaceted contributions to our planet's health and our own wellbeing.

The introduction of conservation credits could be a pivotal step towards honouring and preserving the richness of these rainforests, moving us closer to a future where natural treasures are revered and protected, not for their potential exploitation but for their essential role in sustaining life on Earth.

In this crucial moment, the choice is ours: to continue undervaluing these irreplaceable ecosystems; or to truly recognise that temperate rainforests are far from worthless – that they are, in fact, priceless.

On reflection

If an ancient rainforest falls, and no one is there to sell it, does it have value?

The market has always said no. The overly simplistic obsession with additionality says that a tree in the ground is worthless; a tree in a spreadsheet, converted to carbon, has value. We cannot continue to reward destruction and pay for reinvention but ignore natural processes – the environment doesn't care for our financial instruments.

Since I first wrote this article, a lot has changed. What started as an idea – conservation credits – has evolved into a movement: nature credits. The idea is simple: pay to protect, not just to restore. A rainforest is not valuable because it could be something else. It is valuable because it already is – and it's spectacular!

These ecosystems are more than numbers on a balance sheet; they are living, breathing testaments to time itself. They hold the stories of centuries, the wisdom of adaptation, the intricate dance of species dependent on one another. Every tree, every lichen-lined limb, every moss-covered rock, every drop of rain that feeds these forests carries a legacy of resilience. And yet, we have spent generations looking past them, seeing only what they could be turned into rather than what they already offer.

Imagine a financial system where the most irreplaceable ecosystems aren't invisible. Where the best investment isn't tearing down and starting over, but leaving nature to do what it has perfected for millennia. Where those who choose to protect something priceless are valued more than those who destroy for short-term gain. That future is arriving. And this time, the rainforests might just get the price tag they deserve – not because we've finally learned how to sell them, but because we've learned how to value them.

The Oxygen Conservation Recruitment Process

Written March 2024

The most talented people in every sector have never had as many opportunities and choices about where and how they work. Oxygen Conservation is fortunate to be in the position of having a mission that is both aspirational and inspiring. We're committed to Scaling Conservation and, as a result, are indisputably delivering positive impact for both people and wildlife.

Our playbook

I'm regularly asked how and why we recruit the way we do, so here is a summary of the *Oxygen Conservation Recruitment Playbook*.

Note: when we talk about recruitment, that is shorthand for talent attraction, identification, and development. Development also begins during the interview process!

The fifteen steps in our interview process run as follows:

1. Job description and advert
2. Alternative job title
3. Resource pack
4. Three simple questions and the CV
5. Initial screening (with our early-career professionals)
6. Longlisting (with our Head of People and recruiting manager)
7. Initial interview (virtual)
8. Interview preparation meeting
9. Interview preparation meeting: feedback and coaching
10. Aligning on reward expectations
11. Reference checking
12. Panel interview (always with three people)
13. Group debrief
14. Meet the MD
15. Offer

1. Job description and advert

The first step is crafting a compelling job description and advertisement. This sometimes involves a clear outline of the role's responsibilities and qualifications, and of the value it brings to the organisation.

We build what we call a Workbook Page to support the job description. This is a detailed model of the responsibilities and activities that make up a role, aligned with the management of each of the estates in our portfolio. This page will be adapted and adjusted with the successful candidate, but it provides a fantastic map of how the role fits with and interacts across the company and our individual estates.

The goal is to attract candidates who not only have the skills and experience required but also align with the company's culture and values. We've found the use of imagery, videography, and podcasts hugely helpful in this process. The volume of organic traffic we created in our Estate Management advertisement campaign, with our most recent call for 'professional adventurers', caused LinkedIn to suspend our post because it was attracting too much interest on the unpaid platform.

2. Alternative job title

Most job titles are boring. Conforming to the norm removes any opportunity to stand out from the crowded pages on LinkedIn and on other recruitment sites. When we recently called for 'frustrated accountants wanting to fight climate change', we received more than 250 applications. How did this role stand out when sitting among 2,000 adverts for the position of head of finance?

Please don't think these titles come easily – we're careful to strike a balance between playful and inspiring, and something that sounds silly. The title has to be cool and different but feel authentic to us all. Some people have said playful job titles aren't serious enough for proper businesses, and we completely agree – we're not trying to be a proper business. We're trying to be a better business. We're trying to be the world's first conservation-focused unicorn company, and we understand that if we want to do something no one else has done, we must be prepared to challenge everything.

A perfect added bonus of having a playful job title is that if potential applicants think the title is too playful, they won't fit in with the culture of Oxygen Conservation, and we can all figure that out early.

3. Resource pack

Our work and our portfolio of landscapes give us the ability to produce a resource pack with a significant volume of great content, including photography, videography, and podcasts, as well as long- and short-form thought leadership pieces.

Together with our website, the resource pack is intended to give everyone a comprehensive understanding of the organisation, our mission, values, and the specifics of the role. We also offer guidance about our approach to recruitment, how to perform well throughout the recruitment process, and example interview questions.

4. Three simple questions and the CV

We want to create the biggest talent capture funnel possible. We have therefore worked hard at understanding the balance between making the application process simple and easy, and with us obtaining enough information to make an informed decision in longlisting candidates.

Candidates are invited to submit a CV and answer three simple questions:

1. Why do you want to be part of Oxygen Conservation?

2. What does living sustainably mean to you?

3. How do you pursue a sense of adventure?

These questions are designed to gauge each person's motivation, their technical ability to complete (or redefine) a role, and their alignment with our culture and values.

5. Initial screening (with our early-career professionals)

We believe in including as many members of the team as possible during the recruitment process. This helps maximise the learning potential of every aspect of the process as well as providing candidates with a more complete understanding of the team, our ways of working, and relationships within the team.

As well as using automated screening protocols (for things like the right to work in the UK and, for most roles, a driving licence) we ask our group of early-career professionals within Oxygen Conservation to complete the initial screening of the often hundreds of applications, providing recruiting managers with a group of candidates that meet the desired criteria. Anyone involved in recruitment can suggest a candidate be reconsidered if they find someone that impresses them or that they would like to meet. This helps us find exceptional people who have great character but perhaps not all the credentials in the job description.

Our guiding principle throughout recruitment is to always ask ourselves, *Is this person better than us, in a meaningful way?* Put differently, *Will they be additive to the team in a way that elevates the business?* If the answer isn't a *Hell, yes!*, it's a *No, thank you.*

6. Longlisting (with our Head of People and recruiting manager)

From this list of potential candidates, our Head of People and the recruiting manager collaborate to create a longlist of candidates. This process involves a thorough review of applications to identify those that best meet the criteria and have the potential to excel in the role. The candidates need agreement from both our Head of People and our recruiting manager to be invited to initial virtual interview. Again, if the answer isn't a *Hell, yes!*, it's a *No, thank you*.

It's probably a helpful point to mention here that we're super-fortunate to have one of the country's leading performance psychologists as our Head of People, which provides a distinct competitive advantage in the process of identifying and developing the most talented people.

7. Initial interview (virtual)

We are genuinely excited to meet the candidates invited to interview and are hopeful they will be fantastic teammates, bringing skills, experience, and expertise that will help us Scale Conservation. They are congratulated for their awesome progress so far and invited for a virtual coffee, which is more like a conversation than a formal interview. At this meeting the goal is to understand the candidate's character and experience, and how they align with the role and organisation. Led by our Head of People and another selected member of the team who is functionally or technically close to the role, the meeting allows us to move beyond the application materials and get to know the real person. We do this by asking interesting questions (it's not just us that think they're interesting – candidates tell us this too!) and then diving into their thoughts, feelings, and emotions behind their responses.

What does you ideal working week look like? is fast becoming one of our favourite questions. It allows us to discuss Oxygen Conservation's flexible (but demanding) approach to work, which more and more people seek in a post-pandemic world. It also allows people to share how they see work fitting into their lives, and how a career at Oxygen Conservation would be fulfilling for them, helping them to be happier as a result. If you love what you do, and work can make your life better, then you don't need to seek that work–life balance.

At this point in the process, our Head of People makes a shortlist recommending only people he would be happy to see appointed, and then he removes himself from the assessment process. This is an important step in ensuring he makes a definitive decision. His role is now to help the candidate prepare for the final interview by offering advice and guidance ahead of the panel interview process.

8. Interview preparation meeting

When we call someone to offer them a job, we want it to be a memorable experience. I still remember being offered my first director role and being invited to 'Come and work with me', and that always stuck with me as a wonderful way to be offered a role.

Accepting a job is a big life decision, and it's not fair to expect someone to blindly accept without further discussion. That further discussion (if with a line manager) can be awkward and create a barrier to future relationship building – exactly the opposite of what we want for either person involved. We therefore analysed how we could improve our process and realised we have an amazing opportunity to add value to our candidates, and for us to learn more, with an interview preparation meeting before meeting face-to-face.

9. Interview preparation meeting: feedback and coaching

We tell the candidates what we loved about their initial interview, how we think they could make us better, the areas we think they can improve, and what we haven't seen yet.

This part of the process is led by Andrew (our wonderful Head of People), who loves helping people through coaching, so these conversations are an absolute joy. It's not just self-serving, though. Interviews are pivotal moments in our life, and we don't get enough practice and feedback in these settings, so we decided to pay it forward and offer some support and guidance. This also allows us to test how well candidates respond to and learn from the type of direct feedback given on a daily basis at Oxygen Conservation.

10. Aligning on reward expectations

As a recruiter, how do you evaluate someone's value and put a price on that?

As a candidate, how do you value yourself, decide what you want (often when you have no idea what's possible), and then communicate that effectively with your future employer?

Without a discussion, it's like playing tennis in the dark without a racket. It is important to have an open and honest conversation about salary, the benefits that are offered (both financial and non-financial), and anything else that makes up a total reward package. With this information, our hope is that when an offer is made, the candidate is delighted to accept.

11. Reference checking

Do you find that all the goodwill and amazing relationships you've built up fade when you leave a company? Sure, someone will act as a referee, but what does that person say about you? Do they get the chance to say how diligent, proactive, and wonderful you are? Not normally. Instead, they likely just say how long you worked at your employer in certain roles. What a missed opportunity!

We want to hear from your most vocal supporters about what makes you amazing and how we can help you achieve the next step in a fantastic career. With the candidates' permission, we call a referee before the final interviews. Don't worry, though – we don't expect that to be a current employer. We're delighted to hear from the people that know you best.

12. Panel interview (always with three people)

The most important step in our process is still the face-to-face panel interview. This is an opportunity for candidates to showcase their technical skills, plus their team and culture fit with the rest of the organisation. The panel includes three people, who are most likely their future direct manager, a team member, and a peer working regularly with the role. Online interviews are great, but we love in-person meetings even more – you get another level of information when meeting someone in person, and this works both ways.

The panel interview is also an opportunity to help the candidate meet some potential future teammates. By walking around one of our beautiful sites, or simply having a chat over coffee, candidates get an insight into what the people are really like and whether they want to work with Oxygen Conservation. We continue recruiting and selling the company as much as we're assessing the candidates' suitability to join the team.

13. Group debrief

We genuinely believe that having more people involved makes the recruitment decision better for all. After the panel interviews, everyone who met the candidates has a debrief, where perspectives about each person are shared. We are clear to call out where our opinion is limited and ask others to share their perspective from a different part of the process.

Interviews are a fantastic tool in the recruitment toolkit, but they are limited. They are a single slice of time in a restricted situation. By meeting people in different situations (application materials, virtual meeting, and panel interview), we hope to get to know the person even better, ultimately making the best decision for all involved.

14. Meet the MD

By this stage, a meeting with the Managing Director is often considered a tick-box exercise, but not at Oxygen Conservation. I remain involved in recruitment and intend to for as long as this is practicably possible. It's another opportunity for us to assess the candidate's fit with the organisation, and for them to understand the origins and future ambitions of the business. It's also great to give every new starter time and an opportunity to ask questions that I'm best placed to answer, and for them to decide if they believe in me and my vision for the future.

A note on rejection: Too often, companies do not even tell you that you have not been successful. Infamously, Andrew is still waiting five years on for a decision on a face-to-face interview at Jaguar Land Rover. While it's never nice to hear that you're not what a hiring manager is looking for, that's much better than waiting in hopeful anticipation for a decision that's already been reached. We respond honestly and as quickly as possible to all candidates throughout the process.

15. Offer

The final step is making an offer to the selected candidate. We've paved the way and hope this is an amazing experience for both the line manager and the candidate.

The offer includes all the terms of employment agreed on during the interview preparation meeting. The candidate also gets an offer letter and contract very soon after the phone call. They obviously want to see the details in writing, talk over these points with their family, and, ultimately, sign and start onboarding; so we do not hang about here.

Our recruitment playbook

In wrapping up this deep dive into the *Oxygen Conservation Recruitment Playbook*, let's be clear:

- We're not just in the game – we're changing it.
- Our recruitment strategy isn't just a process – we're redefining what's possible.

THE OXYGEN CONSERVATION RECRUITMENT PROCESS

- We don't just fill roles – we ignite passions by only recruiting people who are better than us, in a meaningful way.

Here's the kicker: we're just getting started. We're talking here to the innovators, the dreamers, and the game changers: do you think you can contribute to our playbook? Bring it on – we want to hear from you. We're here to challenge norms, shatter ceilings, and redefine success. If our journey resonates with you, step up. Share your ideas, critique our playbook, or, better yet, become a part of our story.

At Oxygen Conservation we don't just welcome excellence; we expect it and continue to redefine that bar. Let's set new benchmarks together. After all, in the realm of conservation, it's not just about making a difference; it's about being the difference.

On reflection

Sometimes recruitment doesn't come easily, and you have to get out there and work hard to find talent. We're currently in the process of trying to find an incredible person to be our Estate Manager at Invergeldie. We've written extensively about the challenges of recruiting for a completely new take on a role, in geographically specific and often remote locations. That means we have to work particularly hard to find the right candidate – our very own unicorn.

I'm so delighted that we have the best Head of People in the entire country on our side to make this search possible. Based on Andrew's dataset of the more than 2,000 applicants we've met since starting Oxygen Conservation, we are able to revisit candidates with the right skills and character traits, even though they might not recognise that this makes them suitable to be an Estate Manager. With Andrew providing an updated shortlist for the recruitment managers, we've identified potentially the perfect target.

Now it's my turn to compete. Between editing sections of this book, I've exchanged messages with this person, scheduling an initial meeting. At that meeting, uniquely, I need to sell the candidate the vision of Oxygen Conservation, as they've recently taken a new role with another company. I love the fact that, as I sit writing this, there are two distinct possibilities. The first is that they might never know they appear in this book. The second is that it will be a wonderful surprise for them when I share this section as part of the onboarding process when we welcome them to Oxygen Conservation.

Always be prepared to compete for talent – there isn't enough of it to go around.

Adventure with a Purpose: Oxygen Conservation's Mission to Scale Conservation

Written May 2024

Oxygen Conservation stands as a beacon of innovation and inspiration in the battle against climate change and biodiversity collapse. Founded with the mission to Scale Conservation, we are focused not only on what we do but also on how we do it, with a vision to inspire others to join this crucial fight.

What makes us so different

In this article I'll summarise the main factors that make Oxygen Conservation unique and a brilliant place to work.

Aspirational ambitions

We talk about being the world's first conservation-focused unicorn company because ambitions need to be aspirational and inspirational. If we don't create an exceptional market leader, we cannot hope to be a catalyst for an entirely new alternative asset class.

Emphasising environment, impact, and adventure

At Oxygen Conservation work is an adventure with a purpose. We prioritise environment, impact, and adventure in everything we do. We have been coasteering in Wales, e-biking across the Highlands, freediving in Cornwall, and wild swimming on Dartmoor, on top of many daily micro-adventures. We believe work should make your life better – not that it should be something in conflict with your health, happiness, and fulfilment.

Scaling Conservation

Within just two years Oxygen Conservation has made remarkable strides, acquiring around 30,000 acres across the UK demonstrating our commitment to conservation at an unprecedented scale.

Giving people hope

Our climate is collapsing and we're living through the next mass extinction. Meanwhile, the people that are supposed to be leading the way are making it worse by licensing new gas and oil exploration and making it harder for people to advocate or act for the environment. In the face of fear, people want hope. We're trying hard to give it to them by Scaling Conservation and creating an entirely new, alternative asset class.

Elevating the environment sector

Oxygen Conservation is transforming recruitment in the sector, raising the profile of young environmentalists, and fostering a high-performance culture. For too long the environment sector has been apologetic, nervous, quiet, undervalued, and underappreciated. As a result, the leaders of NGOs and the charitable sector have sought to maintain the status quo, promoting experience over talent, and safety over creativity and charisma. Things are different at Oxygen Conservation. We want to inspire the most talented people into the environment sector. The people who are mad enough to think they can change the world are the ones who probably will, and we've got lots of them!

High-performance culture

Traditionally, performance didn't matter in the environment sector. Excuses were made, difficult conversations avoided, and outcomes never measured. Oxygen Conservation has changed the game. We believe that how you do anything is how you do everything, and feedback is given often and quickly. If you don't want to achieve exceptional standards and levels of performance (and yes, of course that means working very hard), this isn't the place for you. If, however, you want to achieve incredible things, we'd always love to hear from you.

Collaboration and partnership

We want to collaborate and partner with brilliant organisations and are delighted to be working with the following companies and many more: Oxygen House,

Triodos Bank, Burges Salmon, Galbraith Group, Low Carbon, CampWild, TreeStory, CreditNature, Bidwells, WeAreBeard, Earth Minutes.

Sharing and showcasing

We're committed to showcasing the brilliant people and businesses across the developing natural capital economy and love sharing their stories on our *Shoot Room Sessions* podcasts. We will always use our platform and voice to advocate for people, wildlife, and our partners, as well as the organisations we respect and admire.

Radical transparency

We maintain a culture of complete transparency and continuous improvement, openly sharing our mistakes, failings, actions, achievements, and successes. Inside the business, all information is available to everyone. This is really the only way to help the most talented people develop at speed and make the best possible decisions.

Redefining brand identity

Oxygen Conservation has intentionally designed a minimalist, stylish, and elegant brand identity, aiming to disrupt the environment sector and elevate standards through high-quality visual imagery. One of our first hires was a photographer and videographer, and every single image we publish or share has been taken of our land by our team. Authenticity is everything.

Our website was intentionally created without reference to the environment sector, drawing inspiration from high-end watches and sustainable clothes brands like Christopher Ward, Patagonia, and Finisterre. We're intentionally disrupting the environment sector – raising its profile and seeking to make it aspirational and inspirational.

Recruiting for potential

We recruit for potential, not experience. In the process, we have attracted some of the most talented young people working in the environment sector. These people are so talented and so young that they would scare the old guard in the public and charitable sectors. At Oxygen Conservation, though, they now have a place where they can reach their full potential, and we're delighted they've chosen to be part of our mission to Scale Conservation.

Authenticity and inclusivity

We are not going to apologise for being ourselves, for making some people uncomfortable with the pace at which we work, for the fact that we're obsessive about what we do, or for how excited we are about how we do it. Some of us have tattoos, some don't. Some have visible piercings, some don't. Some of us prefer to wear jeans and T-shirts, some like to dress smart. For many of us, most of our clothes are second-hand or, in the case of Chris, wonderfully flamboyant (and quite often his wife's).

Above everything, we're 100% authentically us. We are committed to making diversity of thought and experience not just an advantage but a necessity. We achieve this by only recruiting people better than us, in a meaningful way, and that inherently means you will be different. You will be amazingly you.

We're a team

We're very close as a team. We have a no-dickheads policy and include as many of the team as possible in the recruitment process. We all hug when we meet (Dan doesn't like this); we all share food on road trips (except Fi); and we're supportive, encouraging, and playful.

We're a real team and the most fantastic one I've had the opportunity to be part of or lead.

We've only just started

Oxygen Conservation is more than an environmental business; we're trying to inspire change. Through our ridiculously ambitious goals, innovative approaches, high-performance yet inclusive culture (contradictory, I know), and relentless dedication, we hope to inspire as many people as possible to do everything they can to help in the fight against climate change and biodiversity collapse.

On reflection

Scaling Conservation isn't about looking busy. It's about delivering undeniable impact!

The old guard hesitated; we acted. Reflecting now with more than 43,000 acres and hundreds of millions of pounds of assets under management, we're proving that conservation at scale isn't a dream – it's a reality. The playbook has changed, and we're writing it with every deal, every data point, and every acre brought back to life.

A team should be more than a collection of résumés; it should be a self-improving ecosystem of potential.

We continue to attract those that don't want a job but a mission, something bigger than themselves. If high expectations, rapid iteration, and relentless ambition sound exhausting, this isn't for you. But if you see conservation as a high-performance pursuit – like sport, like strategy, like revolution – then you've already found your people.

The future belongs to those who embrace paradox – radical transparency and strategic precision, wild ambition and meticulous execution. We don't just work in conservation; we're redefining it. Not as a slow, apologetic movement but as an aspirational, high-integrity entirely new asset class. The world doesn't need another organisation explaining why nature matters – it needs a force proving that protecting it is the smartest investment of all.

If this sounds completely unreasonable, I can assure you, it absolutely is, and so are our team.

PS – I'm reflecting on this piece, sat in a T-shirt the team kindly made for me with the words 'environment', 'impact', and 'adventure' emblazoned across my chest.

The Urgent Call to Be Kind: Battling Climate Change, Biodiversity Crisis, and Our Collective Concerns

Written November 2023

In these times of turmoil, as humanity and our fragile planet face the relentless onslaught of climate change and the painful erosion of biodiversity, it's abundantly clear that we all share a sense of dread – a profound fear that casts a darkening shadow over us. Now more than ever, though, we must grasp the power of kindness as a beacon of hope – kindness towards our natural world and the creatures that call it home, and, most crucially, towards one another. This is the call for forging a brighter and more regenerative, sustainable path forward.

There is no more time for fighting

Let's consider the main reasons we need to change our actions, and the areas where we most urgently need to develop ways to be kinder to everything and everyone around us.

The collective fear

In the looming shadow of climate change and the heartbreaking loss of biodiversity, a shared sense of fear is beginning to unite people worldwide. This fear, as diverse as the faces of humanity, manifests in an array of emotions – from outrage to anger, and from melancholy to resilient glimmers of hope.

Our planet, its ecosystems, the creatures that grace it, and the future generations we all hold dear stand on the precipice of peril. In these trying times, our fears can render us motionless, paralysing our resolve in the face of seemingly insurmountable challenges. If we choose to nurture them, though, those fears can also serve as the seeds of positive change and transformation.

Throughout history, humans have risen to the heights of the greatest challenges, and this is the greatest we've ever known.

Kindness towards nature

To confront the existential threats of climate change and biodiversity loss, we must begin by extending kindness to nature – the foundation of our existence. Regrettably, our actions have brought nature to the brink and perhaps even beyond.

The time has come to display acts of kindness towards our world. We must adopt a regenerative way of life, drastically reducing our carbon footprint, embracing renewable energy, and minimising our consumption and waste. We have taken far too much for far too long.

Furthermore, we must become diligent stewards of the finite resources we have left and find new and innovative ways to grow the circular economy. This includes protecting precious places and spaces, preserving and restoring ecosystems, planting trees, and restoring peatland. In this, we return to the Earth its lungs – its very breath – ensuring it remains a sanctuary for generations to come. Kindness towards nature is uniquely a concurrent form of self and selfless preservation, ensuring that the planet can remain habitable.

Kindness towards wildlife

The intricate tapestry of our natural world relies on the participation of every species, each making a unique contribution. Biodiversity's perilous decline endangers countless creatures, also subjecting them to untold suffering. To express kindness towards wildlife is to embark on a tireless mission to protect and preserve their habitats.

Presently, regulations are largely absent, almost completely ineffective, and often unenforced. We must acknowledge that nature is not just a resource to be consumed but a treasury of irreplaceable value. By making the preservation of wildlife habitats a profitable endeavour, we can halt the massacre of creatures great and small, putting an end to the illegal (and legal) wildlife trade.

Support for organisations dedicated to rehabilitating and releasing injured and endangered animals is a testament to our collective kindness, although I wish that support wasn't necessary. Kindness towards wildlife necessitates a fundamental shift in our approach to coexistence, recognising that human interference has distorted entire ecosystems. We must strive for a harmonious balance, where both human and animal life can flourish. In this we must be prepared to make concessions and sacrifices, for we have compelled nature to bend to our will for far too long.

Kindness towards each other

In times shrouded in fear and uncertainty, we must remember we're not alone, albeit that many, especially those who feel unable to contribute to the battle in their everyday lives or careers, feel they are.

Kindness towards one another acts as the adhesive that bonds our communities and societies together. A collaborative effort is imperative to effectively combat climate change and biodiversity loss.

Fostering an environment of mutual understanding and cooperation is paramount. In the spirit of togetherness, we can pool knowledge, resources, and strategies to usher in an era of regeneration. This is one of the main reasons we try to be as open and transparent as possible in everything we do. Kindness has the transformative power to bridge political divides (and we are certainly divided at the moment), unearthing common ground for addressing the challenges that collectively confront us, rewriting the chapters of our shared story for the better.

The ripple effect of kindness

Kindness, like the ripples in a sadly now too often eutrophic pond, has the potential to bring about profound change. When we extend our kindness to nature, wildlife, and each other, we set in motion a chain reaction of positive actions. These acts of kindness inspire others to follow suit, compounding compassion and collective responsibility.

Whether it's in planting a tree, endorsing regenerative and sustainable initiatives, or extending a helping hand or kind word to a friend (or foe), every act of kindness contributes to a future that gleams just a little brighter and is hopefully more sustainable.

World Kindness Day

Long ago I pledged to speak candidly about the challenges besieging our natural world, harnessing my fortunate position at Oxygen Conservation in trying to act as an activist founder. My goal was (and still is) to be a force of change, to Scale Conservation, and to ensure a future for my children.

As we confront the pressing issues of climate change and biodiversity breakdown, let us embrace our fears, allowing them to drive us towards positive change. Kindness – directed towards nature, wildlife, and each other – stands as a potent instrument that can usher in transformation, nurture our environment, and strengthen the bonds uniting us all.

It's time to rise above our fears, working hand in hand to craft a world where kindness reigns supreme, leading us towards a brighter, more regenerative future for generations yet to come.

Happy World Kindness Day from everyone at Oxygen Conservation.

On reflection

I'll leave this here as a reminder to always be a little kinder with each other, and to yourself.

Please Choose My Backyard

Written July 2023

There is increasing awareness, albeit sadly in some part acceptance, that the climate around us is crumbling and that we are in the midst of a biodiversity crisis. We have taken and continue to take more than the planet has to offer, and we are seemingly intent on doing so until there is nothing left to take. The alternative is to adopt a more sustainable (I wish we'd talk about regenerative, but we're sadly not there yet) way of living.

While few still challenge the existence of anthropogenic climate change, perhaps the bigger problem comes from those that recognise the need for change but aren't prepared to adjust their way of life to support that transition.

NIMBYism – Not in my backyard

We need to confront the prevailing culture of Not in my backyard, such that local communities not only welcome investment into green infrastructure but even campaign for it, demanding *Please choose my backyard!*

Here are some simple, positive ways we can all take action to reduce detrimental impact on our environment:

1. Upgrading our power grids
2. Embracing renewable energy
3. Investing in water infrastructure
4. Building affordable homes
5. Preserving nature's space

1. Upgrading our power grids

Transitioning away from fossil fuels requires significant investment in our power networks. The shift towards electric vehicles and technology integration puts a strain on our ageing infrastructure. When it comes to constructing new pylons, substations, and connections, though, objections often arise due to the potential visual impacts on local landscapes.

The solution lies in open dialogue and creative problem-solving. Let's encourage communities to actively participate in discussions about renewable energy opportunities. Rather than merely opposing developments, we should incentivise hosting these projects and celebrate them as significant contributions to our shared sustainability goals.

2. Embracing renewable energy

Renewable energy, particularly wind and solar power, holds immense promise in combatting climate change. Unfortunately, the current planning system, which seeks consensus from local communities, sometimes hampers progress. Consensus is great in theory. In practice, it results in inertia and maintaining the status quo, which, ironically, often no one wants either.

To overcome this obstacle, we should prioritise engagement. By increasing awareness about the broader benefits of renewable energy, communities might be more willing to accept developments.

In the absence of agreement, compulsory development orders should be used to ensure we make the progress to net zero we all require. Obviously, absolute climate breakdown won't do wonders for your view or your amenity either.

3. Investing in water infrastructure

A growing population and a changing climate have meant a regular cycle of drought and flood is now inevitable. We are therefore desperately in need of the creation of new reservoirs and significant upgrades to the existing water infrastructure.

The resistance to sacrificing rural landscapes – including farming land and maybe even villages – for such developments is a significant barrier to progress. It's almost certain all will recognise the need and, increasingly, the demand that additional investment is made in infrastructure development. It's just as likely, though, that people will feel equally sure that it can't possibly happen where they live.

Individual villages, communities, and landowners will be disproportionally affected as a result but, the alternative is that everyone is affected. Finding a consensus simply won't be possible. Instead, we need appropriate leadership (wherever that best suits) to push progress forward and for those affected to be generously incentivised and rewarded for prioritising the greater good. Compensation isn't enough.

4. Building affordable homes

People are being forced to move away from family and friends due to a lack of homes and, worse still, a lack of affordable homes, especially in rural communities. The problem is worsening year after year as house targets continue to be missed.

I'm yet to meet or speak to anyone who doesn't support the building of more affordable homes, or who thinks young people shouldn't have an opportunity to buy or rent their own homes in the communities where they were born and raised. Opposition to new developments in their own neighbourhoods prevails, though, leaving the next generation destined to become a new type of socio-economic nomads.

We can tackle this issue by prioritising inclusive community planning with a mandate to deliver the necessary homes within the local area. If agreement cannot be reached, a local market mechanism should be used to incentivise land to be presented for development. We need leadership, investment in green infrastructure, and activity – not inactivity in the pursuit of consensus.

5. Preserving nature's space

The state of nature in the UK is significantly worse than it has been in living memory, you only need to look at the devastating decline in farmland birds or in any other indicator species. There is increasing acceptance that, if we do not find more space for nature, we will be the last generation to see the vast majority of the UK's wildlife, the result of which will be the collapse of our ecosystem and, ultimately, of life on Earth.

A growing number of people are therefore openly campaigning, and more still are at least recognising the need for more space for nature, including the planting of new woodlands as well as the restoration of peatland and other precious habitats.

Many rural communities are of course pushing back, saying, *Not here – we don't want change. The way the land is managed and looks is part of our culture and just too precious.* This is perhaps the best example of where we need everyone to move beyond self-interest and prioritise the greater good, to recognise that we need more space for nature, and to welcome those seeking to make positive environmental improvements.

This is also where we're already seeing market mechanisms beginning to have a positive impact. Land is being bought for nature restoration, potentially in the face of localised criticism and frustration, but delivering the change we need for the climate and for biodiversity. This change is being fuelled by the potential of natural capital markets offering a financial return for interventions that will benefit us all, especially the generations to come.

Perhaps this also explains the startup culture of the companies leading the way in this growing natural capital economy.

Sadly, we are dealing with parallel problems that act (ironically) like pouring water on an oil fire – it becomes explosive. We have an entitled, self-interested government, ageing local communities that are not prepared to accept disruption to their way of life, and a planning system that requires these exact people all to agree to changes that will only benefit the next generation. It's hardly surprising we're failing – and failing dramatically – to achieve any form of meaningful change.

A way forward?

To address these challenges, we must foster a sense of collective responsibility and prioritise collaboration over individual interests.

I strongly believe in the principle that you can't give criticism if you're not prepared to try and find a solution or offer ideas, so here are mine:

1. Listening
2. Leadership
3. Taxation
4. Incentivisation

1. Listening

We need to continue listening to local communities but also to experts and campaigners who are trying to help us have a future on this planet, not just for ourselves but for the next generations. This consultation needs to be faster and more meaningful; and it must seek to improve, not stop, the proposed development.

Moreover, we should prioritise the voices of young people over those of my generation and the generation before mine. It's young people's future that will be most impacted by the decisions made today.

Following Scotland's example, we should lower the voting age to sixteen and insist on politics, among many other real-life skills, being taught in schools. These skills should replace the archaic memory tests and the joined-up handwriting my seven- and five-year-old children are being taught.

2. Leadership

Consensus is a lovely concept, but in reality, it only achieves mediocracy or – worse still – inaction. We don't have time for consensus. We need action, and we need it now. We need leadership from everywhere, especially from businesses. The existing political system, centrally and locally, is not fit for purpose, and it is too bureaucratic, self-serving, and ineffective to deliver any meaningful change.

Businesses, community groups, and individuals need to lead the way forward. We're trying to do just that with Oxygen Conservation, and our hope is to inspire many more leaders working in and around the natural capital economy. Please do reach out to us if we can help in any way.

3. Taxation

Having shared my thoughts on the ineffectiveness of government – and you can add regulation to that too – I'd ask that what is left of a 'functioning' civil service.

Our civil service needs to focus its attention on creating the taxation measure needed to ensure businesses pay the true cost of the environmental impact of their work, meaning all businesses must have a positive impact for people and the environment. We must then ensure this taxation is invested in the green infrastructure improvements we need to see delivered by the private sector, not only by the public sector.

4. Incentivisation

We must ensure all local communities are not just involved in discussions about where and how green infrastructure projects are delivered, but that they also generously incentivise those most directly affected. The aim is for communities to begin campaigning to provide a home for these projects, much like hosting the Olympics or becoming the next city of culture.

Please choose my backyard

If we put a combination of these measures and likely many more in place, we could one day have a world where people are saying *Please pick my backyard – we want the investment and opportunities change will bring.*

If we don't, then I'd like to be the first to apologise to my children and grandchildren for the fact that we refused to let our lifestyle – and, let's not forget, our views – to be disrupted to give them a chance of a life at all.

On reflection

Reading this piece back almost a year later, I think there is the very real possibility that things have sadly become worse, not better.

As the realities of climate change and biodiversity collapse are becoming more prominent, we're seeing a re-emergence of anti-net-zero rhetoric and governments running from climate commitments, trying to find ways to lower taxes ahead of the elections across the globe.

We need real leadership in the environment sector, we need more of it, and we need it now.

EIGHT
The Interconnectivity Of Solutions

Let's Talk About Lying

Written September 2023

We've had quite a summer of political announcements from the party that has repeatedly committed to being the party of the environment. The Tories reassured us Brexit would not mean watering down environmental protections (Harrabin, 2017). In fairness, it hasn't meant the watering-down of environmental protections – there's been something closer to a biblical flood, intensified by the climate collapse.

We've been told that we need hundreds of new fossil fuel extraction licences to help deliver our net-zero ambitions and provide ongoing fuel security. This was followed up by the claim that anyone not supporting the exploitation (perfect word) of additional fossil fuels is anti-British and pro-Russian, a claim accurately described by one political commentator as the most cynical politicisation of the Ukraine war it's possible to imagine (Mason and Stewart, 2022; Prime Minister's Office and Department for Energy Security and Net Zero, 2023).

We've seen repeated attacks on the move to reduce air pollution in London, which, let's not forget, has been directly linked to increased deaths. In 2013 we saw the tragic death of nine-year-old Ella Kissi-Debrah – the first person to have air pollution listed as the cause of death (Gentleman, 2024).

Earlier this week, the government announced its intention to weaken or remove nutrient neutrality rules (DLUHC, 2023). These rules were originally designed to ensure that any further infrastructure development would not negatively impact the quality of our rivers and streams. What all these rules were trying to do was not clean up pollution – they were to make sure it doesn't get any worse!

By removing these protections, the government is deciding, on our behalf, that pollution is fine as long as we're delivering growth. Perhaps even more dangerously, it is removing the principle of *The polluter pays*.

Who needs clean water?

The government is also wilfully allowing water companies to repeatedly pump sewage into our rivers and streams, openly and non-ironically, stating that rivers aren't meant to be swum in anyway (Defra Press Office, 2023; Laville et al, 2024). It's OK, though – we don't have to worry about telling the aquatic species, as most of them have floated to the surface already!

These actions have caused an impassioned response from across the environment sector, including from the Royal Society for the Protection of Birds (RSPB), which simply and elegantly declared that the government were in fact liars. Their tweet (Butler, 2024) said, 'You said you wouldn't weaken environment protections. And yet that's just what you are doing. You lie, and you lie, and you lie again.' This response was celebrated, praised, and echoed by thousands of people across the country who were proud of the RSPB's honesty, bravery, and leadership. Sadly, as a result of political pressure and bullying, the RSPB have now been forced to distance themselves from the post.

A few weeks ago, I called for the generation of activist business leaders and asked you all to hold me to account for these standards. To the comms professional that wrote the RSPB tweet: if you're reading this, please give me a call. I'd like to buy you a coffee and say thank you. Also, if you're interested, we're recruiting!

One of my favourite sayings in life is 'everybody knows'. Especially in business, everybody knows. Everybody knows who the higher performers are, everybody knows who doesn't work as hard as everyone else, everybody knows who is helpful and kind, and everybody knows who's miserable. That's probably why I didn't decide to call the government liars. I didn't think there was any point, really, because everybody knows.

On reflection

When the time comes around for the next general election, remember it is your opportunity to make your voice heard.

Please vote, and please demand a higher standard of politics and a higher standard of leadership.

Hold Strong Opinions, Loosely
Written August 2023

In a world characterised by an accelerating pace of change and increasing complexity, striking a balance between holding strong opinions and remaining open to challenge can be a difficult task.

Strong opinions

My approach to this is best captured in a concept first introduced to me by the author Nassim Nicholas Taleb: 'Hold strong opinions, loosely' (Taleb, 2007).

This approach encapsulates a mindset that encourages depth of conviction, allows speed of execution, and offers clarity while acknowledging the potential for growth and change. In this article I explore some of the ways the approach manifests itself in our work at Oxygen Conservation and in the way we seek to interact with the many complex and interesting people we meet through our work:

1. Strength of conviction

2. Speed of execution
3. Dangers of rigidity
4. Emotional impact of close-mindedness

1. Strength of conviction

Having strong opinions can be empowering and motivating. When we deeply believe in something, that belief drives us to act, advocate for change, and stand up for our values.

Strongly held opinions can foster a sense of identity, allowing us to connect with likeminded individuals and form communities united by shared beliefs. This is demonstrated in the way we've built the culture of Oxygen Conservation. We have brought together a team of talented individuals around the single goal of Scaling Conservation. To do this we've built a culture that is all about environment, impact, and adventure. In some ways these values serve as a moral compass, guiding us through the many challenges and uncertainties that we face multiple times every day.

2. Speed of execution

The urgency of the climate collapse and biodiversity crisis means that we no longer have time for indecision and inaction. Holding strong opinions creates a powerful decision matrix, allowing for more immediate decisions; faster, more purposeful actions; and, in some cases, inactions.

In a sector defined by talking, procurement processes, bureaucracy, inaction and inactivity, costly feasibility studies, endless pilot projects, endless meetings about meetings, and far too much what-if debate, we are different. Speed of execution is a clear point of differentiation in our approach to Scaling Conservation. This applies to the determination of a site's natural capital potential, to the decision to pass on or acquire an estate, to the immediacy of appointing talented people, and to simple things like responding to the correspondence we receive.

Even the decision to do things patiently is made purposely and as quickly as possible. The best example of this might be our approach to listening and learning from each new landscape we acquire before we begin building a long-term strategy. This can still take months and even years; after all, we're working with nature's clock, not ours.

3. Dangers of rigidity

Unwavering rigidity in our convictions can lead to a host of problems. It blinds us to alternative viewpoints, stifles growth, and can so often lead to mourning the past, even in the face of a potentially better future. Rigidity can foster an environment devoid of debate, resistant to change, and – sadly too often – a lifetime of sadness.

History is rife with examples of industries and businesses that have suffered due to the unwillingness to question and adapt, emphasising the importance of avoiding an overly rigid stance. Many formerly successful businesses like Blockbuster, BlackBerry, Woolworths, and other former household names refused to change with customer demands. We're desperate to avoid their mistakes. While holding strong opinions and seeking clarity and conviction in everything we do, we're therefore always open to challenge, striving to remain curious, and trying hard to adopt a learning and growth mindset.

4. Emotional impact of close-mindedness

On a personal level, we at Oxygen Conservation have had the opportunity to meet a large number of landowners, land agents, and farmers while reviewing land opportunities over the past two years. While I recognise that generalisations are often far too crude to be meaningful, we have certainly found some commonality among people looking to exit farming.

These proud people hold strong opinions that have many similarities, including the way they express those opinions. Almost all have loved but now hate the land they're selling. They are happy to be leaving farming behind, and they are both heartbroken and relieved that their children don't want to follow in their footsteps. They think regulation has caused the demise of farming and that the climate collapse and biodiversity crises are overblown, purely used as a campaign of hysteria by others (but they're never sure by whom or for what reasons).

They don't believe electric vehicles are practical or necessary, and they question the sourcing and ethicality of the materials required to build an electric car, without once questioning the materials or fuel of their diesel 4×4s. They don't like the fact that farming is changing and often don't like the concept of conservation beyond the version they're passionate about – birds, butterflies, bees, or any other specific passion they hold. Often this is accompanied by a belief that nature needs help, but that it can only thrive when being firmly steered by a human hand, usually as part of an agricultural system. They always ask about natural capital and want to understand how the economics of the rural economy are changing. They generally conclude that they don't want that to happen, though, so in the end, they decide it isn't happening.

Whenever we meet people with these views, I listen, seeking to learn. More often than not, I end up recognising fear and sympathising with each of these exceptionally hard-working people who see an industry and chapter of their lives rapidly running out of time. Perhaps this is the same fear we all hold about the future of our planet – that sense of running out of time if we don't change our behaviours and relationship with the natural world.

A note on land acquisition

Interestingly, it is rare that we acquire sites from landowners with the perspectives outlined above, as they're often not ready – either emotionally or practically – to sell, meaning they refuse to engage in the work necessary to complete on large-scale land transactions. Instead, we've been hugely fortunate to work with forward-thinking landowners who are excited by their own next chapters. They have enjoyed their journeys so far but are equally excited about what's coming next, both for them and for the landscape they've passed on to us as its next custodian, often commenting, *We never really own land, do we?* They certainly hold strong opinions, but they hold them loosely, helping share our future thinking and vision instead of carrying old opinions like a burdensome weight.

The virtue of open-mindedness

Open-mindedness is the antidote to the pitfalls of rigid conviction. Having an open mind means being receptive to new ideas, even if they challenge our existing beliefs or make us initially uncomfortable.

One of the most amazing things about the Oxygen Conservation adventure has been the process of becoming more comfortable with being uncomfortable. It involves actively listening, seeking out diverse perspectives, and being willing to revise our opinions when presented with compelling evidence. If you can find a way to be just a little more open-minded, you can become more adaptable and resilient, more capable of navigating the complexities of an ever-changing world, and – maybe, just maybe – happier and healthier in the process.

Our team members challenge each other daily to change their views on everything – from rural land use to property development and redevelopment, technological solutions, resourcing decisions, and – much to my disappointment – the need for more processes and procedures around some decision making, to ensure we're ready to grow and can continue Scaling Conservation.

The balancing act: Holding strong opinions loosely

The concept of holding strong opinions loosely encourages a dynamic equilibrium – an agility between conviction and open-mindedness. This philosophy acknowledges that, while we should be passionate about our beliefs, we must recognise the potential – or in my case the likelihood – that we're wrong. This is so exciting because it offers the opportunity for growth and evolution. It encourages a willingness to engage in thoughtful dialogue, to question our assumptions, and to consider viewpoints that may and should differ from our own in so many ways.

Applications in personal relationships

This principle finds relevance in personal relationships. Disagreements and differences of opinion are natural, but embracing the mantra of *Hold strong opinions, loosely* can transform conflicts into opportunities for mutual understanding. When we approach discussions with a willingness to learn from one another, relationships flourish, and bonds strengthen.

At Oxygen Conservation we only recruit people better than us, in a meaningful way, making it nothing short of nonsense if we don't listen to these people and let our thoughts, feelings, and underlying beliefs be challenged. This level of openness and intellectual flexibility is such a powerful tool in creating a genuinely diverse and inclusive environment, helping everyone develop together, in their own unique ways.

The phrase *Hold strong opinions, loosely* encapsulates a fusion of passion and humility, conviction, and open-mindedness. It serves as a reminder that our opinions, no matter how deeply held, should rarely – if ever – be considered beyond challenge or debate. Please feel free to challenge this thought. By cultivating a genuinely open, adventurous mindset, we can navigate the ever-changing landscape of ideas with enthusiasm, empathy, and intellectual curiosity. Then again, I might of course be wrong...

On reflection

I think the persistent theme running through this chapter is an individual's decision on whether to have a future- or past-focused outlook.

For those stuck in the past, trying desperately to keep the then and now as close as possible, every change can only be thought of as being worse. They are forever in defence mode; it must be emotionally draining. The alternative is to be focused on the future, and on a belief that change can bring something better for everyone.

Perhaps it's because I had a pretty miserable childhood that I was forced to accept the realities of the present while thinking that tomorrow must be better. Ironically, in the last few years, I've learned that there is a name for this mindset. It's perhaps perfectly called the Stockdale Paradox (no relation), named after James Stockdale, an American naval officer that spent over seven years imprisoned during the Vietnam War (NavyOnline.com, 2022). During this time, he faced sustained and brutal treatment, with no set release date or certainty that he would even survive. James realised that he needed to balance an honest confrontation of the present with a steadfast belief that he would survive and have a better future.

On reflection, I think the Rich James (yes, that's my middle name) Stockdale version of the paradox presents itself throughout this book. I am furious at what we've done to the world and bitterly angry at the way so many people refuse to be part of the solution and instead – through ignorance and entitlement – continue to make things worse. At the same time, though, I'm absolutely sure we will find a way forward to a better tomorrow.

Building a Sustainable Future

Written October 2023

Built property is a fundamental part of our mission to Scale Conservation for people and wildlife. If people cannot live, work, and play in the rural landscape, how can we ever hope to inspire them to love, value, and protect it? Over the last two years, we have acquired ten estates in eight counties and three countries, totalling almost 30,000 acres of land. While we have never purchased an estate because of a specific built property, we are delighted to have more than 100 buildings across our portfolio, and each of these is absolutely a feature, not a bug.

The vital role of built property in conservation

In this article we're going to explore some of the reasons we're committed to protecting, improving, and developing built property across our portfolio of landscapes:

1. Stewardship of historic properties

2. Providing sustainable rural homes
3. Repurposing redundant agricultural buildings
4. Using properties as venues for promoting conservation and ecotourism
5. Learning lessons in retrofitting and reducing carbon impact
6. Overcoming challenging planning situations

1. Stewardship of historic properties

When we acquire an estate and become custodians of a unique landscape, we also become custodians of the built environment that reflects the historical culture and context of that estate. These properties may have unique and significant cultural and historical importance, with some being formally listed. By retaining ownership of these properties, we maintain the integrity of the estate, preserving its heritage for future generations.

This commitment to the localities and to their cultural legacy is a marker of our ongoing dedication to the local community, and of our recognition that people and wildlife are equally important to special places and spaces.

That does not mean that these buildings are easy to manage, to live with, and sometimes to love, but we believe we're well placed to accept the challenge to find ways to give the buildings a future that can contribute in a meaningful way to helping us Scale Conservation.

2. Providing sustainable rural homes

We are committed to providing high-quality, sustainable homes for people in the rural community and are working hard to understand how to do this in a cost-effective way. These homes contribute to the sustainability of rural communities, combatting depopulation, and preventing rural infrastructure decline.

Across the Oxygen Conservation portfolio, we have around thirty-five residential tenants and are hoping to welcome many more in the years to come as we repurpose, renovate, and develop buildings and new homes.

3. Repurposing redundant agricultural buildings

Many estates come with redundant agricultural buildings, which can be transformed into productive, sustainable spaces and homes.

These conversions align with our ambitious sustainability and energy efficiency goals. Navigating planning regulations and achieving excellent development standards in this endeavour can be challenging and often prohibitively expensive, though. We are, however, committed to exploring technological developments, innovations, and improvements to make repurposing and retrofitting more efficient and effective, all while sensitively respecting the natural environment.

4. Using properties as venues for promoting conservation and ecotourism

Properties owned and managed by Oxygen Conservation often serve as venues to promote conservation work. Hosting events and activities onsite allows people to better understand the practicalities of conservation efforts and emotionally connect with incredible spaces and places. This not only educates visitors and guests but also opens doors for partnerships and potential funding opportunities.

Additionally, some properties we have repurposed provide exceptional opportunities for ecotourism, promoting sustainable tourism practices that align with conservation objectives. This helps create experiences within the natural environment as well as local employment.

5. Learning lessons in retrofitting and reducing carbon impact

We are acutely aware of the challenges posed by the UK's ageing housing stock, one of the oldest in Europe. Retrofitting these properties and understanding embodied carbon impacts are key challenges. By addressing these issues, we hope to contribute to wider efforts to reduce carbon emissions and create more sustainable living spaces.

We recognise this will be difficult, especially with historically significant and listed properties, but we will do what we can, with what we have, to help move the industry forward.

6. Overcoming challenging planning situations

We often identify tensions concerning the potential for property development in rural environments, particularly in locations perceived as sensitive. Some areas are considered by most to be unsustainable for development due to their location outside of settlement boundaries. However, many of these areas have hamlets and villages, where people have lived in otherwise remote rural areas for generations. Many are now suffering from loss of social infrastructure, at least in part as a result of planning decisions or small protectionist factions of the local community that have sought to 'preserve' those areas.

We believe that there is still a place for sensitive rural development, even within national parks and areas of outstanding natural beauty (AONBs), to help combat rural decline and ageing populations. Such development contributes to local economies, especially where high-quality, sustainable, and 'architecturally beautiful' properties can add to rather than detract from the environment. [Editor's note: beauty continues to be a planning hot topic and is a blog for another day!]

Built property: An asset, not a liability

While many organisations, especially charitable environmental organisations, view built properties as ongoing liabilities and avoid their purchase or seek to exit them as soon as practicable, we hold a different perspective. We firmly believe that, without built property, you cannot holistically manage the land for both people and wildlife. Owning property connects people to a landscape, allowing it to be explored, cared for, and enjoyed. This connection fosters a sense of stewardship and enhances the overall conservation effort.

Furthermore, Oxygen Conservation sees built property as a key part of protecting and growing capital investment. Through the stewardship of historic properties, provision of sustainable rural homes, repurposing of agricultural buildings, and promotion of conservation work, we make a positive impact on both local communities and the natural environment.

These properties serve as assets that not only support our conservation initiatives but also contribute to the long-term sustainability of our mission. They are an essential part of holistic land management for people and wildlife, which underscores our commitment to preserving and growing capital investment in our natural world.

On reflection

Built properties are such an important part of the Oxygen Conservation portfolio and of our ability to genuinely provide positive environmental and social impact. As a result, we currently provide homes to almost seventy people in rural communities where we're fortunate enough to own and manage land. We are also in the process of modernising a number of additional properties, including the farmhouse at our latest addition, Siblyback, which will be made available to the local residential rental market.

In communities where rural housing is in short supply, the addition of our properties to the available housing stock is hugely important and demonstrates our commitment to providing positive social impact.

Our wonderful sustainable tourism offerings at Mornacott in Devon and Manor Farm in Shropham will welcome around 1,000 visitors this year alone and help people better connect with the natural world. We believe that if you want people to love the environment, they need to be able to connect with it and understand it. At both these estates we are also modernising and furnishing the principal properties to make them available to families and corporate visitors.

As part of our acquisitions, we have also secured planning permission across the portfolio for fourteen new-build properties. This will allow us to build new properties with excellent environmental performance standards, thereby providing more homes and visitor opportunities in some of the places that need additional built property the most.

You can read more about our approach to sustainable tourism later in this chapter. If you'd like to experience more, we'd love you to come and visit.

Patient Urgency

Written August 2023

We are a little over six months into our ownership at the Invergeldie Estate in Perthshire – the gateway to the Scottish Highlands. Every time I'm fortunate enough to return, I'm struck by how so little yet so much has changed. Nature is a little like that, I suppose – seasonal sprints become annual marathons and generation ultras; over time the pace drops as more is achieved.

It was always our intention to listen, learn, and engage with each site over the seasons, understanding how it lives and breathes. However, the demand for more immediate change is increasing furiously. The climate is collapsing around us, and we are losing biodiversity at an immeasurable rate. Alongside this, societal demand for change is increasing. Outside of our government system, greater numbers of people, including the communities local to where we work, are calling for change.

Our commitment to patience, listening, and engaging has most often been met with those encouraging us, even if that encouragement often feels like people pushing us to go further and faster. On first meetings, people want to know our plans. They expect our plans to be ambitious, whether those relate to new woodland creation, peatland restoration, renewable energy generation, habitat creation, or the potential of more immediate economic interventions such as employment or potential property developments.

The reality of buying land at scale is that we often know very little about a site ahead of acquisition. Before we even consider receiving an ecological or environmental baseline, we can rarely visit a site more than a couple of times; and we receive little, if any, information about the underlying business activities and economic viability of the site, especially where land uses are likely to change.

While we have ideas, these must be considered, investigated, and tested before being shared to allow engagement in a meaningful way, not just for a rubber stamp. This process is incredibly challenging, not least because everyone means something different when it comes to what *local* is and, moreover, in what they mean by *engagement*. Both words have a tendency of being elastic.

We've felt this pressure to act faster more strongly in Scotland, likely due to the scale of our acquisitions. Invergeldie is no different, however – we are learning so much and so quickly that our ambitions for the estate are changing rapidly too:

- **Sheep numbers:** We have recognised that we must reduce the number of sheep on the hill if natural regeneration and woodland creation are to be successful. With approaching 2,000 sheep across the estate and the grazing pressure being so significant, we have brought forward our plans to reduce stocking numbers over the next twelve months.

- **Deer management:** We've engaged with the Perthshire Deer Management Group and committed to supporting their targets to rapidly reduce growing deer numbers. This will involve us working with a local specialist team of stalkers, remaining authentic to our commitment to working locally, and to try and ensure as much as possible of this sustainable protein reaches the food chain.

- **Wind power:** We hope to one day welcome a wind farm to Invergeldie and as such have partnered with the excellent Low Carbon to explore the suitability of the site for wind. It's early days, but the topography, geology, and environmental considerations look positive. This would deliver a wide range of sustainable benefits, from green energy to additional employment, improved access infrastructure, and opportunities to utilise construction work to support peatland restoration and habitat creation.

- **Built property:** We've made significant progress on our built property portfolio, surveying existing buildings and making improvements to residential properties but with a lot more to do, following an extended period of underinvestment prior to our acquisition.

While we've enjoyed some wonderful interest and support locally, this of course isn't universal; everyone has different priorities and objectives for the landscape. Some just don't want to see change, others want change but not here, some would choose to prioritise specific land uses over others, and others want more change more quickly.

One of the most surprising lessons I've learned relates to deer and also to sheep. I had initially thought it important to maintain a 'traditional' sporting component to the estate, believing this was respectful to the local community. Over the last six months, though, we've learned that for many people in Scottish towns and villages 'traditional sporting estates' are anything but that. Instead, they are reminders of cultural imperialism; of rampant elitism; and of things being taken from rural communities, leaving behind a barren wasteland of an environment.

What else will we learn that we're wrong about in time? Almost certainly a lot.

I'm therefore left reflecting on the seemingly impossible contradiction that we must work faster but also ensure we take the time to make informed decisions and engage on these locally, if I ever figure out exactly what local means.

On reflection

The following article, written just a couple of months after this trip, actually serves as the perfect reflection and update on our journey at Invergeldie.

Wind vs Wilderness

Written October 2023

We no longer have the luxury of black and white; virtually everything we do requires us to operate in a world of grey. Contradictions and compromises are an everyday imperative in our work to Scale Conservation by delivering positive environmental and social impact.

One of the biggest challenges we face is delivering large-scale land use change. The difficult reality for many in the rural economy is in recognising that our collective exploitation of land, for whatever reason, is a big part of why we stand at the threshold of a living hell on Earth, appropriately accompanied by biblical-scale environmental catastrophes now appearing across the globe on a daily basis.

Sadly, however much we all may enjoy our existing way of life, it's no longer sustainable. In fact, we've wasted the window for sustainability – we left that back in the 1980s, alongside awesome music, big hair, and a political doctrine of growth, growth, growth. Actually, ignore that last one. What we need now is regenerative land use change. Doing no harm is no longer good enough. We need to do a lot of good, and quickly.

This is where some of the massive changes we need to make are uncomfortable to those who have for so long enjoyed – either financially, emotionally, or culturally – the status quo. You will often hear we need more or even all land for farming, but that has hugely impacted our natural world, wildlife populations, and water bodies, and not for the better. We have heard and continue to hear that we've always burned the hillside and we've always used the ground for sport, but that has left significant scars – in the landscape physically and on wildlife populations literally. In many ways, we're now left with the land we both wanted and deserve.

The uncomfortable compromises of conservation

Recognising the need for systematic change and being absolutely committed to regenerative land management and restoring natural processes, I'm faced with many uncomfortable contradictions of my own. One of the biggest is that, while I am completely open to exploring the renewable energy potential on our land portfolio, I am acutely aware that we can't build out these huge (and fundamentally important) infrastructure projects without impacting the very environment I'm committed to protecting.

In this article, I'm going to explain our thinking: the advantages we see, the threats we recognise, and the compromises we are (and those we aren't) prepared to make to realise the potential for renewable energy projects across the Oxygen Conservation portfolio.

We believe that wind power, especially in Scotland, where the environmental, logistical, and political conditions are most supportive, must play a significant role in supporting our mission to Scale Conservation. We believe it will do so in several ways:

1. Renewable energy generation
2. Mobilising natural capital investment
3. Funding conservation initiatives
4. Job creation
5. Community infrastructure

1. Renewable energy generation

Wind farms produce clean and renewable energy, reducing our reliance on fossil fuels, which is the most significant threat to biodiversity and conservation efforts worldwide.

If we cannot help in finding a way to end our reliance on fossil fuels, we will no longer have a future on this planet. I wholeheartedly believe that we owe it to the next generations to try everything we can to repay the climatic debts we've created.

2. Mobilising natural capital investment

Revenue generated from wind farm operations will form a key part of the financial returns for investors in the natural capital economy.

If we can prove that it is possible to generate an investment return by delivering positive environmental and social impact, we will mobilise the trillions of pounds needed to help in the fight against climate change and biodiversity loss.

3. Funding conservation initiatives

Revenue generated from wind farm operations will allow reinvestment in conservation efforts, allowing us to purchase more land for conservation. This funding can also support initiatives such as habitat restoration, species protection (and reintroduction), and the transition to regenerative land management practices.

4. Job creation

Wind farms create jobs, during both construction and ongoing operations. Many of the communities where we are fortunate to own and manage land need additional employment if they are to offer a future for young people.

These employment opportunities can bolster local economies, helping to create thriving rural communities.

5. Community infrastructure

Engaging with local communities and stakeholders is crucial in the development of wind farms. This collaboration can lead to the adoption of community benefit agreements and introduce new, accessible infrastructure (especially tracks and walkways). This will make large areas of land, previously locked away, available again to the many, not just the very few.

When thoughtfully planned and executed, wind farms and similar large-scale infrastructure projects demonstrate that economic development and conservation can go together, contributing to a better future for both people and nature in the region. We've seen first-hand that this is possible if there is a vision and willingness on the part of both the landowner and the developer to collaborate, constructively challenge norms, and push boundaries.

It is, however, important to consider the potential environmental impacts of a wind farm, despite its contributions to renewable energy and to our wider conservation efforts. Here are some counterarguments highlighting those concerns as well as the most likely compromises:

1. Limited opportunity
2. Habitat destruction
3. Impact on peat bogs
4. Wildlife collisions
5. Noise and visual impact
6. Turbine manufacturing and maintenance
7. Challenges in decommissioning

1. Limited opportunity

We have a finite amount of land available for anything. Choosing to pursue wind power means prioritising that development ahead of other opportunities such as tree planting and peatland restoration, and the wider restoration of natural processes.

The land available for wind, based on political, social, logistical, and environmental considerations, is in reality a very small proportion of land. We therefore think it's appropriate to pursue the option when it is possible, for all the reasons shared above.

The compromise: We shouldn't prioritise more turbines but instead prioritise turbines in the right place. This means we will work to find the balance between the size of individual turbines and the overall size of the wind farm.

We are committed to wind farms being part of a wider site masterplan that includes woodland creation and peatland restoration alongside wind generation – not one or the other. We're exploring some innovative ways of achieving this balance, including exploring the possibility to plant trees in (traditionally heavily restricted) 'wind protection zones'. We are also using our detailed topographic modelling of an estate to design new woodland areas that have a greater diversity of native tree species around development sites.

2. Habitat destruction

The construction and maintenance of wind farms, including associated infrastructure, can disrupt local habitats and ecosystems. Roads, transmission lines, and the turbines themselves can fragment and degrade the natural landscape, potentially harming wildlife and plant species that depend on these areas.

The compromise: Extensive environmental assessments and wildlife surveys help to inform the design and engineering of a wind farm, such that we can significantly reduce the impact of habitat destruction and disturbance, albeit of course not completely.

We are not, however, prepared to commit to specific environmental improvements at a site by planting trees and then later fell those same trees to facilitate wind development. This is why we commit to developing detailed masterplans with developers and woodland creation consultants to ensure we do not find ourselves in this position. If we make a positive impact on the natural world, we're committed to doing everything we can to protect that.

3. Impact on peat bogs

Some parts of Scottish land contain exceptionally valuable peat bogs, which are essential for carbon storage and biodiversity. The construction and operation of wind farms can disrupt these fragile ecosystems, releasing stored carbon and affecting water flow patterns.

The compromise: The development of a wind farm and peatland restoration both require the use of large-scale plant and machinery, often in hard-to-reach parts of the landscape. We will always try and minimise the disturbance of peat through site selection and detailed planning. Where we disturb peat in the development of a wind farm, we will seek to use those same access routes and that same equipment to restore the entirety of the peatland area of the landscape, not just the area impacted by the wind development.

We are not prepared to touch peatland without a funded commitment to its restoration and ongoing maintenance. We see wind as a potentially significant source of funding to unlock restoration opportunities for some of the more challenging areas of degraded peatland – areas that would not otherwise be funded through carbon credit schemes or government grants.

4. Wildlife collisions

Although sometimes this risk is overstated, it is true that wind turbines can pose a threat to bird and bat populations. Collisions with the rotating blades can result in injuries and fatalities, particularly for species that use the area for breeding, migration, or foraging.

The compromise: Specialist independent bird and bat surveys, alongside wider environment surveys, are be used to inform the precision placement, design, and engineering of a wind farm. While this cannot remove the risk entirely, it can significantly reduce the likelihood of collisions and remove the risk for specific, protected, or vulnerable species.

While I cannot guarantee that any specific animal will not be impacted by any wind development built on an estate we manage, that is the reality of almost everything we do. From regenerative agriculture to ecotourism, property development, and woodland creation, all of the activities we undertake can and do cause harm both in terms of carbon emissions and nature loss. We are committed, though, to designing landscape-level schemes that create much greater positive impacts, thereby outweighing the negative. That's really as much as any of us can do.

5. Noise and visual impact

Wind turbines generate noise and can significantly alter the visual aesthetics of (sometimes, although often not when you look closely!) pristine landscapes and ranging horizon lines. This may negatively impact the experience of tourists and local communities alike, potentially affecting the area's appeal as a conservation destination.

The compromise: Personally, I like wind farms. I think they add something to the landscape. However, this isn't everyone's perspective. My approach is to offer that the local impact felt by a wind farm on the horizon or even the top of the hill is nothing in comparison with that of a collapsing climate and a completely failing biosphere.

We don't have the luxury of ideal scenarios. We have a number of flawed choices, and the time to make those is reducing rapidly.

6. Turbine manufacturing and maintenance

The production and maintenance of wind turbines involve energy-intensive processes and the use of materials such as rare metals. This can result in a significant environmental footprint far beyond an individual wind farm in geographies many of us will never see.

The compromise: This is a question of scale. The impact that fossil fuels have across the globe is beyond individual comprehension and, when considered relatively, the development, operation, and decommissioning of a wind farm offers a fraction of that impact and a vast amount of good in exchange. It's also helpful to consider that wind farms typically repay their embodied carbon within only a couple of years and continue to provide green energy for many years afterwards.

I'm not prepared to compromise on the obligation I feel to try and find a more regenerative way of life. I will continue to believe that wind and other renewable energy form a key part of that process.

7. Challenges in decommissioning

Wind farm decommissioning, which involves the removal and disposal of turbines and infrastructure, will also have environmental impacts, including soil disturbance and waste disposal issues.

The compromise: I hope that we don't even consider decommissioning wind farms until we've developed a fossil fuel-free future. In that world, we have solved the threat of climate change and found a way of regenerating the world around us. In that world, the challenges of decommissioning a wind farm will be so easily solved that this challenge causes me little to no concern.

Contradictions, compromises, and conclusions

In a world coloured by shades of grey, where contradictions and compromises are the currency of progress, the journey towards Scaling Conservation takes us through a terrain as complex as the challenges we face. Wind energy, with all its potential and pitfalls, stands at the crossroads of transformation.

Our landscapes have been shaped by our choices, both past and present. The pristine wilderness we yearn to protect is no longer untouched, and our climate is in chaos. While the road ahead may be fraught with discomfort and uncertainty, we must keep moving forward, for there is no turning back.

In harnessing the power of the wind, we harness the power of possibility. Wind farms, standing as monuments to our quest for sustainability, offer us the chance to rewrite the narrative of our future. They are the visible symbols of our commitment to a world where the balance between human progress and the preservation of nature is not a contradiction but a compromise.

In the end, this is not about absolutes or ideals but about finding a path forward, even if it is through the uncertain world of grey. We may not have the luxury of perfection, but we do still have choices.

On reflection

On Thursday 18 April 2024 we signed the formal option agreement with our wonderful partner Low Carbon for the development of the Glen Lednock Wind Farm. We're so proud to have helped design what we believe to be the most ecologically sensitive and environmentally ambitious wind farm ever proposed in the UK.

Here are some of the things we've done:

- We've worked hard with Low Carbon to agree potential access options and phasing plans to allow us to progress with plans for significant native broadleaf woodland creation and peatland restoration. These plans ensure we will never plant a tree and then be tasked with or consent to removing it.
- We've ensured that the proposal includes planting low-level ecological diverse species within wind protection zones. This is to maximise the potential of new habitat creation and restoration that will form part of the future of Invergeldie.
- We have agreed that the overall impact of the project will achieve positive impact on the restoration of peatland and improve the condition of more peat than may have be disturbed during any construction works.
- We have secured commitments for enhancing environmental and sustainability supervision onsite during works, and for reporting throughout the duration of the development.

In the piece written above, I committed to designing a whole landscape-level scheme, which created much greater positive impacts than any negative impact. If we're fortunate enough to successfully see a wind turbine turn at Invergeldie, I'm sure this will be the case there too.

I'd like to say a huge thank you to Ryan Newall and Merlin Carnegie from Low Carbon, and George Pawley, Chris White, and Dave Keir of Oxygen Conservation, for the progress made to date. I hope this establishes a new baseline for how wind farms are designed and ultimately developed in the UK and beyond.

Education in Conservation

Written August 2023

My summer journey of discovery, touring our portfolio of estates, has helped me gain a better understanding of a wider range of different perspectives and opinions. I recognise that I'm privileged to spend a considerable amount of time in an environmentally focused bubble, and I have a reminder in my to-do-list every Sunday to find a wider range of experiences and opinions.

Several key themes have presented themselves during the hundreds of conversations I've had. One that has caused much reflection has been the role of education in the fight against climate change and biodiversity loss, and by extension, the role of education in our work as we seek to Scale Conservation.

The importance of education

Without a doubt, every single person I've spoken to – whether from the Highlands of Scotland, the lowlands of Norfolk, or the rainforests of Devon – has recognised that there is still so much more to do to educate people about the causes, risks, and realities of climate change.

Over the last two years of the Oxygen Conservation Project, we've seen recognition of environmental issues increasing at a rate much faster than at any other time in history. At the same time, the volume and venom from those that are opposed to a change in their way of life has increased dramatically. Is this possibly the result of a lack of environmental education?*

The next generation

I think education, in the broadest sense, has done an excellent job of teaching young people about climate change. In that envelope, I include the traditional views of education, with people sitting in classrooms or lecture halls, reading from books, or listening to learned professors. I also include activists and campaigners, on social media and, increasingly, on traditional visual and print media. I don't think my or my parents' generation recognises that for large numbers of young teenagers, Greta Thunberg is a rock star!

That's not to say I think several aspects of the traditional education systems could not be enhanced. More time could be spent teaching young people how to learn, and to build successful learning habits continuously through their lives, to:

---

* I'm increasingly sure this is the case, ie that we have a problem in education, awareness, and understanding! While the absence of a price on carbon might be the cause of climate change, a lack of education might be one of the causes of our destructive economic system.

- Communicate better on a personal level
- Follow their passions
- Critically examine the world around them
- Engage in exploratory debate and civilised argument

I think it's important to stress that this paragraph was significantly improved following feedback from one of the country's leading teachers, Colin Hegarty, highlighting the value in leaving formal education to those that do it best.

Overall, I think teachers do an incredibly difficult job well, so thank you.

Lack of education or wilful ignorance?

I can only conclude that where I think education is lacking is with the government, the decision makers, the businesses, and the vast majority of people living in wilful ignorance. If that ignorance isn't due to a lack of education, we can only conclude it's due to something far more sinister, but let's not do that just now.

The horror stories, the fear, and showing anger to those aggressively exploiting and polluting the planet isn't working anymore. We need to engage with, listen to, and persuade those who are the hardest to reach. It's not all doom and gloom, however – I think there is much we can offer from an education perspective in this exact way, including:

1. Education by elevation

2. Education by inspiration
3. Education by culture
4. Education by opportunity
5. Education by necessity
6. Education by collaboration
7. Education by transparency
8. Education by visibility
9. Education by accessibility
10. Education by experience

1. Education by elevation

We are committed to elevating and professionalising the environment sector, creating a business and, by extension, an industry that is both aspirational and inspirational. In this way we hope to tap into a range of emotions that are much nicer to feel, more powerful in their ability to motivate change, and long-lasting – hope, excitement, and pride.

2. Education by inspiration

Our mission is to Scale Conservation, delivering positive environmental and social impact. Generating a profit is a result of what we do, not the purpose. In this way, we will build natural capital to become the world's biggest alternative asset class. We will also mobilise the capital investment needed to combat the biggest problem our planet has ever faced.

Who doesn't want to be part of that mission?

We're fortunate to find more and more people that want to help, including an increasing number from my generation, not just amazingly talented young people.

Money talks, and when we become the world's first conservation-focused unicorn company, we will open the hearts and minds of politicians, decision makers, financiers, and – perhaps most importantly – the many millions of individual investors, including those of my parents' generation. These investors, just like you and me, will have the option to put their pension contributions towards growing a sustainable income for their future, while simultaneously delivering a positive impact and giving us all a chance of creating a future at all.

3. Education by culture

We are also seeking to elevate the entire environment sector by creating a genuinely high-performance culture, based on environment, impact, and adventure. A culture that is achieving in attracting, developing, and – in the future – launching the most talented future leaders across the industry.

Within the short history of Oxygen Conservation, we're delighted to have helped launch and support a number of new environmental businesses, and we hope to be the inspiration or catalyst for so many more. If we can help you with your next startup idea, don't be afraid to connect and drop me a line.

4. Education by opportunity

One of the ways we're helping create the environmental leaders of now and the future is through the development of a wonderful annual, paid internship programme, which will soon start its third year. In the future we also plan to hold annual development camps for passionate environmentalists to learn from our experiences, achievements, mistakes, and adventures. We have already seen two interns successfully secure full-time permanent positions as part of the central Oxygen Conservation team and hope to see that pattern repeated in the years to come. It's important to remember that these people have secured roles because they're better than us, in a meaningful way – we don't sacrifice our performance bar for anyone or anything.

We are fortunate to have far too many talented candidates applying for the limited number of roles we can offer. We would therefore love to explore partnerships with other environmental organisations where there are vacant positions. If you're reading this and that's you, please let us know!

5. Education by necessity

Our work has provided and will continue to present us with an outstanding array of impossible problems, social/political contradictions, environmental compromises, and operational challenges. Some of the most interesting of these challenges have included working to demonstrate that it is possible to:

- Create debt financing facilities backed by natural capital

- Acquire sites with blue carbon potential ahead of the development of an independent blue carbon code

- Find ways to use legal instruments to stop the burning of precious moorland

- Establish agroforestry as part of a regenerative farming system

- Build a recruitment campaign inviting 'the misfits, the rebels, and the crazy ones' to be part of the Oxygen Conservation adventure

6. Education by collaboration

As we rose to meet each of these opportunities, we invited the smartest minds we could find, including those that understood the problem best, and sought to collaborate to find a deliverable solution.

This commitment to collaborative, experiential learning and sharing is as fundamental to our culture as wild swimming and sharing food. That's just who we are as people, and it's not going to change.

7. Education by transparency

In everything we do, we're committed to transparency, accessibility, learning, and sharing as much as possible. This doesn't mean we will give away proprietary information or commercially sensitive materials, but we strive to be as open as possible about everything else.

To achieve this level of transparency, we've invested in elevating the standard of visual media in the environment space, through world-class photography and videography. This is showcased on an elegant and easy-to-use website (all feedback welcome), which is updated regularly and features honest, accessible, and timely content. We've also provided a reference library and recommended books to help people that want to learn more about the environment, conservation, natural capital, and high-performance culture.

8. Education by visibility

In addition to video and audio materials, this year alone we've published around thirty articles capturing our experiences, we've been shortlisted for awards, we've appeared on podcasts, and we've been covered in print and online media. In the coming months we will launch our own Oxygen Conservation podcast, the *Shoot Room Sessions*. This will be filmed at our very own Shoot Room at the Mornacott Estate, giving the heart of a former pheasant shoot new life as our centre for shooting quality visual content. We're oversubscribed for interviews and podcast appearances, but please do contact us if you'd like us to add you to the forward look. We have also recently launched the Oxygen Conservation newsletter, Field Notes, which has been wonderfully well received. You can sign up to receive our newsletter here: oxygenconservation.com/contact-us.*

9. Education by accessibility

It is our intention that all our content inspires people to become more engaged with the natural world, want to find out more, and do what they can to help Scale Conservation.

We also believe that people need to experience the environment if they are to love it, respect it, and want to protect it. We're therefore committed to find the

---

* It is so special looking back reading about our podcast, which has now released more than forty episodes, with another thirty recorded. The *Shoot Room Sessions* have allowed us to showcase many wonderful friends and colleagues and share so much information about their work to help in the fight against climate change and the biodiversity collapse.

right balance between protection and accessibility. At an individual estate level, we have an increased range of ecotourism opportunities, alongside our portfolio of long-term local residential lets. These can be booked with our partner, CampWild, allowing you to experience Oxygen Conservation's landscape up close. Over the coming months and years, we will add more Oxygen Conservation Escapes to our website and hope to see as many people as environmentally appropriate visiting.*

10. Education by experience

We are driven by creating high-quality, luxury ecotourism offerings, which is very much a work in progress as we always seek to better our experience. By targeting individuals, families, and large groups, we hope to attract those hard-to-reach people – ideally those that arrive because of the exclusive experience and want to learn more about and become more involved in conservation. That feels like education.

Educating the harder-to-reach

While we're absolutely committed to creating aspirational and inspirational roles for future generations, our education efforts today are more focused on my and my parents' generation. These people are harder to reach, harder to persuade, and the generations incentivised to choose wilful ignorance over climate action.

---

* As mentioned later in this chapter, in April 2024 we officially launched Oxygen Escapes with our sustainable tourism offerings at Mornacott in Devon and Manor Farm in Shropham. Please do come and visit!

EDUCATION IN CONSERVATION

When we first started Oxygen Conservation, we knew education would play an important part in our work, and, naïvely, I thought that would be about educating the next generation. The reality is that the younger people are already far more engaged, informed, and it's they that are educating us.

On reflection

I am surer than ever that we have a problem in education, awareness, and understanding. It is therefore imperative that all of us share everything we know that might help be part of the solution in fighting climate collapse and the biodiversity crisis. We are not teachers in the conventional sense, we don't want to host classes, and we have no intention of opening up a visitors centre. We are absolutely committing, though, to sharing everything we know and have learned. We believe we are best placed to do that in the following ways:

- This book, and our continued commitment to providing thought leadership pieces
- Our *Shoot Room Sessions* podcasts
- Our monthly newsletter, *Field Notes*
- Our YouTube channel
- Our website

If you'd like to collaborate and together share what we collectively know – and don't know – please do get in touch.

Wild Camping, Wild Places, and Wildlife

Written January 2023

The fury around the legal decision to remove the right to wild camp on Dartmoor, the last place in England where this legal protection exists, is about so much more than the opportunity to spend a night under the stars. In fact, speaking to people who live, work, and – in this case perhaps even more importantly – play on Dartmoor, most have never wild camped, nor are they planning too. Despite this, it's vital to those people that the opportunity is there – not just for them but also for their children and their grandchildren. To me this speaks of wider issues in our relationship with the natural environment, and the loss of hope for the future of our planet and of life on Earth.

We are living at a time of great loss, and it is that loss that so many people are feeling. We are losing species by the day, seeing the next great mass extinction. We are losing acres of important and protected habitats across the globe. Every year we are losing the right to access and enjoy different parts of the natural world. Above all else, we're rapidly losing the potential of a future as the climate continues to crumble.

At Oxygen Conservation we are fortunate to be the custodians of some incredible landscapes, stretching from the Scottish Highlands to the South West of England, including a large area of Dartmoor. The subject of public access and enjoyment is therefore very real to Oxygen Conservation.

It is our belief that we can't hope for people to appreciate, respect, cherish, and even love nature if they can't experience it.

We were therefore delighted to see the areas of Dartmoor under our ownership being included in the land designated by the National Park as available for wild camping. As so many of our team have been inspired by this exceptional place, wondering at the dark skies and the millions of stars above, we hope others find that same inspiration when visiting.

We are also environmentalists and recognise that everything we do has an impact. As considerate and respectful as visitors might be, the very presence of people, especially in larger numbers, has an impact. This is the diametrically opposed challenge we face as responsible landowners and managers – increasing opportunities for public access while also protecting and improving that very environment. Like so many aspects of our relationship with the natural world, it is complicated, and we don't have all the answers. We do, though, have some ideas and are committed to learning so much more, in each of the different landscapes where we are responsible:

1. Making more of the natural world accessible
2. Making sensitive areas less accessible

3. Reaching a wider audience
4. Having more diverse environmental experiences

1. Making more of the natural world accessible

Much of the land across England, Scotland, and Wales is privately held and completely inaccessible. In many ways it's locked away, with little known about its flora, fauna, and funga. Several of the estates we've bought to date do not appear in historic environmental datasets because previous owners have said *Stay out*.

Our approach is different – we say *You're welcome*. We aspire to work with local communities and visitors to understand, protect, and improve these environments, in the process connecting neighbouring landscapes to help Scale Conservation beyond our boundaries. This is a slow process, and it is challenging in a lot of ways, but we're listening, we're open, and we're trying.

Part of this process will be to welcome more wild campers and provide a wider range of visitor and eco-tourism experiences across as much of our land as possible.

2. Making sensitive areas less accessible

We are fortunate to be responsible for some of the most precious habitats, including Atlantic rainforests, salt marshes, historic hay meadows, and some remarkably rare and special species. The impact of every footstep in these habitats is significant, so they must be visited rarely, delicately, and only when it is appropriate to do so; seasonality and weather conditions are especially important. These areas are therefore not suitable for public access.

We recognise this is the compromise we must all make to give nature a chance if we want these habitats to have a future. We hope they will recover to the point that they can one day be visited and enjoyed again.

3. Reaching a wider audience

Recognising that these precious habitats cannot be regularly accessed, we are committed to finding new ways for them to be appreciated in a more sustainable way. We are capturing data, imagery, video, and audio of each of our sites to share widely. Our aim is to share as much as possible and, in the process, reach a wider audience, allowing these special places, spaces, and species to be appreciated and enjoyed, albeit in ways other than in-person visits.

4. Having more diverse environmental experiences

As well as making more of the natural world available to people, we need to provide more diverse environmental experiences. Many people are starved of access to nature, and they are too often drawn to only a limited number of settings. This is unsustainable and results in damage and degradation to the very environment people are so keen to explore and enjoy.

In the same way we all need to reduce consumption, making more mindful choices about the resources we consume and the wider impact we have, the same is true of engaging with the most precious environments. We want to encourage people to step off the beaten track and spread our collective footprint more widely rather than concentrating it. That's why we're committed to

Scaling Conservation and, in the coming years, managing 250,000 acres of land across the UK for people and wildlife.

Creating advocates for nature

We have seen first-hand how experiencing the habitats we manage genuinely changes people. We've heard people's breathing slow. We've enjoyed seeing people relax in the rainforest of Dartmoor, wonder at the dark skies of Perthshire, giggle childlike at the experience of stepping on a saturated peat bog in the Borders, and be visibly moved while running their hands through the long grasses of a historic hay meadow in the Yorkshire Dales.

Every time we invite people to visit these places, we recognise the impact, both on the place and on the people. It makes us understand that one isn't more important than the other and know that we must always try to find the right balance between the two.

We can't hope for people to appreciate, respect, cherish, and even love nature if they can't experience it. We hope that we can create more advocates for the natural environment, and in the process Scale Conservation, by:

- Making more land accessible to people
- Protecting the most precious landscapes
- Finding new and creative ways for a wider audience to appreciate these places in a more sustainable way
- Increasing the impact of visits when we do interact with the environment

WILD CAMPING, WILD PLACES, AND WILDLIFE

On reflection

We've recently welcomed the wonderful Charlie Courtenay, the nineteenth Earl of Devon, to the *Shoot Room Sessions* (Stockdale, 2024c), where he talked passionately about the need to ensure public access. In fact, it was the topic of one of his first speeches in the House of Lords. He also spoke honestly about the realities of being a landowner, including experiencing antisocial behaviour, vandalism, terrorist bombs buried in his woods, and a sheep being bludgeoned to death with a baseball bat. Still, though, he is in favour of increased public access. Charlie recognises that landowners need to be recognised, rewarded, and protected in exchange for this access and that this provision is yet to be made. I recommend, once you've finished this chapter, that you listen to Charlie's *Shoot Room Session*. It – like him – is brilliant.

From our perspective, we've achieved a lot in terms of improving public access to more of the land we own and manage since the original article above. Our partnership with CampWild is giving more people the support they need to be comfortable to adventure more wildly, and their platform now features locations across many of our estates. Please do check them out.

There is still more to do, and there are still more solutions we need to find, particularly around how we improve access for things like mountain biking, fell running, and wild swimming, without exposing landowners to unmanageable risks or liabilities.

As a business, our appetite for risk exposure – especially from a health and safety perspective – cannot be the same as that of an individual landowner. The tools, techniques, and mitigations we need, for us to be comfortable with that

SCALING CONSERVATION

increased risk, are therefore a work in progress. This means I sadly can't invite you all to visit and wild swim in our lakes, rivers, lochs, and ponds, but I wouldn't be upset if you happened to find one of these spots without the invitation.

Oxygen Escapes: Ecotourism Conservation

Written April 2024

In recent years ecotourism has evolved from a niche travel choice to one of the most exciting changes in the travel industry. It is shaping the way we think about rest, relaxation, and our relationship with the natural world. Oxygen Conservation are committed to being at the forefront of this revolution, redefining ecotourism by introducing accessibility, authenticity, and comfort, alongside a genuine commitment to conservation and sustainability. We want to make ecotourism an inspirational and aspirational choice for travellers, particularly in the UK.

This article introduces the concept of Oxygen Escapes – a range of unique guest experiences. We'll outline our thinking about what defines ecotourism and describe our aspirations for redefining what is possible from a conservation-focused ecotourism offering.

Understanding ecotourism

Ecotourism, as defined by The International Ecotourism Society (TIES – lovely acronym), is 'responsible travel to natural areas that conserves the environment, sustains the wellbeing of the local people, and involves interpretation and education' (TIES, 2015).

This definition underscores the foundations of ecotourism, which we believe is built on three fundamental pillars:

1. Conservation: Positive environmental impact
2. Community: Positive social impact
3. Experience: Creating advocates through adventure

1. Conservation: Positive environmental impact

Positive environmental impact is the cornerstone of ecotourism and our mission at Oxygen Conservation. It's about active engagement in preserving and restoring natural environments, to create astonishing destinations complementary to the precious habitat we are fortunate to manage.

We are focused on landscape-level projects to Scale Conservation through habitat restoration, recovery, and creation. This produces a wonderful array of rare, precious, and often recovering landscapes that offer an awesome ensemble of wildlife, creating a magical combination for visitors to experience and enjoy.

2. Community: Positive social impact

The second pillar of ecotourism, community, relates to the socio-economic benefits of ecotourism. By creating unique accommodation and experiences, we can welcome more people to often remote, rural locations and communities. In the process, we can create jobs and opportunities that support and enhance local economies.

Successful ecotourism enterprises ensure that the communities living in and around our estates are stakeholders in conservation efforts and in the growing business that works to improve and protect these environments. This approach not only supports rural communities but also fosters a sense of ownership and responsibility towards environmental conservation.

3. Experience: Creating advocates through adventure

We believe that to love and protect the environment, you have to experience it. In experiencing nature first-hand – whether it's the Highlands of Scotland, the dark skies of the Scottish Borders, the wonderful coast of West Wales, or the magical rainforests of Dartmoor – we can begin to understand it better.

Seeing, hearing, smelling, and touching these superb environments is the best education of all. Education in this sense is about more than just imparting knowledge – it's about transforming visitors into informed advocates for the environment. Our intention is to raise awareness of environmental challenges and opportunities, and to promote sustainable practices. Education in ecotourism fosters a deeper understanding and appreciation of nature, leading to more responsible behaviour among guests and locals alike.

Oxygen Conservation's approach

In the same way that we have redefined what is possible in conservation, we're committed to achieving the same thing in ecotourism through the creation of Oxygen Escapes. By elevating ecotourism and integrating unique accommodation into spectacular landscapes, we hope to offer a blend of authenticity, sustainability, and comfort that will redefine what it means to travel responsibly and maybe one day even regeneratively (we all missed the opportunity for sustainability to be enough).

Environment and adventure

Adding to the excitement of Oxygen Escapes, we are committed to integrating outdoor adventures alongside conservation initiatives.

Adventure seekers can indulge in fell running, hill walking, e-biking, wild swimming, bouldering, kayaking, and paddle boarding, all designed to maximise engagement with nature while minimising environmental impact. These activities not only provide excitement but are also imbued with educational elements, enhancing visitors' awareness and appreciation of the natural environment.

This blend of excitement and environment (ecology, topography, geology, and hydrology) further establishes our role in transforming ecotourism into an attractive, sustainable, and adventurous experience.

Sustainable facilities and comfort

We aspire to create accommodation, facilities, and experiences that are a testament to how sustainability and comfort can coexist. Our accommodation is designed with both aesthetics and environmental authenticity in mind. Often delivered through the restoration and conservation of redundant or derelict buildings, we seek to repurpose as much of the existing structures as possible, embracing circular economic principles as far as is economically viable to do so.

We also offer awe-inspiring glamping experiences by combining sensitively located and specialist-sourced facilities, furniture, fixtures, and fittings.

Across all our ecotourism offerings, we aim to ensure that all operational details and practices – from cleaning supplies to energy provision – are as environmentally friendly as possible. Example of this are that we use solar energy, provide guests with our own carefully selected firewood, and incorporate refillable supplies where possible.

We have by no means solved all the challenges, but we're committed to iteration and evolution, making our accommodation, facilities, and experience less impactful on the natural environment every day.

Premium services and experiences

We are committed to offering wonderful experiences and delivering this through the attention to detail, kindness, and consideration we show all our guests and visitors. Locally sourced, organic ingredients, cooked by wonderfully skilled local experts, combined with exclusive, ecology-focused tours provide a unique experience without compromising environmental ethics.

Aspirational ecotourism and reducing the carbon footprint of adventure

By providing exceptional experiences to a limited number of visitors (too many people will always put pressure on the natural environment), we are committed to making ecotourism an aspirational choice. This is particularly impactful in the UK, where it can increasingly provide a compelling alternative to overseas holidays.

We hope this approach will appeal to those who would normally seek luxury, foreign-travel experiences but who are also increasingly conscious of their environmental impact. With Oxygen Escapes we aspire to reduce the reliance on international travel, thereby decreasing the carbon footprint associated with holidays, adventures, and incredible experiences.

Principles and practices in ecotourism

We are in the process of developing our ecotourism strategy, building on the learnings we've gained since acquiring the beautiful holiday cottages at the Mornacott Estate and the award-winning Wild With Nature glamping experience at Manor Farm in Shropham. As we continue to refine our thinking, we've developed a set of guiding principles, ensuring a sustainable and positively impactful approach:

- **Positive environmental impact:** We strive to deliver positive environmental impact through our work and through our ecotourism experiences and accommodation.

- **Positive social impact:** We work to ensure that visitors, local communities, and the Oxygen team have positive, enriching experiences based on the environment and shared adventures.

- **Positive economic impact:** We believe in prioritising local products, services, and employment, ensuring that the benefits of tourism are widely shared.

- **Direct financial benefits for conservation:** The revenues generated support the conservation efforts on each estate, helping us Scale Conservation and attracting additional investment into the natural capital economy.

- **Educational experiences and adventures:** We believe in offering educational experiences that raise sensitivity to various local (and global) issues, including environmental and social opportunities and challenges associated with our impact on the planet.

- **Gentler footprints:** We are committed to developing sustainable infrastructure and practices, reducing the environmental footprint of our facilities and limiting the number of visitors, such that we continually seek to balance and reduce our impact on the environment.

Launching Oxygen Escapes

We are not just participating in the ecotourism movement; we are committed to actively helping to scale authentic, conservation-based ecotourism. By integrating this authenticity with sustainability and comfort, we hope to offer a new, attractive form of travel that appeals to an increasingly wider audience. We intend that this approach will transform not only how we experience natural environments but also how we contribute to their improvement, protection, and long-term preservation.

Please look out for our new Oxygen Escapes website at www.oxygenescapes.co.uk and get in touch if you'd like more information about the Mornacott Estate (holiday cottages) or Wild With Nature (glamping).

On reflection

Travel isn't just about where you go – it's about how you experience it.

The old tourism model took; ecotourism gives back. Oxygen Escapes isn't about sacrificing comfort for sustainability; it's about proving they can thrive together – another of those wonderful contradictions we encounter on a daily basis. Every landscape we welcome guests into is more than a destination – it's a living, breathing conservation project, one that guests don't just visit, but actively experience.

Nothing connects people to our mission quite like ecotourism. It offers a different emotional connection. Over our first year operating Oxygen Escapes at Mornacott and Manor Farm, we've welcomed almost 1,000 guests, and we're certain to exceed that in year two. Soon, we'll introduce breathtaking stays at Dorback in the Cairngorms and Invergeldie in Perthshire. These aren't just places to visit – they're immersive experiences, woven into the very fabric of Oxygen Conservation. At the heart of it all are our Estate Managers and Rangers, the incredible narrators who bring each estate to life, making every visit unforgettable.

OXYGEN ESCAPES: ECOTOURISM CONSERVATION

If you've read any part of this book and felt even the slightest pull towards the landscapes we work so hard to protect, come and experience them for yourself. Take a dip in our rivers, roam our undulating landscapes and sit under star-painted skies. Our team will go to genuinely unreasonable lengths to make your visit extraordinary, because conservation isn't just about protecting nature – it's about inviting people to be part of it.

NINE
Call To Action!
Navigating The Future

The Green Revolution: How Natural Capital Is Emerging as the World's Most Important Alternative Asset Class

Written April 2024

In the vast, interconnected world we live in, the environment sector has often been sidelined, viewed through a lens of scepticism, and, for too many generations, outright disregarded. It stands, though, as one of the most critical challenges of our time, holding the key to the future of our planet.

The environment sector: A call for urgent transformation

This piece is an urgent call to investors, professionals, and young and talented individuals who feel a deep connection to our world's environmental plight. It's time to transform this sector from an overlooked niche into a central, driving force of our global economy and societal progress. The alternative is the end of life on Earth. Does any one of us want that on their conscience? I don't.

Breaking the stereotype: From fringe to forefront

For too long the environment sector has been unjustly labelled. It's been marginalised, mocked, and ridiculed, with people in the industry often described as tree-huggers, hippies, and eco-warriors. This portrayal has not only undermined its importance; it has also hindered serious investment and engagement.

It's crucial to dismantle these misconceptions and reframe the environment sector as what it truly is: a cornerstone for sustainable development and a prosperous future.

The role of advocacy, the price paid, and the unsung heroes

Throughout history, advocates for the planet have faced ridicule, opposition, and even imprisonment. Their fight against the destruction of our natural world often goes unrecognised, yet it is on these frontlines that the future of our environment is being shaped.

Environmental advocates' sacrifices highlight the urgency and importance of the cause – a cause that demands more than passive acknowledgement. Active support and respect are needed.

Elevating the environment sector through data-driven revolution

In a bid to elevate the entire environment sector, a significant shift is underway. By adopting a data-driven approach, the sector is evolving into a more effective, impactful force. This involves strategic land management, asset acquisition, and the growth of natural capital.

Utilising data not only enhances decision making; it also strengthens the sector's credibility and influence.

Bridging the gap: Business and philanthropy meet environmentalism

The relationship between business, philanthropy, and environmentalism is entering a new era. While philanthropy has played a crucial part to date, the scale of environmental challenges now demands an active role from the business sector, especially considering that industrialisation and business practices have caused environmental degradation and the crises we currently face.

Businesses' involvement in the restoration, recovery, and rewilding of the natural works is not just financially beneficial for all; it is also a moral and ethical imperative. The polluter should pay, and we're all polluters.

Beyond lip service: True collaboration and transparency in environmental efforts

The environment sector's historic call for collaboration has often been a one-sided conversation, with real partnership and transparency lacking. Now there's a movement towards a more authentic collaboration, where diverse voices are heard and actions are taken collectively.

This shift is not about reaching unanimous agreements or delaying actions – we don't have the time for that. It's about fostering a culture where every stakeholder's contribution is valued and utilised effectively, driving real, timely change.

From discussion to action: A new paradigm

The environment sector and, particularly, the public sector, have long equated meetings with progress and arranging further meetings as a success. The urgency of environmental issues demands more than just dialogue, though; it demands action.

The focus is shifting from meeting rooms to the field, where real change happens. Success is no longer measured by the frequency of meetings but by tangible outcomes, impactful interventions, and landscape-scale interventions.

Sharing the authentic, whole story: Successes, failures, and real people

Transparency is paramount in the modern environment sector. It's about being radically honest – sharing not just the successes but also the failures and learnings. This approach humanises the sector, making it more relatable and accessible.

Initiatives like podcasts and open communication channels showcase the real people behind the work, their stories, and their commitment, creating a more engaged and informed community.

Elevating standards: Attracting the best talent

The environment sector is becoming a high-performance field, setting high standards and attracting top talent. This shift is crucial – the challenges we face require the best of the best.

Competitive recruitment processes ensure that only those who are truly dedicated and capable contribute to this vital sector. This is about recognising the value of skilled professionals and offering them the compensation and recognition they deserve.

A new visual identity: Professional, impactful, and appealing

Gone are the days of amateurish branding in the environment sector. The focus is now on professional, high-quality visuals that reflect the sector's seriousness and impact. This involves investing in talented photographers, videographers, and designers to ensure that every aspect of the sector's work is presented in the best possible light.

This new image is crucial for attracting investment, talent, and public support.

Envisioning a successful, lucrative, and impactful future

The future of environmentalism lies in making it both profitable and successful. By creating an economy where it is more lucrative to protect the planet than to exploit it, we shift the paradigm entirely.

This approach will not only sustain the sector; it will also attract more investment and innovation, driving substantial and lasting change.

Join the movement: Engage, contribute, make a difference

If this vision resonates with you, it's time to get involved. Whether it's following our journey, criticising us and contributing ideas, or joining our team, your participation is vital. If you're reading this and think I'm talking rubbish, think things are totally fine, deny the existence of climate change, or just don't like the fact that things are changing, get ready to be really upset. You haven't seen anything yet!

A unified call for change

This article is a call to action. The environment sector is on the brink of a monumental shift, driven by data, technology, collaboration, and a commitment to real, impactful change. By embracing these changes, we can ensure a sustainable and prosperous future for our planet and for generations to come.

How are you going to be part of the solution?

On reflection

Nature isn't an afterthought – it's the economy. The smart money knows it. The old model of extraction and destruction is obsolete; the new model is regenerative and value creating.

Natural capital isn't a trend – it's the most important asset class in the world.

As I stepped off stage at a Blue Earth Summit in late 2024, I was asked why I keep talking about *making* natural capital an asset class. 'You've got more than 40,000 acres and hundreds of millions under management,' they said. 'It *is* an asset class.'

The future belongs to those who are bold enough to be different and willing to be criticised for doing so. Nature is no longer priceless – it's the most valuable thing on Earth.

The only question: will you be part of the future or left in the past?

Activist Leaders and Green Businesses

Written June 2023

Our world is teetering on the edge of a catastrophic environmental collapse, and the need for immediate and dramatic change is undeniable. Around the globe, passionate individuals are raising their voices, expressing their concerns, and advocating for a sustainable future. Peaceful protests have become a powerful tool for these activists, commanding attention to stress the urgency of the situation.

Dictates of conscience

I am increasingly unsure what I think about these campaigners and their tactics and methods. While we often seek simple answers, the complexity of the questions around environment activism requires deep contemplation, vigorous debate, and, ultimately, personal choice.

Supporting the cause

It is crucial to wholeheartedly support the cause of environmental preservation, climate action, and a restorative way of life. For far too long we have been plundering the planet. If we do not swiftly change our ways, it will soon be too late.

Climate protestors deserve our gratitude for the sacrifices they have made. Those people demand change and call for us all to act. Disruptive protests, although they may not align with everyone's preferences, have a proven historical impact in driving transformative change. Movements such as civil rights and gay rights, as well as campaigns against political conflicts and wars, have reshaped our world. It is unlikely we will achieve the change necessary to protect and improve the environment without passionate activists leading the way.

A great recent example of this is the efforts of Surfers Against Sewage (under the leadership of Hugo Tagholm) and the Rivers Trust, as well as wild swimmers, kayakers, and celebrity advocates from across the nation. Together, they achieved an extraordinary feat: obtaining a formal apology from Water UK for their failings in preventing sewage pollution (Lawson, 2023). Additionally, Water UK has pledged substantial investment aimed at enhancing the water quality in our rivers and bathing areas. This is a fantastic achievement, albeit the protestors are realistic that this is a small step in the right direction. Their cause continues.

Disruptive protests and divisiveness

It is important to acknowledge that protest, by its nature, disrupts the status quo and often leads to division. However, our appreciation should be directed towards the vast majority of environmental protestors who choose peaceful means to convey their concerns. Unfortunately, these brave individuals often become victims of aggression and violence. However, their resilience in the face of such challenges – that they are willing to continue to fight the good fight, despite the significant personal cost – only reinforces the urgency of addressing environmental issues.

It is true that a small fraction of protests have unintentionally disrupted public services, including the ambulance service, and caused inconvenience to people's lives. Such consequences are regrettable, and we must continuously strive for more effective and considerate ways to raise awareness and demand change. We must not lose sight of the bigger picture, though. Whether peaceful or disruptive, these protests have undeniably drawn attention and media coverage to the urgent challenges we all face. They have spurred conversations, ignited public discourse, and pushed environmental issues to the forefront of political and social agendas.

While I personally may not choose the same methods, if I were faced with the choice of standing on the frontline alongside peaceful protestors or of suppressing the calls for change, I would unhesitatingly align myself with the former. When my children ask me what I did when the planet was burning, I want to be able to say that I tried.

The role of business activism

Critics may argue that recognising the problem without actively joining the fight makes one a hypocrite. I don't disagree, but I firmly believe that everyone has a unique way of contributing to the fight against climate collapse and the biodiversity crisis.

As an environmentalist and entrepreneur, I have chosen to become an activist within the business community. People yearn for change, for a future on Earth, and – above all – for hope. Through our business, we strive to deliver positive environmental and social impact. Generating a profit is a result of what we do rather than the reason we do it. We are determined to show that business can be a force for good.

One of the most impactful business activists is Yvon Chouinard, the founder of outdoor apparel company Patagonia, who has been a vocal advocate for environmental sustainability for decades. In 2022 Patagonia transferred ownership of its company to the planet by placing 98% of its equity into a non-profit called the Holdfast Collective, which pledged to 'use every dollar received to fight the environmental crisis, protect nature and biodiversity, and support thriving communities, as quickly as possible' (McCormick, 2022). This is a radical example of environmental corporate leadership – one that will have considerable impact.

The need for activist leaders

To effect transformative change, we must become activist leaders – individuals and teams with resources, influence, and an unwavering commitment to urgently drive positive impact.

While divisive in his approach, especially following his purchase of Twitter (now X), it is inarguable that Elon Musk has revolutionised transportation and awakened the world to electric vehicles. By building Tesla into one of the most valuable companies in the world, Musk has played a key role in popularising and advancing battery technology and rapidly accelerated our transition away from petrol- and diesel-fuelled cars.

Oxygen Conservation, founded with the goal of being the world's first conservation-focused unicorn company, stands as a testament to our drive for urgent positive impact. Over the past two years, we have acquired nearly 30,000 acres for conservation and deployed tens of millions of pounds in capital in the fight against climate collapse and biodiversity loss. Our greatest impact, though, lies in us being a catalyst for Scaling Conservation and growing the wider natural capital economy. We aim to inspire others and mobilise resources by demonstrating that investing in natural capital can become the world's biggest alternative asset class. Only through the collaboration of campaigners, activists, and business leaders can we mobilise the trillions of pounds necessary to protect and enhance our natural world.

A personal choice

While I am grateful to courageous activists for sacrificing their civil liberties for the sake of change, I have chosen a different path. I believe that my role lies in creating change through the growth of natural capital and mobilising investments for the protection and improvement of our natural world.

I can only hope to stand on the shoulders of giants like Sir Richard Branson, the founder of Virgin Group. He has been actively involved in environmental initiatives for decades, but he also highlights the many contradictions and compromises associated with sustainability with his involvement in Virgin Airlines and Virgin Galactic. Notably, he launched the Carbon War Room (Branson, 2016), which works to accelerate the adoption of clean technologies and reduce carbon emissions. Branson has also committed to investing billions of dollars in renewable energy projects and pledged future profits from Virgin air and rail interests to the fight against global warming (Milmo and Adam, 2006). He also personally champions projects in conservation and species reintroduction.

My plea remains the same as the activist and business leaders highlighted in this piece: let us all unite in demanding an end to:

- Our dependency on oil
- Deforestation of incredible ecosystems across the globe
- The pollution of our oceans, seas, and rivers

These are some of the most pressing challenges we face, but they all can be achieved with individual and collective will. How many more wake-up calls does our planet need to give us before we realise that our current way of living can only lead to catastrophe?

In these dire times of environmental crisis, our world yearns for leaders who will rise as passionate activists for change. Whether through peaceful protests or innovative green businesses, each one of us has the power to contribute to the journey towards a sustainable future. Let us inspire others; mobilise the necessary resources; and fight relentlessly for the conservation, protection, and growth of our natural capital. Together, we can create hope and secure a promising future on planet Earth for generations to come. Perhaps too, with our collective efforts, we can give others the confidence to lay down their superglue and orange paint as change becomes an unstoppable force for good, reshaping and restoring our world for the better.

On reflection

A few months ago, I sat reading *The Lorax* by Dr Seuss to my daughter, Emma. The book delivers a cautionary tale about environmental responsibility, depicting how the greedy Once-ler's exploitation of the natural world leads to its destruction, despite the protests of the Lorax, who speaks for the trees (Seuss, 1971).

As the book finished, Emma asked whether people were really allowed to cut down trees. I responded by saying that sadly they are, but that we're trying to plant many more than they cut down. Emma paused, looked up at me and said, 'Don't *try!*'

We need this to be the time of the activist founder and the business leader.

I *will* continue to hold myself to this standard!

Will We Be the Generation That Saved or Killed the World?

Written August 2023

In the not-so-distant future, the year 2030 looms ominously as a harbinger of humanity's failure to adequately address the perils of the climate crisis and the mass extinction of the vast majority of biodiversity.

A world heavily impacted by the consequences of our actions is rapidly unfolding before our eyes. This serves as a sobering testament to the urgent need for global action, whereas we seem intent on only making matters worse, pursuing a seemingly suicidal strategy of absolute North Sea oil extraction.

We are now at the decision point where we have to decide whether we will be the generation that killed or saved the world.

What will 2030 look like?

As we peer into this tumultuous future, the ramifications of unchecked climate change are becoming painfully evident, leaving no doubt about the need for immediate and decisive measures to mitigate its devastating effects. Here are just some of the devastating effects we are already starting to experience, which could be inescapable realities by 2030:

1. Global boiling
2. Extreme weather events
3. The great extinction
4. Economics
5. The demise of happiness

1. Global boiling

Rising global temperatures have become an unrelenting force, and global boiling wreaks havoc on our planet's ecosystems and human communities alike. The polar ice caps are almost gone, causing sea levels to surge and coastal regions to be submerged under relentless waves. Major coastal cities such as London, Miami, New York City, and Bangkok are at risk of becoming relics of the past, battered by tropical storms. They could, ultimately, be swallowed by the rapidly rising tides.

Millions of people have already been displaced, forced to flee their homes and seek refuge in increasingly overcrowded inland areas. The harrowing realities of climate-induced migration have become an unprecedented humanitarian crisis, straining resources, and fuelling continuous and sadly increasingly violent social unrest.

2. Extreme weather events

Extreme weather events have become the new norm in this devastated world. Fierce hurricanes, intensified by boiling ocean waters, sprint across almost the entire globe with a ferocity never witnessed before.

The frequency and intensity of droughts and heatwaves have multiplied, decimating agricultural systems and exacerbating food insecurity.

Crop failures have become a grim reality, leading to soaring food prices, widespread hunger, and famine.

The very fabric of our global food system has been irreparably damaged, leaving vulnerable populations in perpetual fear which has fuelled political conflict.

3. The great extinction

Biodiversity loss has pushed countless species to the brink of extinction. Iconic creatures such as polar bears, orangutans, and coral reefs have become tragic casualties of our disregard for the natural world.

Ecosystems once teeming with life and vitality have been reduced to silent wastelands, devoid of their intricate web of interdependence. The collapse of ecosystems disrupts critical services such as pollination, soil fertility, and water purification, further exacerbating the challenges we face in securing a sustainable future for our planet.

4. Economics

The cost of infrastructure damage, disaster relief, and healthcare strains national budgets to their limits. The bankrupt insurance industry faces an existential crisis, grappling with an onslaught of claims and the unprecedented scale of climate-related risks.

The global economy is thrown into a tailspin as supply chains are disrupted, markets destabilised, and industries devastated by the cascading effects of climate-induced disruptions. In many parts of the world, the consequences of hyperinflation alongside climate disasters make money worthless.

The once-thriving tourism sector, reliant on pristine environments and natural wonders, is dealt a crippling blow as destinations become uninhabitable or unrecognisable.

5. The demise of happiness

With the relentless onslaught of environmental disasters and continuous social disruption, mental health issues have skyrocketed. The psychological toll of losing loved ones, witnessing the destruction of homes and livelihoods, and constantly fearing the next catastrophe has become an unbearable burden for many. Healthcare systems are overwhelmed and ill-equipped to cope with the magnitude of this crisis.

The collective trauma of a world torn apart by climate change leaves an indelible mark on future generations. Their outlook on life and hope for a stable future is forever altered. Birth rates have rapidly declined as widespread chemical pollution of our food and water result in serious fertility challenges, and because the pressures of life make many decide that this isn't a world they would want to be born into.

Is this future inevitable?

Is it too late? The honest truth is that it might be. July 2023 was the hottest month on record, with the twenty-four hottest days in a row. Much of Europe sits devastated as wildfires rip across the landscape, yet in the UK we experienced one of the wettest Julys this century. Rapidly increasing ocean temperatures have resulted in 100% mortality rates of coral reefs in Florida, with significant numbers of marine and freshwater fish deaths as water is no longer able to hold oxygen. The global ice caps are melting at an alarming rate and have failed to recover any of their winter ice.

All this is happening while our government continues to renege on environmental and climate commitments, focusing instead on exploiting new gas and oil extraction. This can only be described as knowingly committing global suicide.

Will we hear the wake-up call?

The events of 2023 and this glimpse into the world of 2030 must serve as a powerful wake-up call – a dire warning of what lies ahead if we fail to act decisively. The urgency to significantly reduce greenhouse gas emissions, transition to renewable energy sources, protect and restore the natural world, and embrace a more regenerative way of life has never been greater. It is imperative that businesses, communities, and individuals come together in a concerted effort to address the climate crisis head on.

My promise is that we at Oxygen Conservation will do everything we can to try and save enough of the world to give the next generation a chance, and to put right what we've all done so wrong for so long. Here are the main things we feel it is vital we all focus on:

1. A natural capital economy
2. The role of business
3. Nature-based solutions
4. The way we live
5. Collaboration
6. Education and awareness

1. A natural capital economy

Transitioning to a natural capital economy must be at the forefront of our collective agenda in recognising the true value and impact such an economy will have on the natural world. Investments in renewable energy infrastructure such as solar and wind power must be scaled up exponentially. The shift from fossil fuels to clean and sustainable energy sources not only reduces greenhouse gas emissions but also creates new job opportunities and stimulates economic growth.

Public awareness campaigns, media engagement, and grassroots initiatives can mobilise communities, inspiring them to take action and hold policymakers and businesses fully accountable for their environmental impact. The true carbon and nature-based costs of what we do must be factored into future economic systems if we are to truly value the world around us.

This is one of the many painfully ironic and frustratingly ignorant aspects of the climate crisis. Even for those people who are only financially motivated, there is no business case for the end of life on Earth. Delivering positive environmental and social impact is the only sustainable way to preserve and grow capital.

2. The role of business

The business community has a vital role to play in shaping a sustainable future. Embracing circular economy principles, reducing (and eliminating) waste, and adopting environmentally restorative practices can drive innovation, improve resource efficiency, and create a more sustainable business landscape.

Investors and financial institutions should prioritise environmentally positive investments, rewarding companies that demonstrate a commitment to ESG principles. Collaboration between businesses, future governments, and civil society is essential, to foster a transition to a natural capital economy and ensure a just and equitable transition for all.

3. Nature-based solutions

Promoting regenerative agriculture practices, reforestation, water conservation, and ecosystem restoration can help build the resilience of our food systems and ensure the wellbeing of both rural and urban populations.

Nature-based solutions to carbon sequestration and storage are the only viable option to buy civilisation enough time for future generations to develop a technological solution to capture carbon at scale.

4. The way we live

We must support research and development in innovative technologies that promote energy efficiency, carbon capture, and sustainable transportation. We also need to face the reality that we must consume less, compromise more, and be more mindful of our impacts in every aspect of how we live our lives.

5. Collaboration

Collaboration between nations is paramount at every level, as climate change knows no boundaries. Collective action is the only path forward.

We face a simple choice of a collaborative future working together to protect against the impact of a changing climate, or preparing for worldwide climate wars.

6. Education and awareness

Education and awareness play a pivotal role in this transformative journey. We must empower individuals with the knowledge and tools to make sustainable choices in their daily lives. Education systems should integrate climate change into their curriculum, fostering a deep understanding of its causes, consequences, and solutions.

Perhaps this is actually dated thinking, as every young person I meet is so well self-taught, via the range of material from across the globe available digitally.

The next generation will change politics

You'll note I left the governments out of the list above. It is clear that they have little to no interest in being part of the solution. Until they demonstrate otherwise, I'll assume the UK government at least is largely going to do nothing and that anything they do will not help.

I am also sure that this will be one of the last general elections in the UK that isn't fought almost exclusively on environmental and climate-based issues. The young people voting in the next election will be more engaged, more informed, and more active than any generation before theirs. They will demand a solution to the problems previous generations have caused, and they'll be right in doing so – they will be the ones who have to pay off our debts.

An alternative view of 2030

Ultimately, the world of 2030 need not be a dystopian vision of climate chaos. This year could be a turning point – a moment when humanity rallied together to address the greatest challenge of our time. By honestly embracing the urgency and magnitude of the climate crisis and biodiversity collapse, we have the power to rewrite the narrative and forge a future where sustainability, resilience, and harmony with nature are the cornerstones of our existence.

If we're not going to heed the warning of this month's environmental headlines, or the glimpse into the future offered in this article, then it will almost certainly be too late.

We can all choose to use this moment as a rallying cry for bold and decisive action, not as a distant regret. The world heavily impacted by climate change in 2030 is not an inevitability; rather, it is a potential reality we can prevent. The time to act is now, for the sake of our planet, for the delicate balance of life, and for future generations. If not us, who? If not now, when? Together, we can create a future where the dire consequences of climate change are but a distant memory, and a sustainable and thriving world is our enduring legacy.

Do we want to be the generation that killed or saved the world?

On reflection

I wouldn't change a word of this article. We don't have long left to decide.

Hope Is Just a Four-Letter Word

Written June 2023

In the battle against climate change, it is important to recognise that anger and fear have their place and many of us feel those emotions every day. Above all, though, it is hope that can truly propel us towards a sustainable future. While anger and fear are powerful emotions, they burn hot and fast (ironically, just like fossil fuels), often leading to abrupt and short-lived responses. In contrast, hope offers longevity and resilience, allowing us to overcome obstacles and inspire collective action.

Strength in hope

This piece explores the transformative power of hope in the fight against climate change, highlighting its ability to unite, motivate, and create positive change, ultimately concluding with why it's the weapon of choice at Oxygen Conservation.

The nature of anger and fear

While I know anger and fear are very different emotions, they are often used together when thinking about what we've done to the natural world. I will use both almost interchangeably here.

Anger and fear are intense (and understandable) emotions that can ignite powerful reactions. However, much like fossil fuels, they tend to burn out quickly, leaving us drained and unable to sustain long-term efforts. These negative emotions are also unpleasant to carry, such that our biology often seeks to shed them, leading to a temporary motivation rather than a lasting commitment or drive for change.

Hope, on the other hand, offers endurance and perseverance, allowing us to navigate the challenges of climate change with a sense of possibility and optimism.

From stopping to inspiring

Anger and fear are often associated with a desire to stop or prevent certain actions or behaviours – very much a feature of the Just Stop Oil campaigners. While this is crucial in addressing climate change, and of course we need to stop the use of fossil fuels, hope takes us a step further by inspiring action and innovation.

Hope creates an atmosphere of possibility, encouraging us to imagine and create more sustainable and regenerative solutions. Instead of focusing solely on what needs to be stopped, hope motivates us to think about what can be achieved, driving us towards positive change and a brighter future. Think about the transformative impact of Tesla in the electrification of vehicles and the effect that has on the wider industry.

The unifying power of hope

Anger and fear can be divisive, pushing people away and limiting collaboration. In contrast, hope unites and inspires collective action.

When we share a sense of hope, we can come together, form alliances, and work towards common goals. Hope transcends boundaries and encourages individuals, communities, and nations to collaborate and to pool resources, knowledge, and efforts to address the complex challenges of climate change and the biodiversity crisis. By fostering a shared sense of hope, we can create a global movement for sustainability, amplifying our impact to find a future for this and the next generation.

Endurance of hope

Motivation fuelled by anger or fear is often temporary. It lacks the resilience needed to sustain long-term action.

Conversely, hope has the power to endure, in many ways just like renewable energy. It becomes part of our identity, shaping our beliefs, values, actions, and collaborations. By cultivating hope, we create a lasting commitment to positive change, persevering even when faced with setbacks or slow progress. Hope inspires continuous learning, adaptation, and growth, driving us towards a sustainable and regenerative future.

Choosing hope

In a world filled with reasons to be angry and scared about the state of our planet, some believe that even talking about, never mind choosing hope becomes a radical and courageous act.

We believe in talking about a positive future and about being the world's first unicorn-focused conservation company, knowing that if we achieve this goal, we will have helped create a whole natural capital ecosystem that cannot fail to produce a more regenerative way of life.

By embracing hope, we endeavour to inspire others to do the same, fostering a collective mindset that empowers individuals and communities to take action. Choosing hope does not mean ignoring the challenges we face, or never being angry or scared. It means believing that change is possible and knowing that our actions matter in achieving that change.

Hope at Oxygen Conservation

Every day gives us hope in so many different ways, including:

- The people we've been able to attract to support our ambition to Scale Conservation – both experienced professionals and the talented new generation of environmental professionals who astound me with their knowledge, creativity, and passion

- The scale of investment we've been able to mobilise, thanks to an amazing group of investors; and the multiple offers of additional, transformation investment wanting to help deliver change at a landscape scale

- The interest, positivity, support, and recognition we've attracted from so many individuals and groups, which helps demonstrate the power of momentum and continues to build hope

HOPE IS JUST A FOUR-LETTER WORD

We believe hope is our most potent weapon in the battle against climate change. While anger and fear have their roles in highlighting the urgency of the crisis, it is hope that sustains our motivation, unites us in collective action, and paves the way for a sustainable future. Hope offers endurance, resilience, and inspiration, allowing us to envision a world where humanity and the environment thrive together.

By choosing hope, we reject the notion of helplessness, embracing instead the power of individual and collective agency to build a more resilient and regenerative world for ourselves and for future generations.

It's your choice, but we choose hope!

On reflection

I hope you've enjoyed this book.

I hope you've learned from our experiences and our mistakes.

I hope you're inspired by our achievements and our successes.

Above all, I hope you've decided to be part of the generation that saved the world.

Conclusion

To conclude this book, we have adapted one more article, 'The Organisation of the Nonobvious', written in May 2024, which summarises the main principles and purpose of the work we do at Oxygen Conservation.

In the face of the biggest parallel challenges of our time – climate collapse and the biodiversity crisis – we need an entire new set of tools and techniques to help the natural world fight back against our exploitation and abuse.

At Oxygen Conservation we have embraced this mandate by instituting practices and strategies that many – especially the traditional conservationist – might consider nonobvious.

Addressing the nonobvious

The following ideas, innovations, and actions are fundamental to our work to Scale Conservation, delivering positive environmental and social impact, while generating a profit as a result of what we do rather than the reason we do it.

Natural capital financing

We are leveraging the concept of natural capital to sustain our conservation initiatives. By quantifying the ecosystem services our projects provide, we create a viable finance model that reinvests nature's dividends back into its preservation, demonstrating that economic and environmental interests can not only align but also thrive together.

Holistic restoration projects

Our project portfolio spans a diverse array of initiatives, from peatland restoration to afforestation and renewable energy. This holistic approach ensures we address many more of the challenges associated with environmental degradation simultaneously, showcasing the interconnectedness of our ecosystems and our multifaceted strategy in nurturing them.

Regenerative practices

At the heart of our operations are regenerative practices that enhance soil health, biodiversity, and carbon sequestration. By helping the land heal itself through these methods, we not only restore ecosystems but also pave the way for sustainable land use that future generations can inherit and build on.

Biodiversity advocacy

Our commitment to biodiversity goes beyond mere conservation; it provides advocacy for the intrinsic value of all life forms. We champion the preservation of a myriad of species and habitats, not simply prioritising single species.

Forward-thinking partnerships

Collaboration is key to our strategy, and we choose partners who share our vision and values. This ethos is exemplified by our alliances with businesses like Oxygen House, Triodos Bank, Burges Salmon, and the Galbraith Group, as well as partnerships with charities like the Woodland Trust, the Wildlife Trusts, the Rivers Trust, and many others. We are combining resources and expertise to foster sustainable environmental solutions.

Radical transparency

Radical transparency underpins our operational ethos. By maintaining honesty, clarity, and accountability in our actions, we not only foster trust among our stakeholders but are also trying to reset a benchmark for integrity in the conservation sector. One of the most popular things we've done is organising the list of ways we have been and continue to be criticised.

Knowledge sharing

We believe in the power of knowledge to inspire and enact change. Through our website, podcast, and long-form publications, we organise, categorise, and share our learnings and insights, engaging with the wider community to foster a collective understanding and appreciation of conservation's critical role.

Scalable impact

Over the past four years, we've acquired eleven wonderful estates, totalling just over 43,000 acres. Our model is designed to demonstrate adaptability and replication, allowing us to amplify our impact across different ecosystems and geographies. This scalability ensures that the lessons we learn and the successes we achieve can serve as blueprints for broader environmental stewardship.

Cross-sector engagement

We extend our collaborative efforts beyond the environment sector, engaging with diverse industries to integrate conservation into various facets of society and the economy. This includes:

- Advocating for better access and enjoyment of the environment by working with CampWild
- Supporting regenerative agricultural working with the wonderful Brewer Family at Wood Advent Farm
- Committing to renewable energy development by working with Low Carbon

We believe that cross-sector engagement fosters innovative solutions and broadens the scope of our impact.

Adaptive land management

Our adaptive management practices are responsive to evolving environmental data and research, ensuring our conservation methods are both effective and resilient. This approach allows us to navigate the complexities of ecosystem restoration with agility and informed precision.

Ecotourism initiatives

Integrating ecotourism into our land management practices offers a dual benefit:

- It educates and engages guests.
- It generates funds that are reinvested into conservation.

Ecotourism initiatives exemplify how environmental stewardship can coexist with economic viability. As we develop our own unique ecotourism offerings, we've added beautiful holiday cottages at Mornacott in Devon and the award-winning Wild With Nature glamping experience at Manor Farm in Shropham.

Renewable energy integration

Incorporating renewable energy into our conservation lands not only reduces our carbon footprint but also exemplifies our commitment to helping in the process of transitioning to net zero. This integration demonstrates the synergies between conserving natural habitats and advancing renewable energy technologies. Progress in the environment sector is so often about contradictions and compromises. Advocating for green infrastructure within the natural environment is perhaps the best example of that.

Innovative technology use

We harness cutting-edge technologies to enhance our conservation efforts, utilising data analytics, remote sensing, drones, AI, and other tools to monitor, analyse, and optimise our land management progress. This technological integration and organisation underscores our commitment to precision and efficiency in our mission.

Organising the nonobvious

In orchestrating this symphony of nonobvious elements into a coherent and innovative business model, we've exemplified a pioneering approach to environmental regeneration and conservation. By harnessing big data analytics for enhanced landscape assessment, pioneering unconventional land acquisition strategies, leveraging natural capital for sustainable financing, and implementing holistic restoration practices, we have crafted a greenprint for the future of conservation that is as ingenious as it is impactful.

Our commitment to regenerative practices, biodiversity advocacy, radical transparency, and knowledge sharing not only redefines the conservation paradigm but also demonstrates a robust business model that is adaptable, scalable, and deeply integrated with various sectors. This model not only fosters cross-sector engagement and adaptive land management; it also integrates ecotourism and renewable energy initiatives, positioning our organisation at the forefront of the global transition to a more sustainable and equitable relationship with our planet.

Through these multifaceted efforts, we intend to not only address the critical environmental challenges of our time but also showcase how aligning ecological integrity with innovative business practices can create a resilient, thriving, and sustainable future, as part of a genuine natural capital economy.

The future of wealth is wild

The world is changing – whether we like it or not! Natural capital is no longer a hopeful theory or a distant ambition – it's a reality. We've spent this book dismantling old paradigms, questioning assumptions, and proving that conservation isn't a charitable endeavour; it's an economic imperative. The shift is happening. Land, water, biodiversity – these are now not just ecological assets but real investable ones. They are the foundation of a new economy, one that values regeneration over extraction, resilience over short-termism, and impact over illusion.

We are only at the beginning. Owning over 43,000 acres and managing hundreds of millions of pounds in natural capital isn't just proof of concept – it's a declaration of intent. If the first step was proving that nature is an asset class, the next is to reshape the entire financial system to reflect that truth. The question isn't whether conservation and capitalism can coexist; it's how fast we can make it the default. That is the essence of our next book, *Rewilding Wealth*.

This isn't about doing less harm; it's about creating more value – value that compounds over generations, that restores ecosystems while generating financial returns, and that builds a world where wealth and wellbeing are inseparable. The next frontier isn't just protecting what remains; it's actively rebuilding what was lost and embedding that into our environmental, social, and economic DNA.

For decades, we've heard that protecting the planet requires sacrifice. That wealth and environmental responsibility exist in opposition. That the cost of doing business is environmental degradation. That is not just outdated; it's fundamentally wrong. The most successful businesses of the future will be those that align with nature rather than exploit it. The most enduring investments will be in landscapes, biodiversity, fresh air, and clear water. The companies that thrive will be those that understand that profit is not the enemy of purpose – it is the enabler of it.

Will you cling to the old, extractive economy, or will you help build something new? Will you stand on the sidelines, or will you invest, innovate, and lead? We don't have time for passive participation. The world needs action, ambition, and inspiration. It needs leaders who understand that the future of finance is the future of the planet.

Natural capital isn't just the most important asset class in the world – it is the future of wealth itself. It's time to rewild our thinking, our investments, and our ambitions.

Bibliography

Allen, D, *Getting Things Done: The art of stress-free productivity* (Piatkus, 2015)
Allen, K, 'FT Factcheck: Do we use more land for golf courses than we do for homes?', *Financial Times* (24 October 2016), www.ft.com/content/79772697-54e4-32c9-96d7-5c1110270eb2, accessed 5 February 2025
Associated Press, 'Welcome to the mobile age: NFL conference title games filled with dual-threat QBs' (Fox Sports, no date), www.foxsports.com/articles/nfl/welcome-to-the-mobile-age-nfl-conference-title-games-filled-with-dualthreat-qbs, accessed 27 February 2025
Ballew, M et al, 'The Greta Thunberg Effect' (Yale Program on Climate Change Communication, 26 January 2021), https://climatecommunication.yale.edu/publications/the-greta-thunberg-effect, accessed 27 February 2025
Bechtold, T, 'How the analytics movement has changed the NFL and where it has fallen short', *The Analyst* (2021), https://theanalyst.com/eu/2021/04/evolution-of-the-analytics-movement-in-the-nfl, accessed 27 February 2025

Belsky, S, 'Create, then deliver', *Medium* (2 December 2014), https://scottbelsky.medium.com/create-then-deliver-8968eb23c871, accessed 11 February 2025

Belsky, S, *The Messy Middle: Finding your way through the hardest and most crucial part of any bold venture* (Penguin, 2018)

Blackstone, 'Mondays at Blackstone' (Blackstone, 2016), https://youtu.be/watch?v=k8iZe9NsGto, accessed 9 February 2025

Bock, L, *Work Rules! Insights from inside Google that will transform how you live and lead* (John Murray, 2015)

Branson, R, *The Virgin Way: Everything I know about leadership* (Portfolio, 2014)

Branson, R, 'The story of the Carbon War Room' (Virgin, 28 October 2016), www.virgin.com/branson-family/richard-branson-blog/story-carbon-war-room, accessed 16 February 2025

Brown, T, 'Design principles to solve major problems' (Talks at Google, 2009), https://youtu.be/watch?v=lAd1E8vWEWg, accessed 13 February 2025

Butler, P, 'RSPB criticised by watchdog for accusing politicians of being liars on X', *The Guardian* (14 August 2024), www.theguardian.com/environment/article/2024/aug/14/rspb-criticised-by-watchdog-for-accusing-politicians-of-being-liars-on-x, accessed 15 February 2025

Chapagain, A and James, K, *The Water and Carbon Footprint of Household Food and Drink Waste in the UK* (WRAP, March 2011), www.wrap.ngo/sites/default/files/2020-12/The-water-and-carbon-footprint-of-household-food-and-drink-waste-in-the-UK.pdf, accessed 6 February 2025

Clear, J, *Atomic Habits: An easy and proven way to build good habits and break bad ones* (Random House Business, 2018)

The Cycling Channel, 'Bradley Wiggins: A year in yellow' (18 August 2019), www.youtube.com/watch?v=MASQk7E7O1E, accessed 27 February 2025

Defra, *British Food and Farming at a Glance* (Defra, 2016), www.gov.uk/government/publications/british-food-and-farming-at-a-glance, accessed 5 February 2025

Defra, *United Kingdom Food Security Report 2021: Theme 2: UK food supply sources* (Defra, 2023), www.gov.uk/government/statistics/united-kingdom-food-security-report-2021/united-kingdom-food-security-report-2021-theme-2-uk-food-supply-sources, accessed 5 February 2025

BIBLIOGRAPHY

Defra, *Nature Markets Framework progress update March 2024* (UK Government, March 2024), www.gov.uk/government/publications/nature-markets-framework-progress-update-march-2024/nature-markets-framework-progress-update-march-2024, accessed 03 February 2025

Defra Press Office, 'Government response to "Our Troubled Rivers" documentary', *Defra in the Media* (6 March 2023), https://deframedia.blog.gov.uk/2023/03/06/government-response-to-our-troubled-rivers-documentary, accessed 17 March 2025

Difford D, 'Where does the British public stand on hunting?' (YouGov, 18 November 2024), https://yougov.co.uk/society/articles/50958-where-does-the-british-public-stand-on-hunting, accessed 27 February 2025

DLUHC, 'Land use statistics: England 2022' (Department for Levelling Up, Housing & Communities, 27 October 2022), www.gov.uk/government/statistics/land-use-in-england-2022/land-use-statistics-england-2022, accessed 5 February 2025

DLUHC, 'Nutrient neutrality announcement: Explanatory paper' (Department for Levelling Up, Housing and Communities, 11 September 2023), www.gov.uk/guidance/nutrient-neutrality-announcement-explainer, accessed 19 February 2025

Ebrahim, N, 'Chaos in Dubai as UAE records heaviest rainfall in 75 years', *CNN* (18 April 2024), https://edition.cnn.com/2024/04/17/weather/dubai-rain-flooding-climate-wednesday-intl/index.html, accessed 18 February 2025

Elkington, J, *Green Swans: The coming boom in regenerative capitalism* (Fast Company Press, 2021)

Environment Agency, 'Summary of the state of the environment: Soil' (Environment Agency, 2023), www.gov.uk/government/publications/state-of-the-environment/summary-state-of-the-environment-soil, accessed 5 February 2025

Feedback Global, *Farmers Talk Food Waste: Supermarkets' role in crop waste on UK farms* (Feedback Global, February 2018), https://feedbackglobal.org/wp-content/uploads/2018/08/Farm_waste_report_.pdf, accessed 6 February 2025

Ferriss, T, *The 4-Hour Work Week: Escape the 9–5, live anywhere and join the new rich* (Vermilion, 2011)

Finch, T et al, 'Spatially targeted nature-based solutions can mitigate climate change and nature loss but require a systems approach', *One Earth*, 6/10 (2023), 1350–1374, https://doi.org/10.1016/j.oneear.2023.09.005

485

The Food Foundation, *From Purse to Plate: Implications of the cost of living crisis on health* (The Food Foundation, 2023), https://foodfoundation.org.uk/sites/default/files/2023-03/TFF_Cost%20of%20living%20briefing.pdf, accessed 6 February 2025

Gentleman, A, 'Mother of girl whose death was linked to air pollution sues UK government', *The Guardian* (25 January 2024), www.theguardian.com/environment/2024/jan/25/mother-of-girl-who-died-from-air-pollution-sues-uk-government, accessed 15 February 2025

GFS, 'UK threat' (Global Food Security, 2022), www.foodsecurity.ac.uk/challenge/uk-threat, accessed 5 February 2025

Google, 'Our approach to Search' (Google, no date), www.google.com/intl/en_us/search/howsearchworks/our-approach, accessed 10 February 2025

GOV.UK, 'Natural Capital Committee (NCC)' (GOV.UK, no date), www.gov.uk/government/groups/natural-capital-committee, accessed 17 March 2025

Harrabin, R, 'Brexit "will enhance" UK wildlife laws – Gove', *BBC News* (19 June 2017), www.bbc.co.uk/news/science-environment-40331919, accessed 19 February 2025

Hayter, P and Miller, T, *Cricket 2.0: Inside the T20 revolution* (Wisden, 2019)

Heal, A et al, 'What is the British countryside really for?', *Financial Times* (19 October 2023), https://subs.ft.com/products?location=https%3A%2F%2Fig.ft.com%2Fuk-land-use%2F, accessed 5 February 2025

Heidrich, D and Nakonieczna-Bartosiewicz, J, 'Young activists as international norm entrepreneurs: A case study of Greta Thunberg's campaigning on climate change in Europe and beyond', *Studia Europejskie – Studies in European Affairs*, 25/2 (2021), 117–152, https://doi.org/10.33067/SE.2.2021.6

HM Treasury, *Final Report – The Economics of Biodiversity: The Dasgupta review* (HM Treasury, 20 August 2021), www.gov.uk/government/publications/final-report-the-economics-of-biodiversity-the-dasgupta-review, accessed 14 February 2025

HM Treasury, *The Green Book (2022)* (HM Treasury, 16 May 2024), www.gov.uk/government/publications/the-green-book-appraisal-and-evaluation-in-central-government/the-green-book-2020, accessed 14 February 2025

House of Lords Library, 'Food waste in the UK' (House of Lords Library, 12 March 2021), https://lordslibrary.parliament.uk/food-waste-in-the-uk, accessed 27 February 2025

BIBLIOGRAPHY

Huffington, A, *Thrive: The third metric to redefining success and creating a life of well-being, wisdom, and wonder* (Harmony, 2015)

Jeswani, HK et al, 'The extent of food waste generation in the UK and its environmental impacts', *Sustainable Production and Consumption*, 26 (2021), 532–547, https://doi.org/10.1016/j.spc.2020.12.021

Kano, N et al, 'Attractive quality and must-be quality', *Journal of the Japanese Society for Quality Control* (in Japanese), 14/2 (1984), 39–48

Kerr, J, *Legacy: What the All Blacks can teach us about the business of life* (Constable, 2013)

Kuper, S, *Barça: The rise and fall of the club that built modern football* (Short Books, 2021)

Kuper, S and Szymanski, S, *Soccernomics: Why England loses, why Germany and Brazil win, and why the U.S., Japan, Australia, Turkey – and even Iraq – are destined to become the kings of the world's most popular sport* (HarperSport, 2012)

Laville, S, Horton, H and Clark, A, 'Water companies in England face outrage over record sewage discharges', *The Guardian* (27 March 2024), www.theguardian.com/environment/2024/mar/27/water-companies-in-england-face-outrage-over-record-sewage-discharges, accessed 17 March 2024

Lawson, A, 'UK water companies offer apology and £10bn investment for sewage spills', *The Guardian* (18 May 2023), www.theguardian.com/environment/2023/may/18/uk-water-companies-offer-apology-and-10bn-investment-for-sewage-spills, accessed 27 February 2025

Long, H, 'Head Coach Bill Walsh' (NFL, no date), www.nfl.com/100/originals/100-greatest/game-changers-4, accessed 17 February 2025

Macdonald, B, 'The scourge of the grouse moor', *The Spectator* (11 May 2019), www.spectator.co.uk/article/the-scourge-of-the-grouse-moor, accessed 5 February 2025

Mason, R and Stewart, H, 'Johnson hints UK oil and gas output must rise to cut dependence on Russia', *The Guardian* (7 March 2022), www.theguardian.com/environment/2022/mar/07/johnson-hints-oil-and-gas-output-must-rise-to-wean-uk-off-russian-supplies, accessed 17 March 2025

McCormick, E, 'Patagonia's billionaire owner gives away company to fight climate crisis', *The Guardian* (15 September 2022), www.theguardian.com/us-news/2022/sep/14/patagonias-billionaire-owner-gives-away-company-to-fight-climate-crisis-yvon-chouinard, accessed 16 February 2025

McRaven, WH, *Make Your Bed: Little things that can change your life... and maybe the world* (Penguin, 2017)

Milmo, D and Adam, D, 'Branson pledges $3bn transport profits to fight global warming', *The Guardian* (22 September 2006), www.theguardian.com/environment/2006/sep/22/travelnews.frontpagenews, accessed 16 February 2025

Moore, R, *Sky's the Limit: British cycling's quest to conquer the Tour de France* (HarperSport, 2011)

NavyOnline.com, 'Distinguished graduate: James B Stockdale' (NavyOnline.com, 8 June 2022), https://go.navyonline.com/blog/distinguished-graduate-james-b-stockdale, accessed 15 February 2025

Neveling, E, *Jürgen Klopp* (Ebury Press, 2020)

NFL, 'The rules of the draft', *NFL Football Operations* (no date), https://operations.nfl.com/journey-to-the-nfl/the-nfl-draft/the-rules-of-the-draft, accessed 10 February 2025

The North Face, 'Athlete Development Program' (The North Face, no date), www.thenorthface.com/en-us/about-us/athlete-development-program, accessed 27 February 2025

Parry, A et al, *Strategies to Achieve Economic and Environmental Gains by Reducing Food Waste* (WRAP, 2015), www.wrap.ngo/resources/report/strategies-achieve-economic-and-environmental-gains-reducing-food-waste#download-file, accessed 7 April 2025

Patagonia, 'Environmental Internship Program' (Patagonia, no date), https://eu.patagonia.com/gb/en/environmental-internship-program.html, accessed 10 February 2025

Perarnau, M, *Pep Confidential: The inside story of Pep Guardiola's first season at Bayern Munich* (BackPage Press, 2014)

Polman, P and Winston, A, *Net Positive: How courageous companies thrive by giving more than they take* (Harvard Business Review Press, 2021)

Porter, SD et al, 'Avoidable food losses and associated production-phase greenhouse gas emissions arising from application of cosmetic standards to fresh fruit and vegetables in Europe and the UK', *Journal of Cleaner Production*, 201 (2018), 869–878, https://doi.org/10.1016/j.jclepro.2018.08.079

Prime Minister's Office and Department for Energy Security and Net Zero, 'Hundreds of new North Sea oil and gas licences to boost British energy independence' (GOV.UK, 2023), www.gov.uk/government/news/hundreds-of-new-north-sea-oil-and-gas-licences-to-boost-british-energy-independence-and-grow-the-economy-31-july-2023, accessed 27 February 2025

BIBLIOGRAPHY

Quested, T and Ingle, R, *Household Food and Drink Waste in the United Kingdom 2012* (WRAP, 2013), www.wrap.ngo/resources/report/household-food-and-drink-waste-united-kingdom-2012, accessed 7 April 2025

Rane, J, 'The North Face introduces athlete development program', *Men's Journal* (10 February 2023), www.mensjournal.com/travel/the-north-face-introduces-athlete-development-program, accessed 27 February 2025

Savills, 'Current agricultural land use in the UK' (Savills, 17 January 2019), www.savills.co.uk/research_articles/229130/274017-0, accessed 5 February 2025

Seuss, Dr, *The Lorax* (Random House, 1971)

Shrubsole, G, 'Who owns England's grouse moors?' (Who Owns England, 2016), https://whoownsengland.org/2016/10/28/who-owns-englands-grouse-moors, accessed 17 March 2025

Stanley, V and Chouinard, Y, *The Future of the Responsible Company: What we've learned from Patagonia's first 50 years* (Patagonia, 2023)

State of Nature Partnership, *State of Nature* (State of Nature Partnership, 2023), https://stateofnature.org.uk/wp-content/uploads/2023/09/TP25999-State-of-Nature-main-report_2023_FULL-DOC-v12.pdf, accessed 3 February 2025

Stockdale, R, 'Creating the pathways for private finance' (Oxygen Conservation, spring 2023), www.oxygenconservation.com/news-events/creating-the-pathways-for-private-finance, accessed 12 February 2025

Stockdale, R, 'Ep 36: Evelyn Channing, agency for change', *Shoot Room Sessions* podcast (2024a), www.oxygenconservation.com/podcast/e36-evelyn-channing, accessed 6 February 2025

Stockdale, R, 'Ep 51: Andrew Shirley, investments of passion', *Shoot Room Sessions* podcast (2024b), www.oxygenconservation.com/podcast/ep51-andrew-shirley, accessed 14 February 2025

Stockdale, R, 'Ep 64: Charles Courtenay, the Earl's evolution of Powderham', *Shoot Room Sessions* podcast (2024c), www.oxygenconservation.com/podcast/e64-charlie-courtney, accessed 16 February 2025

Sutherland, R, *Alchemy: The surprising power of ideas that don't make sense* (WH Allen, 2019)

Szymanski, S and Wigmore, T, *Crickonomics: The anatomy of modern cricket* (Bloomsbury, 2023)

Taleb, NN, *The Black Swan: The impact of the highly improbable* (Allen Lane, 2007)

Tesla, *Impact Report 2023* (Tesla, 2023), www.tesla.com/en_gb/impact, accessed 10 February 2025

Thomas, G, *The Tour According to G: My journey to the yellow jersey* (Quercus, 2018)

TIES, 'What is ecotourism?' (TIES, 2015), https://ecotourism.org/what-is-ecotourism, accessed 16 February 2025

UN, 'Sustainable Development: The 17 goals' (UN Department of Economic and Social Affairs, no date), https://sdgs.un.org/goals, accessed 14 February 2025

Van der Zon, J et al, *All-in team Jumbo Visma* (Prime Video, 2023), www.primevideo.com/detail/All-in-team-Jumbo-Visma/0KWF97LALDDVEENFX3YPZC3C06, accessed 13 February 2025

Vivobarefoot, *Diversity, Equity, and Inclusion Policy* (Vivobarefoot, no date), www.vivobarefoot.com/media/wysiwyg/pdf/Vivobarefoot_DEI_policy.pdf, accessed 27 February 2025

Vivobarefoot, 'Sustainability at Vivobarefoot' (Vivobarefoot, no date), www.vivobarefoot.com/us/sustainability, accessed 27 February 2025

Walsh, D, *Inside Team Sky* (Simon & Schuster UK, 2014)

Wedgwood, J, 'Vivobarefoot: A B-Corp transformation journey' (The Happiness Index, 29 January 2025), https://thehappinessindex.com/happy-customers/vivobarefoot-a-b-corp-transformation-journey, accessed 27 February 2025

World Class Advertising, 'Nike – Dream Crazy' (2023), youtu.be/watch?v=mTjcGED1-Ko, accessed 9 February 2025

WWF-UK, *Hidden Waste: The scale and impact of food waste in primary production* (WWF-UK, 2022), www.wwf.org.uk/sites/default/files/2022-10/WWF-UK%20HIDDEN%20WASTE%20REPORT%202022_2.pdf, accessed 6 February 2025

Acknowledgements

Oxygen Conservation has been, and continues to be, the challenge and adventure of a lifetime – an audacious, exhilarating journey that would never have been possible without the belief, trust, and investment of Mark, Roy, David, Lil, Tony, and Adam. For providing the most incredible opportunity to think bigger, push boundaries, and build something that matters, thank you!

Along the way, others have shaped our story in ways both profound and subtle. Matt, Sarah, Ben, and of course Benny – your contributions, counsel, and support have helped and continue to help turn vision into reality.

Oxygen Conservation isn't for everyone, and it isn't for everyone forever. But for those who have been part of it – whether for a moment, a season, a year, or, in the case of some of you, for decades – I am deeply grateful.

SCALING CONSERVATION

You have helped create something previously thought impossible, and something very special. Thank you.

Finally, to Helen, Emma, and George, thank you for letting me do this, and for loving me anyway.

The Author

Rich Stockdale is a transformative leader and pioneering environmentalist on a mission to Scale Conservation. Armed with a PhD in data science, he combines relentless commitment with visionary thinking to redefine our relationship with the natural world.

He founded Oxygen Conservation with Oxygen House in 2021 and has rapidly built one of the world's most impactful natural capital portfolios, valued at hundreds of millions of pounds and actively transforming thousands of acres into thriving ecosystems for people and wildlife.

Rich is determined to make natural capital a mainstream asset class, with the ambitious target of managing over £1 billion in assets by 2030, reshaping how the

SCALING CONSERVATION

world values nature and creating positive impact on an incredible scale.

🌐 www.oxygenconservation.com

in www.linkedin.com/in/richstockdale